450

four hundred and fifty

TANTALIZING

unfinished sentences

to get teenagers talking & thinking

les christie

ZONDERVAN.com/
AUTHORTRACKER
follow your favorite authors

Unfinished Sentences: 450 Tantalizing Statement-Starters to Get Teenagers Talking & Thinking

Youth Specialties products, 300 S. Pierce St., El Cajon, CA 92020, are published by Zondervan, 5300 Patterson Ave. S.E., Grand Rapids, MI 49530.

ISBN: 978-0-310-23093-9

Cover design by Proxy Design
Interior design by Jack Rogers

Printed in the United States of America

unfinished sentences

Other Youth Specialties books
by Les Christie

Have You Ever…?
450 Intriguing Questions
Guaranteed to Get Teenagers Talking

What If…?
450 Thought-Provoking Question to
Get Teenagers Talking, Laughing,
and Thinking

Contents

Acknowledgments

A big thank-you to the administration, faculty, and staff at San Jose Christian College for their encouragement and support during the writing of this book. I always count it a privilege to be working alongside such a wonderful group of people, including Al Hammond, Amy Nistor, Amy Wynn, Barbara Beavers, Barbara Newsone, Becky Gomes, Bev Wiens, Brandon Steiger, Bryce Jessup, Cameron Caruthers, Carl Wohlwend, Clay Baek, Dan Myers, Danielle Brown, Darlene Spangler, Dave Killgore, David Beavers, Dean Smith, Dennis Nichols, Doris O'Neal, Farnum Smith, Glen Miller, Jennifer Leeper, Jim Crain, Joe Womack, Jon McFarland, Kathy Wallace, Karen Lambrechtsen, Kay Llovio, Kelley Miller, Kim Whitt, Kyeong Hea Seo, LaSha Allen, Laurel Hall, Lisa Hulphers, Liz Ortiz, Liz Stanley, Matt Micek, Matt Sampson, May Wu, Merilyn Hargis, Mike Bowman, Nam Soo Woo, Nellie Salazar, Peggy Carlson, Peter Chang, Portia Hassanzadeh, Ralonda Dittmar, Rob Jones, Rob Starke, Rodger Oswald, Roger Edrington, Ronna Phifer-Ritchie, Roy Thompson, Ryan McDaniel, Scott Squires, Stephany Haskins, Susana Quiroz, Sylvia Venechanos, Tim Mandon, Tom Stephens, Tonya Persall, Traiano Nistor, and Treton Mol.

Unfinished Sentences by topic

How to Use Unfinished Sentences

Some of the unfinished sentences in this book are just plain fun; some are even a little silly. Use these questions as crowd breakers or to get conversations going. Other questions are serious and bring teens face to face with tough issues. Some of the sentences are designed to stretch kids and to push them out of their comfort zones. Some of the sentences offer interesting dilemmas, giving youths the opportunity to think, dream, and be creative.

Feel free to change the questions, add details, or ask follow-up questions. For starters, consider these ideas:

Don't let kids finish the sentences with a one-word answer. Answers should include explanations, thoughts, or feelings. Encourage kids to talk about the processes they went through to come up with their responses and to let the sentences be springboards into memories, thoughts, and experiences. Give them opportunity to explore possible responses.

Brainstorm answers together. Think of every possible way to approach the situation. Don't evaluate responses at this point. Later, look closely at the responses and let students choose a course of action and explain their preferences.

Ask what the Bible has to say about certain questions. What would Jesus do if he were faced with the same set of circumstances? Why? What would parents do? Why? What would the minister, youth minister, youth sponsors, or teachers do? Why? What would Billy Graham or Mother Theresa do? Why?

Give kids the option of passing on a question or choosing another.

Use *Unfinished Sentences* on long trips in a car or bus when you want to get the conversation going or break the tension. You may want to start with some of the lighter sentences for the trip out and look at some of the deeper ones during the trip back.

Code your favorite questions. For example, put an **F** next to sentences you think are funny and know will get a laugh. Write a **DD** next to the sentences you know will cause the group to go digging deeper into the conversation. Put a **HT** next to the ones that are hot topics that will cause some heated debate.

Combine *Unfinished Sentences* with a Bible study on a particular topic. There is a convenient index on page 7 to assist you.

Choose your sentences wisely. Avoid questions that are not appropriate for particular students because of sensitive issues or difficult circumstances.

With small groups whose members are intimate with each other, use the more personal questions. Let them wrestle verbally with each other over their conclusions to sentences.

1

The first words out of my mouth in the morning are...

2

When I'm feeling overwhelmed, I usually...

3

When I need to go somewhere to think, I will most often...

4

When I consider the beauty of God's creation...

5

The last date I had was...

6

My parents think I drive...

7

My favorite fragrance is...

8

When I see a beautiful painting, I...

9

My parents make me mad when they...

10

When someone has hurt me verbally, I will...

11

When I'm introduced to someone for the first time, I usually...

12

My favorite time of day is...

13

A family tradition that brings our family closer together is...

14

People would describe my bedroom as...

15

People find it pretty funny when I...

16

I'm looking forward to...

17

I'm most like my dad when...

18

In the last month in my life, God has...

19

I usually pray about...

20

What I like least about my room is...

21

Two things I would like to accomplish in the next year include...

22

My room is cool because...

23

My routine in getting up in the morning is...

24

The most courageous person I have ever met or heard about is...

25

My favorite family tradition is...

26

The best thing about our youth group is...

27

I usually eat a sandwich by...

28

I feel close to my parents when...

29

I enjoy being around people who...

30

I enjoy reading...

31

My favorite food is...

32

One way to improve our youth group would be...

33

What I like best about my school is...

34

The one thing my grandparents taught me was...

35

I can talk for hours about...

36

Time goes slowly when I'm...

37 The animal my personality most resembles is...

38 The thing that drives me crazy about my brother or sister is...

39 The easiest tests for me at school are...

40 The thing I like best about my brother or sister is...

41
My favorite movie is...

42
The movie star people think I look or act like is...

43
My number one advisor is...

44
When I'm feeling sad, I usually...

45

The chore that I hate doing the most is...

46

My favorite way to waste time is...

47

People might be surprised to find out that I...

48

The thing I miss most about my childhood is...

49

My biggest fear about death is...

50

If I could invent a gadget to make my life easier, I'd invent something that would...

51

Just for the fun of it, before I die I would like to...

52

Next year looks better to me because...

53

I will probably never ____ ____, but it would still be fun if I could because...

54

Next year may be a problem because...

55

I have never quite gotten the hang of...

56

I'm a bundle of nerves when it comes to...

57

If I were to describe myself as a flavor, it would be...

58

My name means ________, so I...

59

The object in my home that means the most to me is...

60

I was given my name because...

61

The best news I've heard this week is...

62

My favorite city is...

63

The worst news I've heard this week is...

64

Usually I'm the kind of person who...

65

Something that I will never give up from my childhood is...

66

The best boss I ever had was...

67

The most useless thing in our house is...

68

I want to be the kind of person who...

69

As I grow older, I'm looking forward to...

70

In general people worry too much about...

71

Lately I'm becoming...

72

An emotion I often feel but don't usually express is...

73

The feeling that best describes where I am right now is...

74

Last year at this time I would never have thought God would...

75

Something or someone I will most likely take for granted tomorrow is...

76 The person I'm most thankful for this year is...

77 One of God's attributes that I most appreciate is...

78 If I could just...

79 When I need to relax and unwind, I usually...

80

When I go to a party, I...

81

The quality I appreciate most in a friend is...

82

For fun I like to...

83

A spiritual milestone in my life was the time...

84

My ideal vacation would be...

85

The area in which I would most like to grow spiritually is...

86

I feel happy when...

87

If I were to draw a picture of what it feels like to be depressed, I would draw...

88

When I wake up in the middle of the night, I sometimes worry about...

89

The first thing that comes to my mind when I think of God is...

90

To make me completely content would require...

91

The way I feel about Christ's Second Coming is...

92

The greatest thing that ever happened to me was...

93

The greatest thing I can do for others is...

94

One characteristic I received from my parents that I wish I could change is...

95

One characteristic I received from my parents that I want to keep is...

96 When I was a child, I felt closest to...

97 In general I view life as...

98 Between the ages of seven and 12, I lived...

99 The things I prefer to do alone include...

100

Ten years from now...

101

A skill I have acquired is...

102

My favorite music is...

103

The personal relationship in my life I enjoy most right now is...

104

Music influences me by...

105

I think Jesus would say ____________ about the music teens listen to today because...

106

Today's music groups who have a positive influence on my life include...

107

When I have time to myself on a rainy day, I like to...

108

The best way to eat an Oreo cookie is...

109

My favorite place to escape is...

110

The one thing I wish I could change about myself is...

111

My biggest snack craving is...

112

When I get really tired...

113

Overall, life is...

114

My favorite book is...

115

I feel anger when...

116

The most memorable compliment I have ever received was...

117

A time when I really felt frightened was...

118

The most physically challenging thing that I've ever done was...

119

The best place I have ever gone on vacation was...

120

Participating in sports makes me feel...

121

The stupidest thing I ever did was...

122

If I could play a musical instrument, I would choose...

123

The person who has had the most impact on my life is...

124

My sense of humor is...

125

People say I look like...

126

When my mom or dad hugs me in public, I feel...

127

The one thing that someone has said to me that has stuck with me the longest is...

128 My favorite childhood toy is...

129 If you asked me to tell about myself, I would say...

130 My dream car is...

131 My favorite game to play is...

132 My idea of going camping is...

133

I frequently daydream about...

134

The thing that fascinates me the most in God's creation is...

135

My favorite recurring dream is...

136

When I grow up, I want to be...

137

My worst memory is...

138

The most embarrassing thing that has ever happened to me was...

139

My favorite ice cream flavor is...

140

My first kiss...

141

The one bad habit that I wish I did not have is...

142

The thing I fear most about getting old is...

143

The thing I look forward to most about getting old is...

144

I most regret...

145

One of my favorite childhood memories is...

146

When it's sunny outside, my favorite thing to do is...

147

I'm grossed out when...

148

My favorite TV show is...

149

I view friendship as...

150

At this stage in my life, the area that I need more self-confidence in is...

151

My motivation in life is...

152

I would be willing to die for...

153
The worst rejection I have ever experienced was...

154
My heart breaks when...

155
A weakness can be good when it...

156
My biggest weakness is...

157

People generally say that I'm...

158

My favorite color is...

159

My favorite season is...

160

My favorite holiday is...

161

My family celebrates birthdays by...

162

When I feel a distance growing between a friend and me, I usually...

163

My family celebrates Christmas by...

164

My best attribute is...

165

To me work is...

166

My favorite animal is...

167

My favorite teacher is...

168

At the beach you will most likely find me...

169

What I don't understand about the opposite sex is...

170

An enjoyable date would include...

171

The kind of person I want to marry is...

172

I think God asks us to wait until we are married to have sex because...

173 Sexually explicit movies and songs...

174 My worst date was...

175 I can hardly wait to...

176 The ultimate date would include...

177 My best date was...

178

I learned about sex from...

179

If I were to move to a primitive country, the three things I would miss about my current life would be...

180

The best piece of advice I learned about sex was...

181

I think sexual temptation is different from other temptations because...

182

The largest animal I have ever touched was...

183

The most dangerous thing I would like to try to do would be...

184

Wouldn't it be cool if computers could...

185

If I were at a party where alcohol and drugs were free-flowing, I would...

186

At my school drugs and alcohol are...

187

My greatest fear concerning my friends who use drugs or alcohol is...

188

I try to help my friends who are using drugs and alcohol by...

189

What is most important to me in my life right now is...

190

I think people use drugs and alcohol because...

191

I worry most about...

192

I want God to see me as...

193

When I was a kid, my parents woke me up in the morning by...

194

I see God as...

195

The biggest lie I ever told was...

196

When I'm hanging out with my friends, I like to...

197 The area that concerns me about movies is (choose one: language, violence, sexuality, use of humor, or morals and values) because...

198 The first thing I said today was...

199 The ingredients that make a good movie include...

200 What I like best about television is...

201 What bugs me most about movies and television is...

202 When I'm talking with my friends, we usually talk about...

203 If I found a wallet full of cash on the street I would...

204

If I bought several items at a store and discovered on my way out that I had not been charged for one of them, I would...

205

If I saw someone cheating on a test, I would...

206

The childhood event that taught me my most valuable lesson was...

207

After I die I want people to remember me as...

208

When friends let me down, I usually...

209

If a terminally ill friend came to me and asked me to help him die, I would...

210

The kind of person I like to spend the most time with is...

211

If I came upon a terrible car accident on the highway, I would...

212 The biggest failure in my life was...

213 I would rate my personality as...

214 For me to trust someone...

215 The biggest disappointment in my life was...

216

I'm hoping that...

217

The things I find too personal to discuss with others include...

218

When I receive a compliment, I usually...

219

Before making a telephone call, I will often...

220

If I noticed a self-destructive habit in a friend, I would...

221

The things I value most in a relationship include...

222

The last time I cried in front of another person was...

223

The one thing that is too serious to joke about is...

224

When someone does me a favor, I usually...

225

If I could change one thing about the way I was raised, it would be...

226

The hardest phone call I've had to make was...

227

When I'm walking and see someone begging, I usually...

228

If I planned my own funeral, I would include...

229

The last time I yelled at someone I was upset about...

230

My worst nightmare was...

231

My most treasured memory is...

232

The worst psychological torture I can imagine would be...

233

The thing I really love about my dad or mom is...

234

The one question I've always wanted to ask my parents is...

235

The person I admire the most is...

236

The most important thing I've learned about life is...

237

The thing my parents do that embarrasses me the most is...

238

The last time I laughed so hard I cried was...

239

If I had to live with someone other than my parents, I would choose...

240

The thing I dislike most about myself is...

241

The bravest thing I ever did was...

242

The thing that really gets on my nerves is...

243

If I were to die, my family would miss the way I...

244

If I had to truthfully describe my family, I would say...

245

If a friend gave me a gift I didn't like, I would...

246

On a typical day God...

247

The stupidest rule my parents have come up with is...

248

If I were planning my birthday party, I would include...

249

The thing that scares me the most right now is...

250

The wildest, craziest thing I've ever done was...

251

The hardest thing about growing up is...

252

The last time I laughed at myself for doing something funny or silly was...

253

The last time I told my parents I loved them was...

254

The last time my parents told me they loved me was...

255

If I could pick a nickname for myself, I would choose...

256

When I'm mad at my parents, I get back at them by...

257

I think the opposite sex has it easiest because...

258

If everyone forgot my birthday, I would...

259

If I were to marry someone of another race, my family would probably...

260

The most difficult choice I've had to make up to this point has been...

261

Sometimes it's difficult to counsel a friend effectively because...

262

Some people call listening the language of love because...

263

The city I was born in...

264

The thing that keeps me from being a good listener is...

265

My most unique relative is...

266

The family member who is most inspiring to me is...

267

People fear death because...

268

People think suicide is a solution to their problems because...

269

If a person told me she were going to attempt suicide and had a time, place, and method, I would...

270

My deepest need is...

271

What the world needs is...

272

I wouldn't get lonely if I could just...

273

I'm most lonely when...

274

You could help me when I'm lonely by...

275

The last time I was extremely moody was...

276 One way to reduce worry is...

277 The best way to encourage a moody person is...

278 People don't like being around a moody person because...

279

One way my life could be different is if I trusted God more in the area of...

280

Our society is obsessed with thin, sleek bodies because...

281

The best advice I could give to a friend who has an eating disorder would be...

282

When it comes to putting God first in my life, I...

283

I thank God because...

284

The thing that gives me the most satisfaction is...

285

People follow Jesus because...

286

The most bizarre combination of foods I've ever eaten was...

287

The weirdest food I've ever eaten was...

288

The most food I've ever eaten at one time was...

289

The worst tasting food I've ever eaten was...

290

A time I sacrificed something for someone else was...

291

If I were on a desert island and had to eat the same meal every day for a year, I would eat...

292

If I had more faith, I could...

293

A time someone sacrificed something for me was...

294

One amazing way God has worked in my life this last year has been...

295

It's difficult at times to have faith because...

296

I would describe the meaning of love to a child by saying...

297

The way I need to be encouraged today is...

298

It's difficult sometimes to encourage others because...

299

An unhealthy attitude that appears in people who live for money is...

300

Prayer can be a dialogue with God rather than a monologue by...

301

Prayer brings me closer to God because...

302

The best time of day for me to take a few moments to be with God is...

303

It's difficult for me to have a disciplined, consistent time with God because...

304

Something very few people know about me is...

305

If McDonald's ran the church, it would have...

306

The hardest thing about prayer is...

307

The best place for me to pray is...

308

The greatest thing about prayer is...

309

Prayer is...

310

Some Christians are afraid to share their faith because...

311

Prayer is not...

312

The biggest help in my prayer life has been...

313

The area of my life that is on hold at this time is...

314

The one thing I could do this week to strengthen the spiritual foundation of my life would be...

315

If someone feels dry spiritually and says he feels far from God, I would...

316

The best thing about church is...

317

The worst thing about church is...

318

When I think of church, I usually feel...

319

If I were a pastor, I would...

320

My first memory of church is...

321

If I were to describe church to a friend, I would...

322

The roadblocks that keep me from having greater faith in God are...

323

The most useless gift I've ever received was...

324

The one gift I've always wanted but never received is...

325

The ugliest gift I've ever received was...

326

The smallest gift I've ever received was...

327

The most expensive gift I've ever received was...

328

The most meaningful gift I've ever received was...

329

The most surprising gift I've ever received was...

330

Having a relationship with God means...

331

A time I've personally experienced spiritual warfare was...

332

The most bizarre invention I've ever heard of is...

333

The most useful invention I use regularly is...

334

The time I felt closest to God was...

335 Before I die I hope that...

336 The biggest choice I'm facing this week is...

337 My family solved some of our communication problems by...

338 A spiritual goal I have for my life is...

339

What I appreciate most about my parents is...

340

I could be more helpful at home if I...

341

My happiest times with my family are when...

342

One of my favorite, funny memories about my family is...

343

If I could say one thing to my dad or mom, I would say...

344

To appreciate my mom this week I could...

345

To appreciate my dad this week I could...

346

To get my life back in perspective when it spins out of control, I...

347

The biggest problem I have with my friends is...

348

When I have a problem in a friendship, I usually...

349

I think being made in God's image means...

350

Good friends earn my trust by...

351

I became a Christian by...

352

My friends pressure me to...

353

One way knowing God personally has changed my life is...

354

The best way I've found to build a bridge with my non-Christian friends is...

355

The best thing friends can do for each other is...

356

When I talk to my friends about Christ...

357

When a friend gets mad at me, I usually...

358

I wish I had more...

359

I'm glad I'm a Christian because...

360

Friends can build up one another by...

361

My favorite family holiday tradition is...

362

Friends can show they accept each other by...

363

The time when I needed financial help the most was...

364

If I could raise one person from the dead, I would...

365

The nicest thing anybody ever said about me was...

366

Money is great, but...

367

The most daring thing I ever did was...

368

If I were lost in a big city, I would...

369

The dog that best typifies my life would be...

370

When playing Monopoly, I usually...

371

The thing I like best about children is...

372

The thing I remember most about my first job was...

373

The worst thing my brother or sister did to me as a child was...

374

When I was a child, I wanted to grow up to be...

375

My experiences in learning how to drive include...

376

The worst way I can imagine dying would be...

377

Using football as an analogy, my life is like...

378

Two of the barriers that are keeping me from reaching my full potential are...

379

Most dentists...

380

If I had to choose a job for the rest of my life, I would choose...

381

In my spiritual journey I feel I'm...

382

The best way to eat spaghetti is...

383

I would describe heaven as...

384

The only time I could ever justify killing another person would be...

385

The one image in my mind I wish I could forget is...

386

I would describe hell as...

387

I'm most tempted to say or do something that makes me appear more important in the eyes of others when...

388

The last time I said, "I love you," was...

389

I'm most relaxed when...

390

The areas of my life in which I find it most difficult to trust God are...

391

The kind of person who brings out the best in me is...

392

The last time I said I'm sorry was...

393

People know I'm angry by...

394

The worst job I can imagine having would be...

395

My three greatest strengths are...

396

Three things I'm most thankful for in my life right now include...

397

When I was a child, we expressed affection in my family by...

398

The worst thing that could possibly happen to me is...

399

The best way I can imagine dying would be...

400

The most beautiful thing I've ever seen is...

401

If I didn't watch television for a year, I would probably...

402

The one thing in my life that I care most deeply about is...

403

I choose my friends because...

404

My definition of success is...

405

The darkest room in my house is...

406 I would describe God to a child by saying...

407 My feeling about animals being used in medical research is...

408 Most lawyers...

409 People who domesticate wild animals...

410 It seems like every time I go to the beach or lake...

411 Animal rights activists are...

412 Forgiveness is difficult to give (or receive) because...

413 Most chefs...

414 I feel people who beg on street corners...

415 The last time I went camping...

416 I think beauty pageants are...

417 I like to buy my clothes at...

418 Teenagers today are reading...

419 My idea of shopping is...

420

When I get embarrassed, I usually...

421

Most doctors...

422

A great encourager in our group is...

423

The last time I exaggerated was over...

424

A person can tell when I'm exaggerating by...

425

The major thing that causes a heart to break is...

426

When I see someone who's really happy, I often wonder...

427

Most teachers...

428

It's more difficult to receive a gift than to give one because...

429

The sickest I've ever been was...

430

When I get a headache, the best thing for me to do is...

431

What has been most helpful to me in remembering people's names is...

432

The last time I really had fun was...

433

I think the worst kind of lie to tell is...

434

I think capital punishment...

435

To help someone reach her full potential, I would...

436

When I was a child, I was given the nickname...

437

One way to overcome racial problems would be...

438

What causes me to get overwhelmed by life is...

439

I would prefer to take a shower (or bath) because...

440

When the Second Coming of Jesus occurs, I think most people will...

441

My routine just before going to bed at night is...

442

If I were to draw a graph of my spiritual journey, it would look like...

443

To be successful I would have to...

444

Most of my conversations on the telephone tend to center around...

445

Instead of using standardized tests, a better way to measure how well students are doing would be...

446

I start getting really silly when I...

447

What tires me out the most is...

448 Tomorrow I need to...

449 The worst physical torture I can imagine would be...

450 I wish the writer of this book would have included a sentence about...

Oh, yes, Cassie thought, devouring the sight of Daniel standing before her. She more than missed him. She longed to be with him, to touch him, something she'd done constantly when they were together. Simple caring touches, like cleaning and filing his nails just so she could hold his smooth brown hands between her own. In her mind, Cassie relived the feel of his body resting between her thighs, his back against her breasts as she brushed the short tight curls on the top of his head, running the brush, then her fingers, along his scalp, massaging, breathing in his scent. She'd never experienced anything so erotic. Miss him? She couldn't begin to say how much.

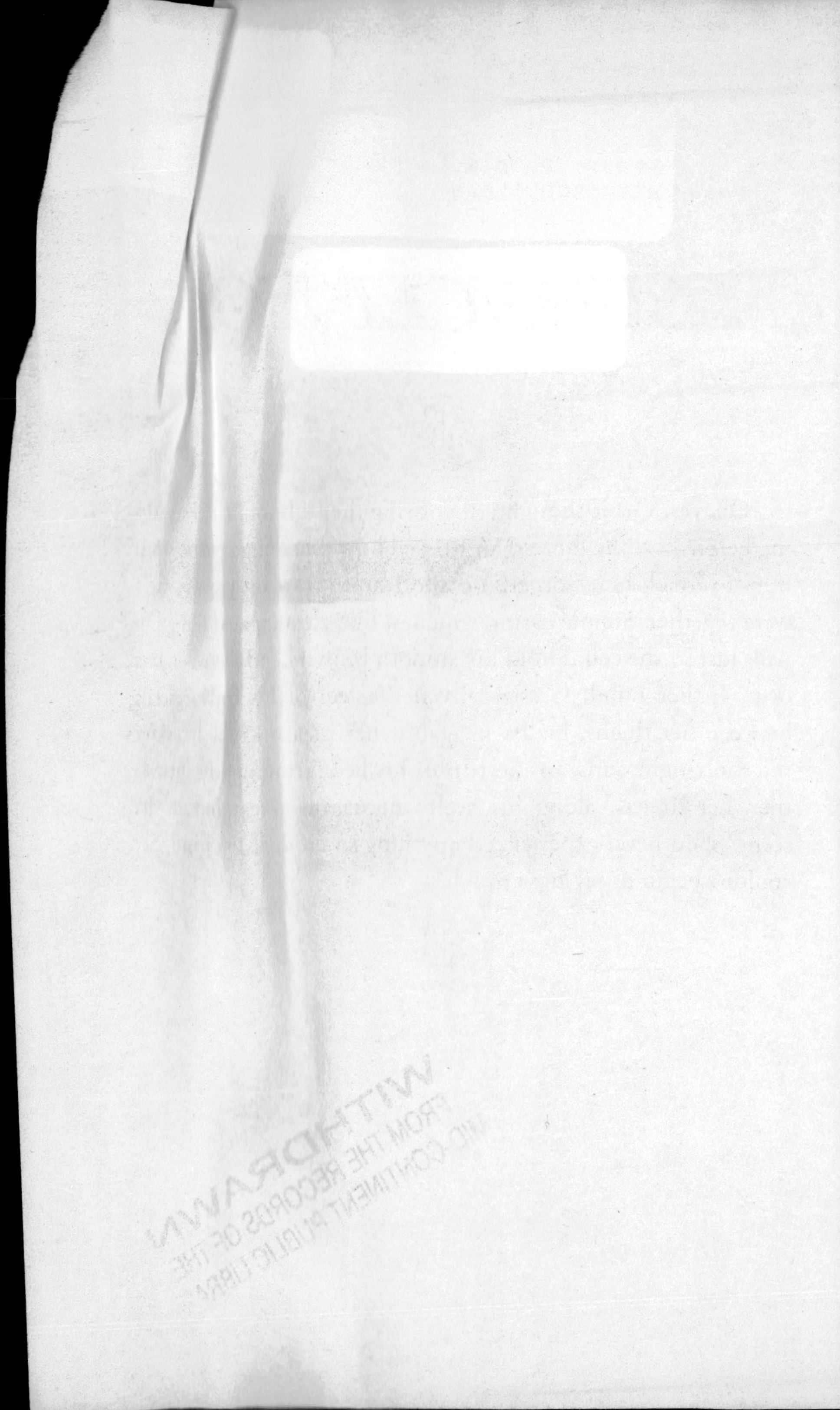

MISCONCEPTIONS

PAMELA LEIGH STARR

Genesis Press Inc.

Indigo Love Stories

An imprint of Genesis Press Publishing

Genesis Press, Inc.
P.O. Box 101
Columbus, MS 39703

All characters in this book have no existence outside the imagination of the author and have no relation whatsoever to anyone bearing the same name or names. They are not even distantly inspired by any individual known or unknown to the author and all incidents are pure invention.

ISBN: 1-58571-117-9
Manufactured in the United States of America

First Edition

Visit us at www.genesis-press.com
or call at 1-888-Indigo-1

For my children…

BJ, Tab, and Kait,

May no misconception of thought or deed

Pull you away from your dreams.

PROLOGUE

She was beautiful. The classical lady in red. Cassie twirled around the room before making a spinning beeline for him. Daniel stood completely still, watching as she came closer. As always, his entire body reacted to being near her. His fingers pulsated with their usual urge to touch her. The blood rushed through his body, spreading the need, heating his insides, elevating his desire until it settled and throbbed. In a barely visible move, Daniel shifted to the left as he watched her move closer and closer toward him. He shifted slightly again, this time to the right. The movement brought no relief. Knowing they didn't have time to indulge in the various pleasurable activities that were filling his head, Daniel attempted to rein in his desire.

Impossible.

One huge twirl and she was standing in front of him. We don't have time for this, Daniel thought, attempting to exert rational control over his completely irrational body.

Cassie stood right under him, full of spirit and just plain happiness, as always. Why the hell was she with him? Daniel asked himself for the thousandth time. What did she see in him?

Cassie looked up at him. "Party time."

"I know," Daniel answered. They were going to a friend's birthday party, though, he wished they weren't. She was beautiful. Her long black hair was twisted into a fancy knot on the top of her head. The deep V in the front of the red dress gave him a glimpse of the firm sweetness he knew well. Daniel shook his head slightly. He couldn't think about that now. Somehow he willed his thoughts to scatter. Unfortunately, they settled on a conversation he'd had earlier that day with a co-worker.

Was Roy right about her? Could Cassie be faking the feelings she claimed to have for him? Daniel watched as the bright smile slowly faded from her face. Roy, a pilot he worked with on a regular basis, had given Daniel his *unsolicited* opinion of Cassie. Though he should have discounted Roy's words, they had easily reinforced Daniel's own constant doubts. Could she really love him? For that matter, could anyone love him? His own mother hadn't loved him enough to stay in his life. How could he expect Cassie to?

He'd known from the beginning that it was a mistake to get involved with her, a mistake to let her get close to him when she was certain to leave him one day.

Wouldn't she?

As Daniel gazed at Cassie's sweet face, Roy's voice echoed in his ear. "Man, don't let the innocent face fool you. It's all an act. Women like her want something. And it's not love. They're looking for what's in ya' pants or what's in ya' pockets. Watch it!"

Of course she would leave him. There was something about him that repelled those that he loved. Didn't his own mother desert him, desert him *because* he loved her so much? His brow raised with the sharp pain the memory brought to mind. That was why he'd cut all ties with his aunts, uncles and cousins before they began to look at him differently, to realize that they were better off with him out of their lives. For sure, he was better off being a part of no one's life. That was how he had lived his life. That was how he'd liked it.

Until Cassie.

Her soft fingers at his temples massaged away the frown he felt taking control of his face, then trailed to each side of his face, tracing his jaw line. "Do parties make you frown now?"

"No, not at all." As he kissed her lips, Roy's voice, as well as his frown, faded away. But the doubt that had begun when he was ten years old, doubt of his worthiness to be loved, remained. If he didn't deserve to be loved, how could he even imagine that Cassie could love him? That thought grew in a dark corner of his mind, even as he pulled her closer, pressed his lips harder against her soft, giving ones. He hugged her close, letting her feel his desire, trying to erase his negative thoughts. Daniel was determined to concentrate on the fact that right now, this sweet, giving woman wanted him, wanted him *now.*

But for how long? Your own mother got sick of you. Why should anyone else be different? In his mind, Daniel heard his own voice push past his attempts to accept Cassie at face value. Was Cassie really the sweet, funny woman who claimed to love him? He pulled back.

"That frown should have vanished by now." Cassie's voice broke through his thoughts. "You won't get another kiss until that anti-party face has completely disappeared."

She put her hands on her hips when his only response was to keep frowning.

"Daniel, you can't walk into a party with your face turned down like that."

He wanted to push the negative thoughts back, force them to disappear.

"This is how you look right now." She drew her eyebrows together and molded her mouth in a straight line of disgust.

She was adorable. A grunt of a smile made its way to his face, then a real one.

She always made him smile. Doubt and all, he couldn't remember being this happy in a long time. The past few months had felt like heaven.

"I can walk into a party any way I want," he told her. Daniel lifted a long, steady finger to trace a line from the nape of her neck to the base of her spine. She shuddered, and then fingered the buttons on his shirt. "How about walking in completely naked?"

Daniel's smile widened. Her weakness, he'd discovered, was a simple caress. A touch could turn her into living fire in his arms. "I'll save that show for you."

"Then let's get going. I want to make it back early. I can't wait to view that limited engagement."

He'd needed that reassurance. Physically, he could always tell that she wanted him. Anything else, Daniel simply didn't know for sure. All he could do was wait. Time would tell if she was playing him for a fool. Would she dump him, as his mother had done? If he ever suspected that she was even thinking of such a thing, he would end it first. Cut all ties to protect himself, just the way he had with his relatives. No questions, no begging, no long drawn-out explanation. It would just be over.

CHAPTER 1

Cassie Villiere stiffened as she stood in the middle of the busy Ticketing Center at Houston's Hobby Airport. What was he doing here? Daniel didn't have a flight today. She had checked the flight schedule. Suddenly, Cassie realized that she was out in the open and quickly hurried back to her station behind the counter, knocking her friend sideways.

"What's wrong?" Melanie asked.

"Nothing."

Melanie stared at her a minute. "Don't try that with me. You're mighty tense for it to be nothing," Melanie whispered from the side of her mouth as she completed a transaction with a customer. "Thank you, have a pleasant flight."

Melanie turned to look directly at Cassie. "It's all over your face. There's only one person I know that makes you look and act like this." She swung her head around, her long braids following. "Where is he? He's not supposed to be here."

"I know," Cassie answered, not bothering to continue the lie.

"Then what's he doing here?" Melanie asked, her hands on her almost nonexistent hips. She was shaped like a bean pole, a bean pole that oozed confidence and sensuality.

"I don't know."

"Excuse me, miss. I'd like to board the plane before it takes off."

"The flight attendant wouldn't allow such an injustice to happen to a handsome man like yourself." Melanie fed the line to the short, bald man on the other side of the counter, without missing a beat.

He stuttered, finally muttering, "Th-th-th-thank you," before taking the ticket from Melanie as if it were a gift from the gods. Melanie had that effect on men. Most men, that is. Daniel was another story. Melanie and Daniel couldn't stand each other.

Daniel's arrival and departure from Cassie's life was an emotional book filled with the most precious and the most hurtful times of her life—almost three years worth. Cassie had no intention of adding any more chapters. The last addition had taken its toll on her. She nervously watched as he walked toward the phones on the far end of the wall. Daniel wasn't on the flight schedule, she was sure of it. And according to her calculations, he had reached the limit of the hours regulations allowed pilots to fly, right down to the last second. This narrowed the reason for his presence to two things.

He knows. He somehow found out and has come looking for me.

Or Daniel was actually flying out of Houston as a passenger.

The second reason was unlikely, but she prayed that it was the one. She watched as he paused in front of the phones. If she left now, while his back was turned, she could make it to the ladies' room. Melanie would cover for her.

"You are not running!" Cassie's best friend told her. Melanie gripped Cassie's wrist, holding it motionless. The red-coated nails of her other hand tapped against the counter. "It's too late anyway. He's on his way over. If you move now, he'll see you."

He *was* coming this way with a deep look of concentration on his face, seemingly completely oblivious to anything around him, including her.

"You have to look the devil in the eye, sister," Cassie heard Melanie say. "Put him behind you. Face him down. Bite the bullet."

"Enough, Melanie," Cassie hissed. "I'm not going anywhere. I'm okay. I can handle this."

"That's the plan. You quit your job as a flight attendant

because of Daniel, and you've been avoiding him for months." Melanie waved her hands for emphasis as she completed another transaction with a customer.

"That's not entirely true."

"You arrange your schedule to avoid working when he has a scheduled flight in or out of Hobby, just so you won't run into him." Melanie flung the words at her with a toss of her long braids. "Now's the time to be strong, sister." She patted Cassie's hand, a brief look of understanding flashing across her face before her normal sassy expression locked back into place.

Melanie was a lifesaver, a good friend. Often Cassie wished that she *were* Melanie's real sister. If not by blood, then at least by race. If she had that much in common with Daniel, then he would probably still be hers now. Unfortunately, fate had not blessed her with the same distinct features and skin coloring as her soul mate. Cassie's black hair and olive complexion were as close to being black as she was going to get.

Cassie sighed, and then plastered an artificial smile on her face before opening her line to help the next customer. She had no real desire to change who and what she was. Cassie would rather know what went wrong. The sad part about her whole relationship with Daniel was that she had no idea why things had fallen apart. The only thing she knew for sure was that she hadn't gotten over him, not in the last two and a half years. In fact, the last five months had been the worst.

He was coming closer, Cassie could feel it. Methodically, with false cheer, she continued to sell airline tickets, tag luggage, and wish passengers an enjoyable flight. Those were the steps she concentrated on. Ticket, luggage, cheer. Ticket luggage, cheer. Ticket...

"Melanie," he said.

"Daniel," her friend replied. "What are you doing here, Fly Boy?"

"Flying." Daniel's answer was short, gruff, and clearly annoyed. He hated being called "Fly Boy," which explained Melanie's reason for using the name.

Melanie's opinion had always been that Daniel was a fly-by-night jerk, here one minute, gone the next. Cassie had never believed it, not then, and not now. There had to be more to their breakup. So much more she didn't know because every letter, every phone call, every e-mail message he'd left unanswered. If by chance they met in the terminal, he completely ignored her, refusing to even talk to her. Cassie had given up trying to find a reason and had simply tried to survive living without him, and, therefore, planned her work schedule so that it wouldn't coincide with his. It had been better than seeing him all the time and getting no response, absolutely nothing.

"Miss, my luggage," the customer reminded her.

"Sorry ma'am," Cassie apologized, continuing to eavesdrop as Melanie taunted Daniel with questions that he studiously ignored.

Why didn't Melanie get moving? Daniel hadn't noticed her at the far end of the counter and probably wouldn't if Melanie would finish those three simple steps : ticket, luggage, cheer.

"Ain't that the truth? Huh, Cass?" Melanie nearly shouted, turning demanding eyes toward her, directing Cassie to stay cool, bite the bullet.

Cassie felt Daniel's gaze on her. Melanie was going to pay for this. Her friend refused to allow her to take this one step at a time. Seeing Daniel from afar without being noticed would have been a good first step.

"Cassie," he said, his voice sliding through her ear canal, vibrating the tiny bones and in turn every muscle, every body part. Cassie was amazed that she was still standing.

"Daniel," she answered, taking a step closer to the counter.

"It's true, isn't it, Cassie?" Melanie asked. "That's how it is sometimes."

"What?" Cassie asked, having missed part of the one-sided conversation Melanie was having with Daniel.

"What we were talking about just now—missing people," Melanie prompted.

Oh, yes, Cassie thought, devouring the sight of Daniel standing before her. She more than missed him. She longed to be with him, to touch him, something she'd done constantly when they were together. Simple caring touches, like cleaning and filing his nails just so she could hold his smooth brown hands between her own. In her mind, Cassie relived the feel of his body resting between her thighs, his back against her breasts as she brushed the short tight curls on the top of his head, running the brush, then her fingers, along his scalp, massaging, breathing in his scent. She'd never experienced anything so erotic. Miss him? She couldn't begin to say how much.

"What do you think, Cassie?" Daniel asked, his gaze intent, almost pleading.

Cassie stared, stunned. He was actually directing a question to her "Miss people?" she asked. "Yes, it's true."

He flinched, and his face hardened. He obviously didn't want her to miss him.

"That's good to know," he said, and was gone.

Cassie sighed. At least now she knew that he hadn't found out. He wasn't here to see her. For the first time in years, he was leaving Houston as a passenger.

Daniel settled into a seat, feeling awkward as he adjusted to being a passenger rather than the pilot. He stared hard at the flight attendant. She was going through the standard procedures for emergencies. Having piloted for over four years, he knew the routine by heart. But boredom with the usual speech was not his reason for staring so rudely at the young woman. She nervously went through every step, darting glances his way every few seconds. It was obvious she sensed his hostility. The poor woman couldn't help the fact that she reminded him of Cassie. Unfortunately, it didn't take much to remind him of Cassie. Feeling remorseful, Daniel ignored her, opening the letter he'd been reading earlier.

The letter was from his cousin, Ness, full of news about her husband and kids. This letter was the catalyst that had softened his resolve to stay away from Cassie, to even speak to her. He couldn't seem to concentrate on the words before him as memories of his time with Cassie began to fill his head, particularly the unforgettable memory of that night when he'd given in to his desperate need to make love to her just one more time. It had left him hoping, wishing, and dreaming, fool that he was. But any hope or wish was nothing but a dream. Cassie had said as much. She didn't miss him, didn't want anything to do with him.

Melanie, Cassie's cheeky, smart-mouthed friend, had made sure he knew it. A replay of Melanie's exact words at the ticket counter went through his mind. "There are some people in life you forget almost instantly, and you can't miss what you don't remember."

Cassie, so completely beautiful, and so obvious in her attempt to be invisible, had unashamedly agreed with Melanie. That she had shouldn't tear at his gut so much. Not after the lesson he'd learned three years ago, when he found out he'd been used as an experiment. That first bit of evidence was all it took. It was all he needed to confirm what he knew to be true. No woman could love him enough to be a part of his life forever.

The crinkle of paper brought his focus to the letter he held in his hand. Well, Ness, his favorite cousin, still cared about him. She had convinced him to end his self-imposed exile from New Orleans and the rest of the family. Loneliness had been getting to him, not to mention the trauma from the close call with the plane he had nearly crashed. Those things were enough to convince Daniel that he needed to visit the people he had cut himself off from. He had come to realize that he shouldn't have broken away from his family, at least not from family who truly cared. He could easily strike his mother from that list. The pain of her desertion was still a burning sadness. And the pain of Cassie? She had been planning to hurt him, just as he suspected. So he'd dumped her before she could dump him. He had thought he'd be over her by now.

But he wasn't.

Daniel realized now that he'd been a prime candidate for her games. His cold, hard exterior kept him from making friends easily or entering relationships with women.

Only the bold ones approached, and they assumed he was being choosy when he turned them down.

His cousin Vanessa and Aunt Joyce were the only people in the world who could reach his true self, the real man inside. But because he had stopped going home to New Orleans, his hard exterior had become almost impenetrable.

Cassie had gotten beyond it, though. From the first time she was assigned as a crew member on one of his flights, she'd unnerved him with her innocent smile, kind words, jokes—she was always telling jokes. Then there was the touching. Cassie always had her hands on him. He couldn't stop her from giving him these little gifts of herself. At least that's what he'd thought they were at the time. Daniel hadn't wanted them. He'd tried to discourage her with his cold reactions, but for some reason, she'd continued to chase him, pretending that she liked him, somehow becoming a regular crew member on most of his flights. When she wasn't, Daniel missed the humorous ad-libs Cassie added to the dull emergency drill. Her laughter, her smile, her jokes and the special attention she gave him with her soft touches eventually caused him to cave in. Cassie was smooth. She'd had him fooled. He would have never guessed that Cassie was a calculating game player, but the words he'd heard with his own ears confirmed that she had never really loved him.

Daniel couldn't stop himself from remembering the night his trust in Cassie, in relationships, died. They had been dating for months and had come to a friend's birthday party together.

Cassie, he remembered, had been wearing a red dress made of some slinky material. It moved on her body in waves. She'd worn her long black hair up, because she hated the way it stuck to her neck in the heat of summer. Daniel loved it when she wore her hair up because he knew the trace of a single finger from the nape of her neck down her spine was enough to make her whimper. He remembered his hand reaching toward her neck many times that night.

Cassie, a sucker for helping someone in need, had introduced him to one of her lost birds, a new employee at work, who was fresh out of flight attendant school. She was silly and young and had stared wide-eyed at him as Cassie introduced him. The young woman had worn an expression that seemed to say, "What are they doing together?" He'd often seen that exact expression on many people's faces when they were introduced as a couple.

Daniel had laughed and left Cassie to explain. He went to the bar to get a beer and a drink for Cassie. The man whose words he had been trying to knock out of his head was standing at the bar.

"Look who's here! Just the person I wanted to see."

"Roy." He nodded quickly, telling the bartender what he wanted. He had no intention of having a conversation, long or short, with Roy.

"I have some interesting news for you."

"Some other time," he told him, though not quick enough because Roy was now standing directly in front of him.

"After the cold look you gave me when I tried to tell you about your woman, I should have known you wouldn't be open to hearing some more truths."

The aftermath of their previous conversation still hanging at the back of his head, Daniel wasn't in the mood for more. Cassie was here with him. She had looked into his eyes with sweetness and what he hoped was love before the party, on the ride here, and not more than three minutes ago. *Don't let Roy's ramblings get you*, he told himself. Daniel grabbed the drinks, taking an extra beer for Cassie's friend since he hadn't asked what she wanted. "Hang on to those truths," he told Roy, turning to walk away.

"Then I guess you know about the bet."

Daniel froze at his words. He didn't want to hear what Roy had to say. He knew he would regret it, but he felt himself turning around, heard himself ask, "Bet?" And that one word was enough to get Roy going.

"So you don't know about the bet." He inched closer. "It seems that a year or so ago when you were playing hard-to-get, a bunch of female flight attendants and even one male, if I heard right, decided you needed to be broken. It seems that you were viewed as a challenge, and a bet was made. There were a dozen or so participants, a hundred dollars apiece, winner take all and have you, too."

Daniel had known he would regret listening to Roy. His words released the flood of doubts he had been trying to hold in the back of his mind. He didn't want to believe them but *knew* them to be true. She couldn't really love him. He had known it wasn't real and that it wouldn't last. She'd made a fool of him. She would leave him. But not if he left her first.

On the other hand, what if it wasn't true? His insecurities

could cause him to ruin the best thing to happen to him in a long time. He'd talk to her. He'd ask her about it.

Not giving Roy another thought, Daniel moved to do just that.

"Don't believe me?" he heard Roy say behind him. "Then go kiss her feet and beg to know if it's true."

Begging? Daniels feet slowed. Was that what he'd been doing? No, he wouldn't beg. Begging wouldn't help. It didn't help him keep his mother, and it wouldn't help now. He had too much dignity to beg. He just needed to know. Daniel paused. He leaned against a nearby wall for a second, holding one of the bottles of cold beer to his forehead. He needed Cassie. It was dangerous to need someone as much as he needed her.

Daniel went to find Cassie, taking the roundabout way back to give himself a minute to get it together. He found his route blocked by a group of guys trying to spout a keg of beer, almost directly behind Cassie and her new cause. He couldn't get past the guys but could easily hear their conversation. At the words coming from the silly girl, Daniel had stopped dead in his tracks.

"So, is it true?"

"Is what true?" Cassie asked.

"What they say about black men. Do they 'do it' better?"

Daniel stood his ground, closing his eyes as he awaited Cassie's answer. Stunned, he heard no reply. Her head didn't so much as move with a show of denial or exasperation at such a stupid question.

"Come on, you can tell me. We're friends, remember. Their 'things' really are bigger, right?"

Still, nothing from Cassie.

"I want a taste of that one day myself. You know, I want to be able to say that I've experienced them all. Black, Hispanic, Asian, Indian, Caucasian, I want variety. I not only want to see the world, I want to experience all the men of the world."

Cassie shifted. Was it in agreement or annoyance? When was she going to tell this girl how foolish she sounded? When was she going to say she loved him and nothing else mattered? Let her say she loves me and nothing else matters. Please let her say it. This on top of Roy's revelation was making it very difficult for him to stay calm and rational. He heard a crack, felt liquid dripping down his arm to his elbow. Without realizing it, he had squeezed the plastic cup. He didn't care. He could wash his arm and the shirt he was wearing. The most important thing at the moment was Cassie's answer. The words that would come out of her mouth had to be the right words. Words that would disprove his doubts. He needed to hear that love was the reason she was with him. He needed to hear that there was no other reason, that she loved him as much as he loved her.

"Of course," the girl went on, "before I get started I could use some background information. So tell me, is he good?"

Watching and listening to the girl burned a hole in his stomach. Witnessing Cassie do and say nothing burned a hole in his heart. The fear he held deep down that no one really wanted him for himself worked its way to the surface. After a long silence, Cassie finally did say something, but not one word from her lips gave a bit of evidence that she had any love in her heart for him. Her words were soft, almost unemotional, so soft Daniel almost missed them. But he did hear and they allowed cold anger to take over, destroying his love and trust for good.

"Better than you'll ever know," was all she had to say.

"Then he's worth keeping, not to mention that you won the bet."

"Oh, the bet—"

Those were the last words out of Cassie's mouth that he heard before he backed away.

She knew about it. She had participated. And what exactly did she mean by, "Better than you'll ever know?" She had chosen those words to show how she felt about him. It was all clear. She didn't mention love because she had never loved him. An intense feeling of betrayal exploded within him. He could almost feel it on his skin. He put what was left of the drinks down with controlled fury and went outside into the darkness where he replayed the scene over and over. Cassie had proven that his doubts were real. This was the bit of evidence that showed that she didn't love him—that she did not want him for himself. He was a bet, a prize. She would desert him when she got tired of him.

No, she wouldn't get the chance.

It was over.

Hours later, Cassie found him, her innocent facade firmly in place, and they wordlessly left the party. Daniel slept with her that night. He wouldn't call it making love. No, he slept with her and left when he was done without offering any explanation. Cassie knew what she'd done. He'd let her figure out exactly when and how he had found out. What was important was that *he* knew and had taken action to protect himself and his pride. For over three years now, his pride had been his only comfort. He wouldn't count that lapse with Cassie a few months ago as anything more than a release of sexual tension.

CHAPTER 2

"Why did I do it?" The question zigged- zagged across Cassie's brain, bringing her to full consciousness.

Why?

It had happened just a few months ago. Cassie felt, once again, the overwhelming relief of discovering Daniel alive after that miraculous landing at Hobby, despite last minute problems with the landing gear. Over a hundred people owed him their lives.

Home that day, Cassie had seen the footage on TV. After a frantic trip to the hospital, she had been relieved to find Daniel sitting on a stretcher in the emergency room. The only evidence of any injury was a bandage covering a long row of stitches that closed a wide gash across his forehead. She'd felt almost giddy with relief.

Surprisingly, Daniel had accepted her offer to drive him home, probably due to a combination of the doctor's threat to keep him overnight and the pain medication he'd been given. Cassie's plan was to put him to bed then go home, but he had been so groggy and disoriented, she had decided to spend the night. In the middle of the night, she'd awakened on the sofa to find Daniel wandering around the apartment.

"I want—"

"What?" she had asked, somehow knowing what he wanted because she wanted it, too.

"I want you," he had said.

Amazing, she'd thought. It had to be the medicine talking. The fact that he had actually spoken to her and ridden in her car had already been too much to believe. Cassie had decided to let the night happen. She couldn't deny Daniel because she wanted him too, more than wanted him. She needed to touch him, to feel him one more time. As if it were yesterday, she remembered it all.

"I need you, Cass," Daniel had said in a whisper.

Cassie had followed him, not thinking twice about her actions. It had felt so right, so natural to be with him again. The gentle pressure of a single finger moving from the nape of her neck, down past her shoulders, completely froze her body, then melted it as her muscles changed from solid to a malleable semi-liquid form that Daniel could and did shape at his leisure. The night had been exactly what she wanted. Cassie hadn't started it, but she'd known what she was doing. She had been trying to get her heart back.

Now, wide awake, she lay in her bed and thought about her current situation. Up until now, she'd stayed away from Daniel, had been doing a good job of it, with Melanie's help, of course. Today had been a shock to her system.

Having a sudden craving for milk and Oreos, Cassie got up and went to raid the kitchen, not bothering to turn on any lights. Melanie's penchant for neatness guaranteed that there was no chance of stumbling in the dark hallway.

Using only the light from the fridge, she found a glass and rummaged in the cupboard for Melanie's stash of Oreo cookies. After following a healthy diet for the last few months, her body demanded a sugar fix tonight.

She had just finished off the first sinfully delicious chocolate confection when Melanie walked in with her arms full and laughing as she slammed the door on what looked like a gorgeous giant.

"Go back to work," Melanie laughed through the closed door.

There was a quick succession of knocks, then the sound of heavy footsteps retreating from the door.

"Cassie, what are you doing up?" Melanie charged into the kitchen, full of obvious energy.

"Couldn't sleep."

"Finally broke down, huh?" Melanie asked, setting a bag on the kitchen counter and snatching an Oreo for herself. "All that healthy eating is great, but you gotta live once in a while."

"That's exactly what I told myself. But look." Cassie lifted her half empty glass high. "I only broke down halfway. Milk, it does a body good!" she quoted the often heard phrase on TV.

"How about going all the way?" Melanie asked, lifting a half gallon of rocky road ice cream from one of the bags. "I bought some of the fat free stuff, too," she added, taking the other half gallon out of another bag.

"Mel, don't tempt me."

"It's got milk in it." She waved the carton. "Calcium for strong teeth and bones."

"...and marshmallows, and nuts loaded with fat."

"Don't forget the swirls of heavenly chocolate syrup that land on your tongue with every spoonful."

That did it. "I can't resist. Hand over the good stuff."

Melanie found two spoons as Cassie opened the carton. They dug into the ice cream with gusto, pausing to enjoy an Oreo now and then.

"Too much. I give," Cassie surrendered. "All that chocolate is going to put my body into shock."

"You're entitled. One shock to counter the other."

"M-m-m-m," Cassie answered, grabbing a bottle of spring water from the fridge.

"M-m-m-m, is all you have to say? My friend, I know what seeing Daniel did to you today. I'm not blind."

Melanie flipped the switch, flooding the kitchen with light.

Cassie covered her eyes against the bright flash and kept them covered longer than it took for her pupils to adjust. She needed time for her brain to adjust to the shift in topics. She would never consider Melanie blind to anything. Cassie's love for Daniel—now that was blind. But her love was also true and strong and causing her even more heartache.

"I don't want to talk about Daniel," Cassie told Mel, grabbing an Oreo, twisting it apart and scraping the cream with a finger.

"I know you don't. That's why tomorrow you're going to join me at my parents' house for Thanksgiving dinner where you won't have to think about him for one minute."

"Wait a second, Mel. You told me to face him. I still haven't completely forgiven you for what you did to me. You forced me to bite the bullet."

"At the time, it was exactly what you needed to do. Now you need to put Fly Boy out of your mind, let thoughts of him lay low until you're ready to deal with him again."

"That's the problem. I don't want to have to deal with him. Not now, not ever."

"Cass, you'll have to eventually."

"Not necessarily."

"Don't lie to yourself, my friend. I've helped you run away from him long enough."

"We're back to biting the bullet again."

"You have to do it, Cass."

"Why? Everything inside tells me to run away from him."

"Because you don't want to run away from him."

"Ha!" Cassie gave a short laugh, throwing the empty water bottle into the trash, her back to her best friend to hide the lie on her face.

"If you did, you'd be gone already."

"Where?"

"Back to New Orleans. Back to your aunt and uncle."

"I have a *job* here, friends—"

"—and a man you can't seem to forget."

Cassie sat at the kitchen table. "A man I can't seem to forget," she slowly repeated.

Melanie sat across from her. "I can't figure out what you find so good about Fly Boy, but I guess there's gotta be something there."

"There is," Cassie admitted.

"Then you know what you have to do."

"I know."

"Bite the bullet," they said together.

"Now, ya' talking. Did I tell you about the new security guard downstairs?"

Melanie asked, pulling Cassie down the hall for a chat session.

"The one you slammed the door on?"

"That's the one. Wasn't he fine..."

For the next hour, Cassie enjoyed Melanie's graphic description of her encounter with the security guard. Oreo cookies, rocky road ice cream and thoughts of Daniel mixed and churned, keeping her up long after Melanie's attempt to divert her mind.

CHAPTER 3

"Daniel, you didn't forget that box Mama packed for you, did you?"

"What do you think's in that huge canvas bag Scott's pulling out of the van?" Daniel asked his cousin Vanessa. He lifted his leather carry-on onto his shoulder.

"It was good to finally see you again, cuz," Ness told Daniel, giving him a hug that sent shots of guilt through him. Vanessa, known as Ness by all their family, was his favorite cousin. It had been nearly three years since he'd seen her last, at her wedding, a wedding he had warned his cousin would lead to a disastrous marriage.

He couldn't have been more wrong. Scott and Ness were happily married. The doom Daniel had predicted for their interracial marriage was way off the mark. Scott and Vanessa proved that some couples can make a life together despite difficulties or differences. Daniel had made a special trip to New Orleans to stop Ness from marrying a white man. He was glad she hadn't listened to him.

"I hope you had a good time. The family, especially Ness, was glad to see you again," Scott said, shaking Daniel's hand with a gray-eyed stare, one that suggested the beginnings of a wary friendship.

He couldn't blame the guy. Daniel hadn't made his feelings a secret back then. This visit home put to rest any concerns Daniel had that Scott might hurt his cousin the same way he himself had been hurt. He wouldn't want Ness to have gone through the same feelings of being used.

"I'm glad I came. It was good to see everybody." He wrapped his arms around Ness for a hug. "Especially you, Ness, and it gave me a chance to meet my new cousins." He had four new cousins in all. Vanessa was a step-mom. Scott's girls, Vicki and Megan, from a previous marriage, waved back enthusiastically from the van. The babies Kacey and Kyle were fast asleep and couldn't see the smile or the wave Daniel gave before turning back to his cousin. Scott and Ness were the proud parents of identical twins. The boys were obviously loved by their parents and everyone else in their huge family. The babies had been passed back and forth on Thanksgiving Day at his Aunt Joyce and Uncle Cal's house. Daniel had even had a turn with Kacey, or maybe it was Kyle. He couldn't tell. They both had curly dark brown hair and gray eyes like Scott. Their turned up noses and wide mouth were from Ness.

Daniel had enjoyed holding the baby, making silly sounds and playing with him, but it had made him wonder what a child made by him and Cassie would look like. Who was he kidding? He threw that daydream away in a hurry.

"You could try to come back more often," Ness was saying.

"That might be a good idea," he told her, not committing to anything.

"Christmas would be a good time."

"Maybe."

"Then there's Mardi Gras in February."

"Mardi Gras?"

"Yeah. You remember: the floats, the bands, the partying. You can stay with us next time instead of a hotel."

Daniel glanced at Scott who'd climbed into the van. "How does your husband feel about that?"

"Scott? He wouldn't mind. He doesn't hold grudges. Besides, you're family."

"I'll let you know."

"I'll take that as a yes. If you don't come at Christmas, you have to be here for Mardi Gras. Monica will have the triplets by then."

"That's right." Daniel shook his head in amazement, still surprised at coming home to find his "I'll never marry again" older cousin Monica not only married, but expecting.

"No promises, Ness," he told her, putting on the hard look he hadn't worn since leaving Houston four days ago.

"I hate when you screw your face up like that, Danny. I'll call you and talk you into it. Have a safe trip." She kissed him on the cheek and hopped into the van.

Daniel gave a short wave. The hard mask melted as he watched Vicki and Megan blow kisses to him through the back window.

As he checked his luggage, a replay of the last time he'd done that clicked into his mind. Daniel knew that he shouldn't want to, that he shouldn't need to, but he hoped that he'd see Cassie again, talk to her without that friend of hers around. He had already broken that vow of never talking to her again, and seeing Scott and Ness together—well—it was giving him ideas.

Hope?

Maybe.

He made his way to Concourse B, his leather carry-on planted on his shoulder, a feeling of complete comfort settling over him. Not that he hadn't been comfortable during his visit. He had been as comfortable as you could get with dozens of aunts, uncles, and cousins, even the little ones, questioning his single status.

He didn't regret coming home for a visit, he could even go as far as saying that this was the first real Thanksgiving he'd had in years. His usual Thanksgiving was a turkey dinner "to go" from one of Houston's fine restaurants and a solitary day of watching football on TV. He wondered how Cassie celebrated the holiday.

They hadn't been together long enough to share a Thanksgiving, not that it mattered.

Walking through the crowd of travelers, he soaked in the essence of the airport terminal. An airport terminal had been home to him for a long time. Whether he was at New Orleans International Airport or Houston's own Hobby Airport, it didn't matter. Wherever he flew, the bustle in the terminals, the farewells, the looks of satisfaction when people departed and anticipation of others upon arrival, was a high. Energy pulsed everywhere.

Airport workers were special people, friendly and open. It probably had to do with having the opportunity to meet so many people from so many different places. He didn't know. What Daniel did know was that it was all part of his world.

Finding his way to Concourse B, Daniel was annoyed to discover that he was having problems keeping a stoic expression on his face. He stood in one place for a minute, concentrated, and when he was satisfied that he had regained some control, slowly walked in a semicircle, studying the stores at this end of the terminal. He read the signs as he moved, his eyes intent on each name. W.H. Smith News and Gifts, Wilson's Leather Goods, a restaurant called Bag-a-Beignet. None of them interested him. His eyes landed on a sign that was purely New Orleans, The Creole Kitchen. A large display of Godiva chocolates caught his attention. Cassie would love those.

This was crazy. Every and anything was throwing Cassie into his head. He must be a glutton for punishment, he thought. His eyes scanned a music store, The House of Blues, and Water Stone's Booksellers. Daniel didn't think he could deal with reading a thing right now.

His short journey ended at a tiny shop tucked away in a corner. The store, Scenes of New Orleans, drew him like a magnet. Both he and Cassie had been born in New Orleans. As soon as he walked into the small store, he knew what her reaction to this tiny store would be. "Pure bliss." Her words, not his.

On the walls were beautifully framed woodgraph reproductions of nostalgic New Orleans. They were wood carved pieces placed inside a frame to create unique scenes that were not painted, but carved. The detailed carvings jumped out at him, pulling him into the essence of the old city.

"Good morning, sir," a young woman at the register greeted him.

"Uh, morning," Daniel grunted, absorbed in the recreation of so many familiar places of long ago and today. There was a carving of a woman holding an umbrella and a child wearing an old-fashioned bonnet, strolling past the St. Louis Cathedral and the Cabilldo. The Old French Market was depicted, along with free people of color and slaves selling and trading goods. Cassie would love this store, these unusual wood-carved figures and scenes. He stared with deep appreciation at a jazz duo, trumpet and sax, playing in a classic French Quarter Courtyard surrounded by huge green leaves and flowers and a gurgling fountain.

The carvings were so familiar and so lifelike, Daniel couldn't wait to see the next one. There were wood carvings of Arnaud's, Antoine's, and Brennan's, all famous New Orleans restaurants.

Daniel's favorite was a large carving named *When the Saints*... The image of a large jazz band sprang into life. The brown faces of the trumpet, cello, banjo, and piano players were frozen with a look of pure enjoyment of the music bursting from their instruments. The audience was depicted only by hands that appeared to be clapping and heads that he could have sworn were bopping to the tune.

"Can I help you with anything?" the clerk asked directly behind him.

Daniel, without turning around answered. "No, thanks, I'm just looking." He felt too vulnerable to gaze into a stranger's face.

And he looked some more. In a corner he found a woodgraph that stopped his wandering eye. A dark green cable car sat on the tracks of the street car line. It seemed to be impatiently waiting for a passenger, a girl in a long, old-fashioned dress. Daniel could almost hear the engine roar as the girl, frozen in time, hopped on board for a forbidden ride. This seemed to be a day of dwelling on everything Cassie. She had told him about the secret street car rides she took with her cousin T every Sunday; rides her aunt and uncle, who raised her, would have forbidden.

Cassie and her cousin would hop on the St. Charles street car less than a block from their house and ride all the way downtown and back. They'd sneak back into the house without being missed. It was the thrill and the risk she had enjoyed. Daniel figured that's why she'd gotten involved with him, the thrill and the risk.

Despite the hurt, despite the pain, there were other memories and emotions he had covered up a long time ago that were now rising to the surface. The memory of a stormy Sunday evening flooded his senses. The darkened sky had turned day into night. Cassie had spread cocoa butter lotion on her hands and massaged his temples, his scalp, his neck, shoulders, every single body part that was his. Cassie had said that she wanted to touch all of him. She had, in more ways than one. She was the only woman who had ever touched his soul. He should thank her for that at least. She *had* given him the best six months of his life. But he also wanted to curse her for it.

Daniel took a deep breath. He could almost smell the scent of the lotion she had rubbed all over him that long ago Sunday just before they'd made love all evening long. Afterwards, they'd shared secrets, as most lovers do. The woodgraph before him reminded him of that unforgettable evening of love and shared secrets.

At that moment, Daniel realized that even though Cassie had

hurt him, he could never hate her. He'd tried, but he couldn't.

"Have you found one you like, sir?"

"Yes," he answered without turning. "I'll take this one."

He held the woodgraph securely wrapped and bagged in his hand as he walked to his gate. Not until after the plane landed in Houston did he tuck it carefully inside his leather carry-on.

Cassie was doing great. She hadn't thought about Daniel the whole five minutes it took to walk to the restroom in the terminal, use the facilities, and walk out the door again.

She took three steps forward and froze. He stood not ten feet from her, leaning against a wall, engrossed in what looked like a stack of pictures. Her body refused to move. Cassie knew there was some reason she should avoid him, but, at this moment, that reason was being pushed aside by the overwhelming need she had to stare at him, to take in the beauty and strength of his face. She stood, wishing that she were free to erase that frown, change it into the easygoing smile he had once allowed to develop whenever she'd joke with him. Or the seductive "come to me grin" after she'd spent an hour massaging him from head to toe. That was the one she loved the most, because it was exclusively hers.

Standing here, in the middle of the busy ticketing center, Cassie unashamedly longed for that smile. That longing kept her stuck in Houston. As she stood rooted, her mind opened to other memories. Memories of the sweet lovemaking that had always followed that smile. Lovemaking that had gotten her in the bind she was in now. Cassie looked down. She closed her eyes and groaned at her own stupidity. The reason for avoiding him was more than clear again. If she were lucky, she could get away without Daniel noticing her.

Lifting her head and slowly opening her eyes, she met his green gaze. His expression still looked hard, but his eyes seemed to change. They shone bright with pleasure. Was he *pleased* to see her? Then his eyes did something Cassie wished they hadn't. They looked down then grew as wide as the blue skies Daniel loved to fly.

Now he knew.

Cassie stared right back at him a whole two seconds before doing the only thing she could think of. She spun around and ran back into the restroom, the only available sanctuary.

Cassie's pregnant, and that's my baby! Daniel felt the pictures slip through his fingers as he watched her go. That look of guilt and the mere fact that she had run confirmed it.

Without a second thought, he followed her into the heavily populated women's restroom.

"Undercover airport security," he announced. "Everybody please exit the restroom," he boomed. "Sorry about the inconvenience, but there are other facilities available for your use." The room quickly emptied, with the exception of Cassie and one insolent woman who took her time exiting a stall. Daniel moved over to her and whispered. "This is a matter of life or death. I suggest you leave."

The short round woman slowly looked him up and down before calmly turning her back to him proceeding to wash her hands.

"Then why is she still in here?" the lady asked, nodding her head toward Cassie. "And why is she grinning from ear to ear? Looks like a lovers' spat to me."

Daniel turned and saw Cassie at the far end of the restroom, and, sure enough, she was doing exactly what the woman had said.

His frown deepened. What did she have to grin about?

Probably the joy of dropping such a bomb on him. Unbelievable. This was all completely unbelievable. At first surprised, now he was furious. So furious he felt a growl gather deep in his throat. It must have come out, because Cassie stopped grinning and the round woman glanced over her shoulder with a touch of concern.

Good.

Let them both worry: the woman, because he wanted her gone; Cassie, because she deserved to. How could she keep such a secret and stand there grinning?

The round woman finally turned the faucet off. Daniel leaned in closer. "Looks can be deceiving. That young woman over there appears to be pregnant, but in truth, she may be carrying millions of dollars worth of stolen drugs. The people she stole it from could walk through this door any minute. You don't want to be caught in the middle. As smug as she looks, she probably thinks she's going to get away with it, too."

The round woman was gone before Daniel could say another word.

Cassie narrowed her eyes at him, holding her head high. She'd obviously heard every word and didn't appreciate it. This was the Cassie he was used to, not the woman who had run from him a few minutes ago. Though he was relieved to see her stand up to him, that relief didn't ease his anger.

What he didn't appreciate was discovering in the middle of the airport ticketing center that he was going to be a father. Now that he thought about it, he was lucky to have found out at all. He could feel his face tighten, his frown deepen, if that were possible. Taking two long strides he stood before her.

"How could you do this to me?"

"What choice did I have?"

"What choice? What choice?" he repeated. She was talking about choices. Well, he wasn't giving her any.

"You're right, Cassie. You don't have a choice. We're getting married."

"When hell freezes over and every inhabitant repents and grow wings!" Cassie answered without hesitation.

He laughed.

Cassie couldn't believe it. The anger that had filled the restroom with tension had deflated with the sound of his laughter, though remnants were still there. Daniel had always been quick to lose his temper, but also quick to cool down.

At this moment, Cassie's emotions were a mess. She had gone from desire the moment she set eyes on him, to fear when he discovered her secret, and to amusement at the lengths he went to to clear the restroom. But she was not amused enough to join in with his laughter. The subject was too serious. Marry him? That was exactly what she had always wanted, but not like this.

"It wasn't that funny, Daniel."

"What you just said? Yes, it was. This whole situation? I can't find one thing funny about it," he said in a soft whisper staring down at her.

"Neither can I," Cassie answered in a voice just as quiet, wishing she were tall enough to stare down at him.

"That's my baby you're carrying."

"I never said it wasn't."

"You never opened your mouth to say that it was either."

"Daniel, I was going to tell you."

"When?"

"When? Why does it matter? I don't matter to you, so what difference would it have made?"

"It matters. Everything matters."

For a second, Cassie took that statement to heart. Everything mattered, even her? But no, Daniel hadn't meant her. Of course everything else *would* matter. He was the type of man who took care of what was his. That was the reason she'd hid from him to begin with. Cassie didn't want to face the fact that Daniel would want his baby but not her.

"I know it does," she whispered so softly that she could feel Daniel move in closer to hear her.

It was strange. He stood over her, his closeness somehow easing some of the heartache that he'd caused by his desertion. Cassie didn't move. She couldn't even if she wanted to. Daniel was where she wanted him, standing over her, offering comfort, offering marriage, but not love. That last thought loosened her limbs, and she stepped back just as a long finger made its way from the nape of her neck down to her back and across her shoulder with a gentle, familiar touch that created an explosion of sensations.

Cassie heard her name as Daniel leaned forward to find her lips. She felt breathless as he drew the love she felt for him forward. Every part of her, every bit of love she felt for him went into that kiss. He pulled it all out of her with gentle nibbles and a long, deep connection.

"You lost some things, Fly Boy," Melanie said, casually leaning against the door, holding his leather carry on in one hand and a photo envelope in the other.

Her friend's intrusion ended the kiss, but Cassie didn't move away. Neither did Daniel.

"... and you scared a whole lot of people out there," Melanie told him, walking over to hand him his things.

"I told you to *bite* the bullet, not kiss it like you're never gonna let it go," Melanie whispered to Cassie.

Cassie gave her friend a weak smile.

"Thanks, you can go now," Daniel told her.

"I intend to, but you might want to do the same. Some woman ran out of here in hysterics. She's talking to security. I think they're out there calling for backup or something. Now that's something you created and have to deal with, Fly Boy." Melanie turned to Cassie. "Check you later, my friend," she said before walking out the door.

"Thanks, Mel." Cassie understood loud and clear her friend's double meaning.

Daniel grunted. "She doesn't like me."

"You don't like her either."

"Untrue. I don't like her smart mouth. You always chose the strangest people to hang around with, Cass."

"I chose you."

"Yes, you did," he agreed, pulling away with a frown.

What did she say wrong? Did his reaction mean he wished she'd never chosen him? Cassie didn't want to know. "Bye, Daniel, I have to get back to work."

"You can't go yet."

"Mel's covering for me. She can't do that forever."

"We still have to talk."

"I'm sure we will," Cassie told him, a sadness in her voice at the loss of the tender look he had given her earlier.

At this moment, he looked like the Daniel of old, the Daniel who didn't laugh or smile or know how to live life to the fullest.

"I meant what I said, Cass. We're going to get married."

"And I meant what I said. I haven't seen any angels rising yet." Cassie moved toward the bathroom door as she spoke.

Daniel was right behind her. His hands landed on either shoulder. He turned her around, his fingers reaching for the base of her neck. "Listen to me, Cassie. You can't raise a baby alone without a father. Especially this baby."

"What do you mean by 'this baby?'"

"You know exactly what I mean. You can't raise a black child alone."

"Correct me if I'm wrong, but I'm white. This baby that I'm carrying is half mine. That makes him or her half white."

"That's not the way society looks at it!" he yelled, throwing his hands up high, causing the pictures that he had been holding to fly into the air and across the restroom floor.

A voice invaded the room. "Airport security. Come out or we're coming in."

Daniel moved to the door. The fact that he knew the men on the other side was obvious. Cassie distanced herself from the conversation taking place at the door. She stood in the middle of the restroom, clasping against her chest a few of the pictures that had come raining down on them. She looked through them now. The first was of a large group of people of almost every age sitting around a huge table. These were obviously pictures taken during the Thanksgiving holiday. There were a few others of people laughing, one of a group of kids and adults dancing. All with Daniel smiling in the background. There was one picture in particular that disturbed her. Daniel was hugging a beautiful woman. She was almost as tall as Daniel something Cassie could never claim to be. She had a pair of amazing, laughing eyes. Eyes that looked up at Daniel with love. Jealously hit her hard because Daniel was looking at the woman in the picture in the same way. The woman had skin the color of caramel and short black hair. Was she the reason Daniel had gone home? Could Cassie compete against such a beautiful black woman? Did she even want to try?

Attempting to block that picture out of her mind, Cassie turned to the next one in her hand. The woman was in this picture, too, but instead of hugging Daniel, she had her arms around a handsome white man with curly, dark blond hair. Each of them held a baby with curly, dark brown hair. They were obviously children of mixed parentage. Two adorable little girls, who were white, also stood in the photo. They looked like a beautiful family, definitely different, but beautiful just the same.

A sudden sense of relief relaxed her entire body. Daniel wasn't involved with the beautiful woman. The woman, if she had gotten it right, was married to the man in the picture. They even had a set of twins. The little girls, she wasn't sure of.

The last picture Cassie turned to caused her heart to pound, and her eyes to water. Daniel sat in a porch swing holding one of the babies in his lap and looked to be fast asleep. He must have been rocking the baby, but the swing seemed to have lulled the wrong person into slumber. The baby was reaching for a prize, the last button on Daniel's polo shirt, as someone snapped the shot.

This baby was the product of an interracial couple. From the picture, Cassie couldn't help seeing signs of care and concern Daniel showed for the baby in the firm grip he had on the baby, even as he slept. Would he do less for their baby? Whatever racial barrier Daniel had in his mind hadn't stopped him from holding and caring for the little baby in the picture.

Going through the pictures again, Cassie studied each one. There were both white and black people in the pictures, sharing the holiday together, and Daniel was in the midst of it all. Was this enough to conclude that he didn't have a problem with white people, only her? Cassie wished she knew.

"Give me two minutes," she heard Daniel say, "and we'll clear out."

Daniel turned back toward her. Cassie didn't know what to say. She didn't know what to think. They were at a standstill.

"Here are your pictures. I couldn't get the ones on the floor."

"I wouldn't expect you to. That's not good for you or the baby."

"That's nice of you to say so."

"It's the truth." Daniel paused as if he didn't know what to say. "Look, Cass, we have to get out of here, but we need to talk. We need to discuss the baby, our marriage. I'll pick you up at eight tonight."

"I don't have any plans to marry you, Daniel."

"You don't have a choice."

"I do. To be fair, I'll see you tonight, but you need to come prepared."

"Prepared? Prepared for what?"

Cassie walked to the door, this time not allowing him to stop her. "Prepared with reasons why I should even *consider* marrying you."

CHAPTER 4

Reasons! She wanted reasons! Reason number one, I love you. Reason number two, my life hasn't been the same without you. Reason number three, fool that I am, I want to spend the rest of my life with you.

But what kind of man would want to spend the rest of his life with a woman who had used him as an experiment, had used him to win a bet—one who was a glutton for punishment. Whether or not he wanted to be, a fool; Daniel knew he'd never be able to trust Cassie, but still, he loved her.

Why else had one glance at her as he sat in the emergency room been his undoing. She had been wearing shorts and a t-shirt and had her hair up and her neck bare, waiting to be caressed. The crash, a near disaster, had rattled him, and suddenly, she had been there for him. He had wanted her, as always. What had happened that night had been inevitable.

And because of that night, they had a baby on the way. Reason enough to get married, he'd say. It was the reason he was going to give anyway. He'd get her to marry him and make sure his baby was going to be loved by its father. The only thing that could possibly keep him away would be his job. Being an airline pilot meant spending much time away from home. But maybe he could do something about that.

Dressed in jeans and t-shirt, Daniel left his apartment and hopped into his Stealth. He'd have to get another car. A man with a family needed a much larger vehicle. Just remembering all the stuff Scott and Ness had with them on Thanksgiving Day made him shudder. Ness, he suddenly realized, would get a kick out of his situation. Daniel, her favorite cousin, who had claimed he would never get married, who had tried to convince her not to marry a white man, was going to do whatever it took to marry a white woman that he had been crazy in love with for three long years. Almost as long as Ness had been married herself. Life is ironic, he thought, parking the car and going into the apartment complex.

As Daniel waited at the elevator, he heard rapid words in Spanish coming from the apartment behind him. Cassie lived close to Hobby Airport in a neighborhood with a strong Hispanic culture. She seemed to love to be around people who were different from her.

When the elevator arrived, luck was not on his side. Melanie slid out of with her arms wrapped around a giant of a man. He nodded at her in greeting as he moved into the elevator. Though she was flat chested and skinny as a bean pole, she oozed sexuality. It was that part of her personality that had always made him step back.

"Hey, Fly Boy."

And the fact that she persisted in calling him that stupid name.

"Daniel. It's Daniel," he muttered through clenched teeth.

"That's the first time you ever told me that."

"It's about time, don't you think?"

"Yes, it is. It's about time for a lot of things. Don't hurt my friend anymore than you already have Fly—Daniel."

The elevator doors shut off any other piece of advice she had for him. Hurt Cassie? Melanie had her information all wrong. The elevator took him to the third floor in no time, and his feet automatically led him to the right door. This was familiar territory.

Daniel hoped his tongue would just as easily form the right words. He rang the doorbell.

"Who is it?" Cassie's voice came through the door.

"Daniel."

The door opened, and Cassie stood before him barefoot, wearing, his mind registered, one of her favorite hang around dresses. It had to be at least four years old. It was wide enough to fit her expanding stomach, but so short it barely reached her knees. She wore no makeup, and her hair was in a careless ponytail. Cassie didn't look like she was ready to go anywhere. She looked tired, beautifully tired.

Daniel stopped himself from pulling her toward him, comforting her, and kissing her as he'd done earlier today. He wanted to erase that look of exhaustion from her eyes and replace it with desire. If there was anything she had ever felt for him, it was desire. That he was sure of.

Daniel followed her inside. "I take it that you're not ready to go."

"You should take it as I'm not in the mood to go anywhere or do anything tonight."

"You're not sick, are you?" he asked, suddenly worried about her and the baby's health. There were a lot of things that could go wrong during a pregnancy. He had heard about them, or seen it on TV or something.

She sat down on the sofa in the small living room. "Just tired. I can't deal with going out tonight, Daniel. Let's just talk and get this over with. What are your reasons?" Cassie was more than tired. She was exhausted.

"You don't sound like you're ready to hear reasons. You don't sound as if you're even open to the idea of marriage."

"I'm about as open as I'm ever going to be on the subject."

"That's not good enough." He frowned down at her.

"It's going to have to be. I'm pregnant, and I'm tired from standing on my feet all day. And stop frowning down at me like that. That's all you've done since I saw you earlier this week."

Daniel felt his facial muscles relax. "That's not all I've done," Daniel answered his tone lowering an octave as he sat next to her. He hadn't meant to say that. His tongue was moving in the wrong direction. He only wanted to give her some cold, hard facts, the reality of being a single mother. But seeing Cassie like this, so tired, so exhausted, so grumpy, so unlike herself, he all at once wanted to do something for her.

"Lie back, Cass, so that I can massage your feet."

"That's not necessary," she answered, sitting completely straight, her toes reaching for the floor.

"I think it is. It'll help you relax. Then we'll talk, and I'll be on my way."

She looked up at him, studying his face, probably wondering if he had an ulterior motive.

"Okay," was all she said.

Daniel scooted over to the far end of the sofa. Cassie leaned back on her elbows at the other end, stiff as a board. Why had she said yes? Allowing Daniel to touch her was a big mistake. A whatever-you-do-don't-stop-because-this-feels-too-good mistake. Cassie laid her head on the arm of the sofa, and her whole body slowly eased into relaxation. It started at the tips of her toes, moved up her legs, even eased the tension in her stomach muscles that were clenched with anxiety, and then branched out to the rest of her body in no time. Cassie was so loose, so comfortable, she felt as if she were floating, watching the scene from above. Beneath her closed lids, an image of Daniel massaging her feet became sharp and focused in her mind. He held her foot firmly, gently kneading up and down, using his long, brown fingers to create a path of relief that was quickly turning into desire.

Desire?

What did she desire?

She desired that Daniel forget about her feet. Daniel moved his hands up her calves and behind her knees, lingering for a minute or two, his fingers brushing side to side before caressing her thighs, reaching higher and higher to find her—The baby moved.

"What?" Daniel asked, a startled expression on his face. When Cassie didn't answer, he said, "You said something just now. What was it?"

"I didn't realize I said it out loud. You were doing such a good job of relaxing me." More than relaxing, she thought.

"So, what did you say?"

The baby moved inside her again. "The baby moved," she whispered, a satisfying feeling filling her heart with the opportunity to say that to her baby's father.

"It did? Has it been doing that a lot? Too much? How often is normal? What does the doctor say? The books? Books, Cassie, we need to read lots of books." He spit out the questions rapid fire, staring at her stomach, retaining a death grip on her toes.

"Daniel!" she squeaked, "my toes!"

"Mm-m," he answered as he slowly released his painful grip, keeping his eyes trained on her stomach.

"You won't be able to see the baby move. Not through my clothes anyway. Not that I'm taking them off or anything."

He looked up at her face then. Cassie felt so stupid. Here sat the love of her life, who had touched every part of her body, yet she was nervous because she didn't want to give him the wrong idea. What was the wrong idea? She didn't know anymore.

All she wanted was to be loved. She wanted Daniel to love her. She wanted Daniel to love their baby. As if in complete agreement with her thoughts, the baby moved again. Cassie took both of Daniel's hands and placed them on her stomach. His eyes lit up. There were no frown lines marring his face. At that moment, Cassie knew she was lost to him. She'd marry Daniel and they'd raise their baby together. But along the way, she would discover what had taken him away from her and kept them apart for so long.

"Cass," Daniel whispered. "This is my reason. Our baby. *Our baby*, no one else's. We need to put our differences aside and think about our baby."

Cassie couldn't stop her hand from reaching out to touch his face, the tips of her fingers grazing his jaw. "Exactly what are our differences, Daniel?"

"We'll have a lot more to contend with than most people."

"We will," she agreed.

"But we can deal with it, if we tackle one thing at a time."

"I agree."

"What are you saying?"

"That I agree."

Daniel slowly leaned over Cassie, placing an arm on either side of her. "You agree to what?"

His entire body hovered over her, surrounding her without touching. They were talking. The hurt was still there, but they were talking, and actually knew what they were talking about. At least she thought they did.

"I agree to marry you, to raise our baby together. But Daniel, we have to work on us."

"We can do that. It might not be easy."

"Nothing with you has ever been easy, Daniel."

He gave a short laugh. "It might not be easy, but I can't say it won't be enjoyable." He planted a kiss on the side of her neck. Cassie closed her eyes, waiting for more. When there wasn't anymore, she opened her eyes and discovered Daniel staring down at her, a frown once again plastered on his face.

"Why are you frowning now? Didn't I just agree to marry you?"

"I was frowning again?"

"You *are* frowning. I see that I'll have to break you of that habit all over again."

"I have a feeling that you can."

Cassie nodded. "What's the reason?"

"I gave you my reason."

"The reason for the frown."

"I realized that I shouldn't start something that we wouldn't be able to finish."

So, he didn't want to make love to her. Cassie didn't question this, simply said, "Oh."

"I'll make all the arrangements. City Hall sound okay to you?"

"Umm, yes." Daniel sounded as if he were making a dental appointment.

"I'll be in touch." Daniel leaned over to plant a kiss on her forehead. "Don't get up. Stay here and rest. I'll put the lock on the door when I leave." He stood over her a few seconds more, a frown still on his face. Then he was gone.

At the sound of the closing door, silent tears began streaming down her face. She had promised to spend the rest of her life with a man who didn't love her. What had gotten into her? Cassie swiped at her face with the palm of her hand.

And she was crying.

Cassie never cried.

She went into the bathroom, dried her face and made a promise to herself. She would know everything before she gave up on the life she wanted with Daniel. If it meant marrying him before he even mentioned love, then she'd deal with it.

CHAPTER 5

One week later Cassie became Mrs. Daniel Adams, and she moved all of her belongings into Daniel's apartment. Unpacking her things and finding room for them beside Daniel's felt natural. She had all but lived in this apartment during their six month relationship.

Now here she stood in that same apartment. The wedding and the small reception Melanie had gotten together was over. Cassie glanced around at the familiar surroundings, yet felt unsure of herself and her future with Daniel. She didn't like this feeling. For that matter, Cassie didn't care for the excess of emotions she'd been experiencing since becoming pregnant. She was grouchy, she cried. She was nervous, she cried. Her emotions were in constant upheaval. What she hated the most was flying from one emotion to the other in front of Daniel.

He had been a very understanding, caring and compassionate fiancé this past week. His actions toward her had been very husband-like. While Daniel hadn't offered to rub her feet again, he had been very solicitous, opening doors for her, taking her out for dinner twice and calling her from the hotel when he had an overnight layover for one of his flights.

Cassie felt cared for, which was a start. She just prayed the care Daniel was showing was for her as well as the baby. He talked about nothing except the baby. Of course, the baby was a safe, mutual topic, but Cassie wanted so much to get back to what they had before. Hours of talking about everything and nothing. Cassie missed touching him and being touched. She would love it if Daniel added some lover-like qualities to the husbandly caring he'd shown. But maybe he didn't want to have anything to do with that part of their relationship.

The doorbell rang. Cassie checked the peephole to discover a wall of silver and white wrapping paper. She opened the door for Daniel. He had gone downstairs to get the presents they had gotten from the few friends who'd come to the reception held at her old apartment.

Neither of them had had any family members present. Cassie would have loved to have her aunt and uncle there. They had raised her after her parents died. And her cousin T was missed, too. Though nine years older than she, he'd taken the responsibility as older cousin/big brother seriously. They'd always kept in touch until recently. Every one of them would be disappointed. Which wasn't a first. No one, not her aunt, uncle or even her cousin had approved of her choice of careers. She'd studied to become an emergency medical technician, despite her Aunt Margaret's protest that she was too short, that constant bending and lifting of patients would ruin her back, not to mention the possible exposure to every disease imaginable. Despite them all, she'd become an EMT but used her certification to help her gain employment as a flight attendant. Airlines were quick to hire people with medical training. So Cassie had fulfilled her need to help people and broken away from her family, for the first time, to live on her own in Houston. This, of course, had disappointed her family even more.

Her wedding hadn't been the sterling silver event they would have wanted. She was five months pregnant, something she hadn't shared with her family yet, and her husband was black. Cassie was going to be full of surprises. But her family would adjust, as they had done before, just as long as she was happy. Man, Cassie wanted to be happy.

"We got quite a number of presents for such short notice."

"We certainly did," Cassie agreed, staring at the huge stack

Daniel placed on the recliner.

"This one," he said, selecting a small gold wrapped present on top of the pile, "is from me to you."

"Oh, Daniel," Cassie said, taking the gift and holding it against the bodice of her cream-colored wedding dress. "I didn't get anything for you." Cassie felt the tears forming in the corners of her eyes. He must have seen them, too.

"You didn't have to, Cass," Daniel told her, hesitantly reaching for her and awkwardly holding her in his arms.

Cassie burrowed into his embrace, clenching the square box between them. It felt so good to make physical contact with him. She wanted to bury herself in his arms.

"Don't get all upset. This is something I found in a shop in New Orleans. It reminded me of you."

"You bought this in New Orleans?"

He nodded.

That was before he knew she was pregnant. Her hopes for happiness rose. She felt more secure, more confident of their future.

"Are you going to open your present, or crush it between us until the paper tears?"

"No, I'm going to open it." Her eyes dried and her spirit lifted. Cassie moved to the sofa, and, not wanting to lose contact, grasped one of Daniel's hands as she sat. Using her lap as a table, Cassie tore the paper away and opened the white box all with one hand. Inside was a wood carved figure of a girl getting ready to hop onto a St. Charles Street Car. The army green cable car seemed to be waiting impatiently for its passenger.

The tears that had disappointed her earlier came back, their need for release too strong for her to control. "You remembered that story. The one I told you about my cousin and me. That was so long ago."

"I remembered," Daniel said, his voice a soft whisper.

The memory of the day she'd told him surged through her brain. "It had been raining, no, storming all morning, and our flight was grounded."

"So you decided to take out the cocoa butter lotion." His voice held a husky quality.

"I love the smell of cocoa butter."

"I do, too," he told her.

More tears filled her eyes at that admission.

"It had better, since you used almost an entire bottle massaging me from head to toe."

"I enjoyed touching you, feeling your muscles beneath my hands."

"That's not all we did," Daniel reminded her.

"No, that's not all," she said. Suddenly she was in his arms. They held her tight. She sighed against his chest. Cassie felt his arms shift and move. Her hair, which she'd taken down after the ceremony, was slowly lifted from her shoulders. Daniel pressed a kiss on her cheek, then the side of her neck. His warm breath softly moved the small hairs at her nape. A lone finger played with the tiny hairs before making its way down her spine. She shuddered.

"I'd like to spend this evening massaging you from scalp to toe. I might even be interested in other things."

"I'd like that." Cassie said a silent thank you for the return of Daniel's lover-like qualities. He had always teased and played with her during lovemaking. It was exactly what she wanted.

"And afterwards, we could share more stories and secrets."

"I'd like that, too."

Daniel stood, towering above her with the same I-love-you-let-me-show-you-how-much look that had always sparked Cassie with an energy to show him how much she loved him. Still grasping his hand, Cassie stood and shifted to keep her balance.

Daniel's face fell, and he dropped her hand. "Cassie, you

don't have to do this if you don't want to." The lost of contact was hurtful. The rejection in both his voice and eyes too much.

"Do what?"

"Sleep with me."

"Is that what we were going to do?"

He nodded. More frown lines formed on his forehead with each passing second.

"Funny, I thought we were going to make love on our wedding night."

"Love?" he questioned. "I didn't think that word had anything to do with what has been going on with us. Desire, wanting, that's about it."

Cassie stood staring up at him. Her gaze fell to her expanding stomach. She was going to love him. She was going to pull Daniel out of himself by showing him how much he loved her. It was the best thing she could do for them. The best thing for their baby. She had no other choice.

Cassie gently placed the woodgraph on the glass coffee table, her thumb tracing the raised figure of the girl. She was that girl, daring and bold as she snuck away on a forbidden ride with her cousin. Drawing strength from that memory and ignoring the part of her that wanted his love out in the open at this very moment, Cassie, instead, drew in her jumbled emotions.

"Daniel, that is exactly what I want to do." She didn't wait for an answer. She didn't stop to study the stunned expression on his face, or take much note of the instant disappearance of frown lines. She led him down the small hall into the bedroom.

Cassie peeled away the long-sleeved dress shirt Daniel had worn with the navy blue suit for the wedding. He wasn't muscular but solid, his muscles as firm as she remembered. The pleasure she was gaining from this tactical exploration was as erotic as she remembered. For a few minutes, Cassie had the freedom to explore and reacquaint herself with his hard, smooth body.

Then Daniel stepped back, away from her touch. Cassie's hand froze in mid-air, level with the waist band of his navy blue pants.

"I can take care of the rest. Meet me on the bed," he rasped.

Cassie hesitated. This was a first. Daniel had always encouraged her to undress him. She sighed inside. Another ploy to stay distant from her. Well, he couldn't make love to her and *stay* distant.

She watched as he attempted to release the clasp on the pair of dress pants. His hands were actually shaking. Cassie moved toward him, ignoring a raspy grunt as she deftly released the clasp slowly, sliding the zipper down. Her hand lingered.

"Cassie," he said through clenched teeth. "You know what you're doing to me."

"Yes, and I don't intend to stop."

"Good," he told her, dropping his head to kiss her.

It began in a frenzy, sending the message, "I want you" and slowed to a steady "You are mine, and I'm yours" kiss that evolved into a gentle tug of war, mellowing into an "I love you, I cherish you kiss." The connection lasted so long Cassie thought she had forgotten how to breathe. But at the soft brush of Daniel's fingers grazing the nape of her neck, air gushed into her lungs. The loving, cherished feelings intensified with the overwhelming need to have Daniel inside her.

Cassie's hands slid down his back, her fingers moving under the elastic of the navy jockey briefs he wore. Matching underwear, she absently thought. Her Daniel. Her fingers moved down his firm rear. At the same time, Daniel found her zipper and wasted no time in sliding it down, all the way down. His hands matched the movements of her own as she caressed and kneaded. Daniel's warm breath at the nape of her neck sent a hot chill down her spine. Her hands stopped as she savored the feeling.

"I win," he whispered smugly, never pausing, never stopping.

"What were we playing? Who could make who lose their concentration first?"

Daniel didn't answer. He, instead, relieved her of her dress, bra, and panties. He laid her carefully on the bed and proceeded to make complete, true, honest love to her. It was pure bliss.

Cassie soaked it all in. His touch, his kisses, the feel of his body surrounding her, filling her, fulfilling her. Then the gentle way he cradled her in his arms after they'd shared the most complete gift of love.

Cassie needed this as a confirmation of the love Daniel had in his heart for her. She would need this to remember when the frown lines and evasive ploys appeared.

She lay beside her husband, his arms around her, cradling her close to him as he slept.

Sighing, she slowly drifted off to sleep as she tried but failed to find a word that would describe exactly how she felt.

Their first week as a married couple couldn't be described as blissful, but it wasn't horrible. Daniel had been assigned non-flying duties the second week in December. He normally had a schedule that caused him to accumulate a large number of flight hours quickly. He was limited to no more than one hundred a month, a standard for most airlines.

Without the hours of flying keeping him away, they were able to spend a lot of time in each other's company. It was what Cassie had hoped for, a situation Daniel dreaded.

They drove to and from work in Daniel's car and spent every evening together. Between them stretched a silence Cassie was finding hard to fill. Daniel barely looked at her or said anything unless they were discussing the baby. Cassie couldn't imagine a man more excited about his child than Daniel was. Cassie decided to use that excitement to pull him closer to her. After all, she *was* the one carrying the baby.

If the baby moved, she made a point of grabbing his hand so that he could feel it. Even if he was across the room. The first time Cassie ran to him and claimed his hand, Daniel nearly snatched it back. His brow furrowed deep with frown lines, until he realized what she wanted. The contact she craved had lasted only seconds. The next time his hand had lingered, waiting for another chance to feel the baby move inside her. Progress was slow, but at least she was making it.

What kept Cassie positive was the nights in his arms. If he avoided touching her during the day, he more than made up for it at night.

Early one morning, Cassie turned to face Daniel, studying her husband's face. He was handsome, almost uniquely so. He had a long face, not narrow, merely perfect for his head. His chin stretched out, narrowing his face even more, but ending with a defiant edge.

Cassie traced from one side of his jaw to the other with the tip of her index finger. Her way of waking him.

His eyes opened, "Cass, oh, morning, baby," he said, pulling her closer to him.

Cassie loved this time of morning. Daniel was not quite awake and without realizing it, was his most affectionate. This was the tender side of him she missed. Each morning, Daniel was letting a little more of his old self slip out. Cassie never said too much, merely allowing him to share as much as he wanted.

"How are you and the little one this morning?" he asked, moving a hand to cover her stomach.

"Fine."

"Good, I was hoping," he kissed her temple, "that I wasn't too rough on you."

"No."

"Then how about a repeat of last night."

"Sounds good," she yawned. More than thrilled with the idea.

"What about an early night in. We can watch a video or two, order dinner . . ."

"Yes, it's a date."

She said yes, Daniel repeated in his head for the thousandth time today as he walked toward the ticketing center. She had said yes as if she meant it. It scared him. What kind of game was she up to now, playing sweet and loving all the time, just like before. Did she think he was going to fall for that innocent routine again?

Ahh, but he had. Why else had he suggested that they purposely spend time together? Six nights straight of having her in his arms had clogged his brain. Six nights straight of loving her, yet hiding from her that what they shared was more than sex. He'd gone off the deep end by making love to her. Every night he showed her that he loved her. He loved her with his hands, his kisses, his body. And she let him. But did that mean she loved him back? Was it just sex to her? Expecting that she was actually willing to give anything more was too risky.

Daniel spotted her talking to Melanie. Cassie's hair was tucked under a Santa Claus hat, her neck exposed and waiting for his touch. The urge was strong, but too risky.

"Come on, Cass. Time to go." He couldn't hold in that touch of annoyance.

"Whatever you say, Daniel." She grinned at him as if they shared some secret and went behind the counter to pick up a large box. He lifted it out of her hands.

"You know better than to try to carry a box this big." He frowned down at her.

"I love it when you remind me," she told him, ignoring his grouchy mood. "That's why I do it."

"Let's go," he growled, shifting the package as if it weighed a ton.

"Looks like Mr. Newlywed is anxious for his date tonight."

"Date? What is she talking about, Cass?" Daniel asked, looking from Cassie to Melanie.

"Don't listen to her, Daniel. Melanie is all mouth," she said, attaching herself to his arm.

Daniel casually dodged her touch and whispered, "Don't discuss our business with her, Cassie. It's ours and no one else's."

"I understand," she said after a second's hesitation, hurt in her eyes. "Bye, Mel, I'll see you next week."

Cassie walked on ahead of him, not even looking back to see if he was coming. What was he now, her lap dog?

Despite that feeling, Daniel wanted to call her back. To apologize for his rudeness. But, instead, he kept his mouth shut. This was just the way he wanted it. He didn't want Cassie all over him, touching him whenever she wanted. It would make it even harder to deal with losing her if things didn't work out. He shifted the heavy box and went to follow her.

"Daniel," Melanie's voice stopped him.

"What?" he asked, turning his head slightly.

"I think you've earned a new title, immature boy."

Daniel grunted, a part of him knowing it was true.

He found Cassie at the car. She was leaning against the passenger door with her arms folded at her chest. She looked so small and tired.

He wanted to know what she was thinking but didn't ask. Instead, he unlocked the door with one hand while balancing the box with the other. "What am I supposed to do with this?"

"I don't know, you figure it out." Cassie made herself comfortable in the passenger seat.

Daniel spent the next ten minutes trying to stuff a box the size of a small TV into the cramped space in the trunk. He really needed another car. Some rope held the box in place; hopefully luck would keep it there.

Daniel got into the car. Though the silence was exactly what he wanted and expected, he found himself completely uncomfortable with it.

After navigating the airport traffic, his curiosity was too strong to ignore. "What's in the box?"

"A gift."

"From who?"

"A frequent passenger."

"Oh."

He wasn't going to ask. He didn't need to ask. "A man?" he asked anyway.

"Yes."

Daniel breathed in deeply and slowly. He could feel the anger build in seconds. He didn't like this, he didn't like this at all. He exited the interstate and pulled into a shopping center parking lot.

"I don't like this, Cassie."

"Oh."

"I don't want you accepting gifts from men."

"I understand."

A sense of relief relaxed his entire body. He was glad he hadn't let his temper fly. "Then it's settled."

"Yes, it is. I'll accept presents from whomever I wish and you'll not like it."

"That's not what I meant."

"But it's how it's going to be," she told him, looking straight into his eyes. She had beautiful eyes. Right now they were angry with a touch of sadness because of him.

He slammed his hand against the steering wheel. His childish reaction reminded him of Melanie's new name for him, and his anger died as quickly as it had come. He was a man, not an immature boy. He needed to act like it.

Daniel started the engine and drove home, attempting to act like an adult. As soon as he parked, Cassie opened the door and was inside the apartment building before he knew it. Daniel fought with the box, cursing it and the man who'd given it to her. He made it up to their floor, but when he got inside the apartment, Cassie was nowhere in sight.

He dumped the box on the sofa as soon as he entered. Relieving himself of that physical burden forced the emotions inside him to intensify. Guilt, guilt, guilt. He felt guilty for hurting Cassie's feelings and dousing her good mood. He felt guilty for trying to tell her what to do. Did he have the right to demand anything from her when he let her think all he wanted was sex and to be a father to his child? Daniel knew he didn't, but that couldn't stop him from wanting it all.

He walked through the apartment, searching for Cassie. She wasn't in the living room, kitchen or their bedroom. Before going to search the extra bedroom, he sat on the edge of the bed. As he bent to slip off his uniform shoes, he heard a splash in the bathroom. The light wasn't on, that's why he hadn't checked there. He needed to ask her what she wanted for dinner, he reasoned.

Daniel went to the door. At the last minute, he stopped himself from knocking. Instead, he turned the knob and walked in, opening the door wide. Then he came to a dead stop, the knob in one hand, his shoulder resting against the door jam.

Cassie stood before him completely nude. Her compact body

was perfectly shaped. One foot was poised over the tub as she leaned against the tiled wall for support. His gaze traveled over her body, taking in every feature, and resting a few seconds longer on the swell that was their child. He was suddenly deeply moved by that thought. Then his gaze moved to her face. She looked so tired.

"Can you close the door? I'm about to take a bath."

Daniel stepped inside, shutting the door behind him.

"I meant for you to be on the other side of the door."

"I know, and I'm sorry."

"For what?" she asked, sliding carefully into the tub. "For barging in on my personal quiet time?"

"No, for losing my temper," Daniel admitted as he stooped near the edge of the tub.

Cassie stared up at him with serious eyes. "I accept your apology."

"Why do you say that so solemnly?"

"Because it's a first. It's the first time you've apologized for your rude, irrational behavior."

Daniel laughed. For some reason, the insult didn't hurt. "Let me make it up to you, Cass." The tips of his fingers skimmed the surface of the water, moving toward and away from her full breasts, the tips of which were peaking above the surface.

"How are you going to do that?"

"I can start by bathing you. You look exhausted."

"I am."

"So how about it?" he asked as he used a washcloth to make a swirling trail across the water. "Come on," he pressed when she didn't answer. "I'm dying to make amends."

"Sure." She gave him a tired smile.

Daniel lifted one of her arms. He gathered the soft cloth in his hand and slowly squeezed, dropping ringlets of warm water on her arm. He repeated the motion with her other arm.

Mesmerized, he watched the small waterfall land on her arm, the droplets calling to him.

He kissed a water drop, then another, his tongue sipping the moisture on her skin. First one arm, then the other. Daniel leaned back on his hunches, his breathing harsh. He'd never get through bathing her at this rate.

"Daniel, does this bath include *soap* and water?"

A rough chuckling sound vibrated from his throat before he could stop it. Cassie always made him laugh. And he loved—No, he wouldn't got there.

"Soap coming up." He kneeled at the side of the tub once again, a bottle of body wash in his hands. "Berry Bliss," he read the label. "A blissful bath for you, my wife."

Daniel carefully dotted every part of her body above the waterline, her neck and shoulders, arms and elbows and some special attention to the tips of her breast floating half in and half out of the water. He massaged and washed those first. With a thumb he, gently spread the thick soap around each nipple, making ever widening circles until each breast was foamy and berry-scented. Concentrating very hard on the pink nipples, raised and asking to be touched, kissed, Daniel gently splashed, rinsing the suds away. With their blatant invitation, he couldn't resist leaning forward to taste the freshly cleaned body part. One arm eased under the water, supporting her, drawing her closer to his waiting lips.

Despite knowing that his caresses might reveal that there was more than sex between them, Daniel wanted to please Cassie. The caress with deliberate and slow moments at the nape of her neck was meant to excite her. The attention he had given her breasts was to please her. His actions weren't only for himself.

He continued to bathe Cassie's arms with long gentle strokes, his movements those of a man in love. He was powerless to hold back. He repeated the caress again and again. Cassie shuddered and sighed.

With each caress, a voice inside his head said, "I love you, Cassie." Finally, Daniel stood and peeled off his wet clothing.

"Are you joining me?" Cass asked.

"No, you're joining me," Daniel answered, bending to lift her wet body out of the tub.

She laughed at that. Her sultry eyes open to anything he had in mind. With that look he could almost believe she loved him as she had once claimed.

Daniel lowered them both to the floor with Cassie on top of him, his mind exploding with the excitement of having her above him, controlling the rhythm, the pleasure. He trusted Cassie to bring them both pleasure, and she did with a mind numbing explosion drumming through even the smallest part of his body.

She lay on top of him, their bodies wet with water and sweat. His nostrils were full of the blissful smell of Cassie, berries and sex. Then he realized that he had actually made love to her. She had to be blind not to realize how he felt about her. They were moving in a direction he wasn't ready for.

"Daniel, I—"

"—want to tell me what you want for dinner."

Cassie slowly, carefully, sat up at this, steadying herself by laying her hands on his chest. She stared at him as if he were out of his mind. "That's not what I wanted to say."

"But it's what we need to think about. We have to feed the baby. Get up, Cass, I'll order something.

Her face was full of hurt again, but he ignored it as he stood, instead, staring at himself. The fact that he was still rock hard was proof enough of all the issues he didn't want to think about.

Daniel grabbed a robe. "Chinese sound good? Okay, I'll order what you like."

He had escaped. But for how long?

Cassie couldn't believe what she'd heard. After sharing such pure bliss with her, all he had on his mind was *dinner*? He frustrated her. That's what the man did. Frustrated her beyond belief. Cassie slipped back into the tub and took a quick wash, trying to ignore the still sensitive parts of her body. That happened to be every inch of her skin. She threw the washcloth across the room. Its soft texture reminded her too well of Daniel and the things he had just done to her. The splat the cloth made as it hit a wall and slid into the hamper gave her a sense of satisfaction. She carefully stepped out of the tub and opted to air dry, brushing her teeth for no other reason except that it allowed her to take her frustration out on her pearly whites.

When she dropped her toothbrush back into the holder with a clank, it leaned against Daniel's.

Daniel.

He had shown her so much love and passion and then had done a complete turnaround. Cassie had thought that he was ready to hear her declare that she loved him. But after the most intense lovemaking they had ever shared, what did he want to discuss?

Food!

Cassie wasn't going to stand for it. Daniel had revealed too many of his feelings to revert back to the stilted, dry relationship they had developed this past week.

Going into the bedroom, she found panties and one of her favorite hang around dresses. This one was colorful with a Mexican theme, and unlike the others, reached past her knees.

That was fast, Cassie thought as she entered the living room.

Daniel stood at the front door paying a teenager for the delicious smelling food coming from the white cardboard box in the middle of the coffee table. Cassie took in the carefully arranged plates, napkins, forks, and Oreo cookie centerpiece and smiled. He knew her weakness. And despite his rapid retreat, Cassie felt that she was getting her Daniel back.

Yesterday, she couldn't have even imagined Daniel doing this. Cassie decided to save her attack for another time. She would retreat and see where Daniel was headed.

It didn't take long to find out. Daniel's focus, once again, was the baby. From the moment he informed her that the restaurant he ordered from guaranteed food without MSG, and that she should eat some of the egg foo young because it was high in protein, to the moment he touched the play button on the VCR, it was clear that the focus had shifted from love-of-my-life to mother-of-my-child.

As she ate the high protein meal and refrained from commenting on the fat content of eggs, Cassie wondered what her next step should be. When they were dating, their relationship had been free and natural. So far, she had experienced the attentive fiancé, the disgruntled husband, the amazing lover and the happy father-to-be. Daniel was making her crazy. She got the feeling that he was being what he thought he should be and not who he was.

Her thoughts were interrupted when he removed the empty plate from her lap and settled her between his thighs. He stretched back on the sofa, his arms surrounding her. The tape played on, announcing the importance of healthy eating during pregnancy.

She sighed and stuck with her decision to wait and see. This was the first time Daniel had deliberately held her in his arms when he was wide awake. It was promising. She stayed awake through the first tape, but felt herself drifting off during the second. By the time the narrator reached the fetal development of the third trimester, Cassie found herself doing more than drifting. The last image she remembered was of skin cells stretching to eight times their normal size to accommodate the growing baby. *This is what I have to look forward to*, she thought as her chin fell forward.

Daniel pressed the stop button on the remote control. He had seen these tapes at least five times. He'd bought them right after discovering Cassie's pregnancy and watched them over and over again. Tonight, they had been his salvation. He didn't want to admit his feelings, and he didn't want to go back to being the uptight jerk he had been all week. So, he had opted for something in between.

The baby was a safe subject. The only safe subject. He was on shaky ground with Cassie. Daniel looked down on her, his wife. But for how long? How long would she enjoy the novelty of being married to a black man? Daniel didn't know the answer to that and didn't want to think about it. He stood with Cassie in his arms and carefully carried her into their bedroom and tucked her in, grazing the side of her check with a soft touch.

Today had felt so close to old times. But, he had to remind himself, it wasn't real then, and it wasn't real now. He knew he couldn't handle another night like this. It gave him hope, and he didn't want that. Daniel, suddenly, made a decision that was best for their situation. He picked up the phone and dialed. It wasn't much of a plan, but it would give him time to figure some things out.

CHAPTER 6

Cassie left the urine sample in the usual place and went back into the exam room. Daniel stood with his back to her, studying the charts on the wall. Cassie had a feeling that he could teach a course, Fetal Development 101, with no trouble at all. When he turned toward her, seeing him dressed in his airline uniform brought back the complete disagreement they'd had that morning.

Daniel had decided that it was a good idea to accept a schedule that would take him away for over a week, returning on Christmas Eve. The fact that Cassie didn't agree with the plan hadn't stopped him. Now he stood there quiet and calm, as if he weren't leaving in a few hours.

"You don't have to be here, Daniel. You can leave now. I'll get Melanie to take me home. I've gone to all my other visits alone."

"I want to be here."

For the baby, she finished for him in her head.

Cassie changed into the hospital gown and lay on the table, waiting for the doctor. The silence between them was not uncomfortable, yet not exactly easy.

"So Cassie." The doctor walked in, loud as usual, studying her chart. I see you're a Mrs. now. Congrats to you," he said, raising his head from the chart. "And you must be Mr. Adams, the proud father-to-be."

"He certainly is that."

Both men looked at her strangely.

Cassie shrugged her shoulders.

"Everything's fine. Your weight gain, your urine."

"Good," Daniel answered.

"You're in luck, Dad. We have scheduled just for you today, an ultrasound. You can hear and see your little prodigy for yourself. But let's take your pressure first, Cassie."

With quick movement, the doctor attached the cuff to her arm. As Dr. Jay pumped, Daniel watched over his shoulder. As usual, her arm felt as if it were being squeezed in a vise. Then the pumping stopped, the air was released and it was done.

"That's strange," the doctor said.

"That's high!" Daniel yelled.

"What's wrong?" Cassie asked. "How high?"

"Calm down, now. Let me try your other arm. The reading could be wrong."

Cassie took a couple of deep breaths. "I'm calm."

"Calm." Daniel slowly shook his head.

The doctor pumped again. Daniel stared, and Cassie tried to relax as the vise-like grip was repeated on her left arm.

Both Daniel and Dr. Jay frowned.

"What is it?"

"It's 145 over 95, not too bad. We haven't seen any other signs of problems, so let's not get too upset. Why don't we take a look at this baby then check again."

High blood pressure. That was a sign for all kinds of complications. What could be wrong?

Cassie looked over at Daniel. From his eyes, she could tell that he knew it, too. He sat down beside her and held her hand.

"It's going to be cold," the doctor warned.

"Freezing cold, Dr. Jay, you should have said freezing cold," Cassie joked, trying not to worry as he spread a gel substance on her stomach. She didn't need to worry. Daniel was with her. For now anyway.

Almost immediately, they heard a heartbeat amplified by the equipment.

"Sounds loud and strong," Daniel said.

"It does, doesn't it?"

"And there's the baby!" Dr. Jay announced, pointing to the baby's head. "Hey, your little one's waving. Look at that arm move."

Cassie stared at the screen. Daniel's head was right beside hers as they watched the movements of the little miracle they'd made together.

"The baby's waving at us, Cass. Everything's going to be fine," he whispered to her.

Cassie had to believe that was true.

Dr. Jay took her pressure again. "It's still too high for comfort, Cassie. Has anything happened recently to upset you, any major changes since your last visit?"

"I got married."

"Yes, that's right. Planning a wedding can be stressful." Cassie and Daniel looked at each other. The wedding hadn't been stressful, but their week old marriage was something else. Cassie watched as the frown lines reappeared on Daniel's forehead.

"This is what I want you to do. Take a few days off work, better yet a week, and see me again by the twenty-third."

"Okay."

"I don't care what you have to do to take the time off. To prevent any complications, you need to rest now. Then we'll do a follow up."

"Don't worry, doctor, we'll follow your orders," Daniel assured him.

"With the two of you frowning at me, I don't think I have a choice." Cassie laughed, trying to lighten the mood rather than going overboard with worry.

"Then I'll see you in a week."

They were in the car and on the way home before Daniel

finally spoke.

"I know you don't want me to leave, but I think it's the best thing for you and the baby. Your pressure is up because of me."

"That's not true."

Daniel merely frowned at her a second before turning his eyes back to the road.

"Okay, it's partly true in an indirect way, but not how you're thinking."

"Then that settles it. It's my fault."

"Daniel, that's ridiculous. We have to talk."

"I agree. We'll talk when I get back. If we get into some heavy discussion now, it might make things worse. I refuse to upset you any more than I already have."

Before she knew it, Daniel had parked the car in front of their apartment complex. They went up in silence. The elevator car felt cold and empty. Daniel opened the door to the apartment and went straight into the bedroom, returning almost immediately with a leather shoulder bag. His self-directed frown was still in place.

He stopped in front of her, placing both hands on her shoulders before pulling her close to lay a gentle kiss on her forehead.

"Rest, I'll call you." He paused. "No, I won't call you. Christmas Eve, I'll see you then."

He got as far as the front door before he turned around and added, "If you really need to, the airline knows how to get in touch with me."

The door closed behind him. Maybe this would be good for them, she thought. Maybe they needed the time apart. Then why were these silly tears falling from her eyes? Pregnant hormones. She'd never cried this much before. This wasn't good for her or the baby. The baby moved in agreement.

"Alright, little one," Cassie said aloud to the baby. "We'll rest and straighten Daddy out if we have to hijack his plane and force him to fly to a deserted island."

Melanie called that night, and even though her friend could sense her unhappiness, Cassie only went as far as telling her the doctor's orders. Melanie promised to come by to pick up the form with the doctor's restrictions to take to their supervisor.

She longed to call her aunt and uncle, to speak to her cousin, but she didn't give in to the urge. The whereabouts of her cousin T were a mystery, and she didn't want to burden her aunt and uncle. The surprises she'd sprung on them a week ago were enough for now.

Melanie came over with lunch and even dinner for later, her famous vegetable lasagna. "Well, hello there, my friend, and you, you wonderful little person." Melanie patted Cassie's stomach. "Give your mother a break and stop causing so much trouble."

Cassie laughed.

"You can laugh now, Cass, but the real trouble starts once they come out into the real world. Then you'll have to deal with diapers, potty training, bullies, homework, dances, proms, driving, and college."

"You've just gone through my child's entire life in less than thirty seconds."

"I sure did, didn't I? Believe me, it's gonna last a whole lot longer than that," Melanie assured her, waving her arms around.

Cassie spent an enjoyable few hours with her friend. They watched an old movie on PBS and played a game of Scrabble. Cassie had missed Melanie this past week.

Seeing her at work wasn't the same as living with her.

Before leaving, Melanie promised to come back to check up

on her during the week. Cassie had told her that Daniel would be out of town, omitting how she felt about that. Melanie even went as far as putting the lasagna in the oven and setting the timer before leaving to get ready for her date.

"Fly Boy's not putting on the immature act again, is he?"

"Naw, nothing to worry about, he's just being a man."

"I understand that. Call if you need me, Cass."

"Thanks a lot. I will, friend."

Cassie let out a huge happy breath. Having Melanie over had been good for her. She hadn't thought about Daniel and their problems the entire time. And she was going to keep it that way. What was the use of worrying about something she couldn't fix until Daniel got home anyway? Determined to rest and take care of herself, Cassie refused to worry. She put thought into action by stretching out on the sofa and promptly falling asleep.

The simultaneous ringing of the phone and the kitchen timer jarred her out of a deep sleep. Cassie picked up the phone, the closest noise maker.

"Hello." Her voice came out with a raspy edge.

The buzzer in the kitchen rang on, demanding attention. "Hold on a minute please," she said without waiting for an answer.

Cassie went into the kitchen, and with the press of a button, she ended the annoying buzz. She quickly pulled the casserole out of the oven then went back to the phone, the scent of cheese, veggies and Melanie's special sauce following right behind her.

"Yes, how can I help you?"

"I'm not sure, but I think I dialed the wrong number," a woman with a friendly voice answered.

"That depends on who you're looking for."

"I was trying to call… " The voice recited Cassie and Daniel's number.

"You've got the right number." The tempting smell of the

food was distracting Cassie.

"It seems that way."

"Then the question is still..." Cassie paused. The scent pulled, tugged and almost dragged her back into the kitchen. Her stomach growled. Why was she wasting time talking to a complete stranger when her body was demanding nourishment?

"The question is still… " the voice asked.

"The question is still who?" Yes, who? Who was this woman? Please don't ask for Daniel, Cassie prayed. They didn't need another complication. Feelings of jealousy were already beginning to stir.

"I'm looking for Daniel Adams."

"This is his wife speaking," Cassie answered, immediately letting the woman know her position. "He's not here right now. Would you like to leave a message?"

"Wife? Did you say *wife*?"

"Yes," Cassie answered with pride. Despite their disastrous beginning, she was still proud to be Daniel's wife.

"Monica," Cassie could hear the women's muffled voice yelling to someone. "Daniel's got a wife!"

On the other side of the line, Cassie unashamedly listened to the disbelief, denial and excitement in their conversation. Who were these people? Cassie wasn't getting off the phone until she found out.

"Is she still on the line?" Cassie heard one of the voices ask.

"Oh my goodness! She *is* still on the line!"

Cassie couldn't help laughing. Whoever these people were, she liked them already.

"Hello?"

"I'm still here," Cassie answered.

"I am so sorry. I'm normally not this rude. You took me by surprise."

"I think I guessed that much."

"I'm Vanessa, Daniel's cousin from New Orleans."

"The one in the picture?" Cassie blurted without meaning to.

"If you mean from Thanksgiving, the answer could be yes. There were an awful lot of us there."

"I noticed," Cassie answered, recalling all the people in the few pictures she'd seen.

"I was able to get Daniel to stand still long enough to take one with me. That particular one and the picture I was able to sneak of him holding one of the babies were the best two."

"I saw that one, too."

"Wasn't that a good picture?" The woman on the other line went on as if she had known Cassie all her life. "Daniel looked as if Kacey belonged in his arms."

"I would have to agree."

"Am I talking too much? I tend to do that when I'm excited. Can you tell I'm excited? Daniel was just down here. He didn't say anything about getting married or being married."

"We've only been married for about a week."

"That explains it. But he could have called us with the good news."

That was the problem. It obviously wasn't good news. Judging by his cousin's reaction, Daniel hadn't told anyone.

"When Daniel gets home, tell him to call his cousin Vanessa immediately—"

"Um, Vanessa," Cassie interrupted. "He won't be home for awhile. He's got a busy schedule with quite a few layovers. He won't be back until Christmas Eve."

"Is that right?" The woman paused as if searching for something. "I've got a great idea, Cassie. Why don't you fly over and meet the family. Between the two of us, we can drag Daniel to New Orleans."

"Vanessa, I don't think that's a good idea."

"Call me Ness, everyone does, and you're probably right.

Daniel will be more interested in spending Christmas with his new bride, not a bunch of relatives, especially since he has to be away from you so soon after your wedding."

Cassie wished that were true.

"I could sit here and talk to you for hours, but listen. Can you hear that wailing in the background?"

A second later, Cassie could hear the demanding cries of more than one baby coming through the phone line loud and clear. "Those are my boys, waiting to be fed. I must do my maternal duty. I'm breast feeding, it's the best thing."

"Mmmm," Cassie said, a bit overwhelmed by Vanessa, or Ness as she said, and all the information she was giving.

"Hey, but you're a newlywed. You don't want to hear about motherhood. Not yet anyway." If only she knew, Cassie thought.

"Here, say hello to my sister Monica, Daniel's *older* cousin."

Cassie barely had a moment to say goodbye before another friendly but more serious voice came on the line.

"Hello, Cassie. You'll have to excuse Ness. Since getting married, she has been trying to make sure everyone finds wedded bliss."

"I understand."

"I can't complain. She helped me along the way. Daniel, I see, went about it without Ness's help."

"Yes, he did."

"I won't keep you. I only wanted to say hello."

"That's very nice of you."

"Not at all, we're family now."

If these two women were an example of what Daniel's family was like, Cassie was in love with them already.

"Cassie, do you mind taking down my number? I know we're hours away, but Ness says Daniel's out of town. I want you to feel free to call if you need to."

"Sure."

"Besides," Monica chuckled deep and long, "if the number's on hand, Daniel won't have any excuse about returning the call."

Cassie jotted down the numbers for both Monica and Ness.

"Don't be a stranger," Monica said before disconnecting.

Those were nice people, Cassie thought, but she wouldn't be calling them. They were Daniel's family, and it was clear that he didn't want her to have anything to do with them. He hadn't even told his family that he was married.

A wave of depression washed over her. Daniel sent out so many conflicting signs, she wasn't sure about anything anymore.

The vegetable lasagna didn't taste as good as she thought it would. Her taste buds were as depressed as she was. Cassie forced herself to drink a tall glass of skim milk. An image from the video she and Daniel had watched of calcium being drained from a women's bones to strengthen the baby's developing skeletal system was too scary to let happen.

Cassie took a bath. Afterwards, she flipped the channels of the TV as she tried to relax in bed. Unfortunately, she found that there was nothing good on this Saturday night.

As she lay on her back, giving in to the urge to have an early night, images of the past week flowed through her head. She thought the evidence of Daniel's love for her far outweighed any other emotion he was trying to convey. Cassie looked around the room, missing Daniel, his presence, his touch. She had already proven before that she could live without him, but she didn't want to. Not unless he told her outright that he didn't love her.

Didn't love her. Ha! Her gaze landed on the woodgraph Daniel had given her on their wedding night. Her body suddenly felt completely relaxed, her depression gone in an instant. Their baby was going to be fine, and Daniel would open up to her. Cassie fell asleep with ease.

Beginning her first relaxing morning at home with a breakfast of toast, fruit, and a tall glass of milk, Cassie read through the entire Sunday paper delivered to her door, comics first, of course, to start her day off with a laugh. If a comic wasn't funny enough for her, Cassie normally rewrote the script in her head. With nothing but time on her hands, she went a step farther. Cassie found herself at the kitchen table tracing the drawings and adding new script. She wasn't an artist, but her tracing efforts weren't half bad.

Suddenly, inspiration struck. Cassie decided to put a new twist on her tree decorating this year. Christmas was only days away, and she hadn't done much to decorate the apartment. Every year previously, Melanie had helped her decorate their apartment, turning it into a Christmas haven even Santa would be proud of. This year, a wreath on the door was as Christmassy as she'd gotten.

A tap on her speed dial, a few rings later and Melanie, her savior from boredom, provider of countless favors and forced confrontations, was on the line.

"Melanie, I need a tree."

"Say what?"

"It's Cassie and I need a tree."

"I know who you are, my friend. That's not the problem. The time of morning is, and your request could be the other."

"This can't be Mel."

"Give me a second."

Cassie hummed the tune of "Jingle Bells" as she waited. Melanie was back before she started dashing through the snow in a one horse open sleigh.

"Alright, Cass. Elm, birch, or maple? What kind of tree do you want?"

"Real funny, Mel." Cassie laughed. "I need a Christmas tree."

"I knew that. What size do you want, a ten, eight, a six foot tree, or maybe one of those cute little Charlie Browners you always guilt me into buying?"

"If we hadn't bought them, who would have?"

"The 'Peanuts' gang."

"You know what I like, Mel. Please pick one up for me. Maybe you can get that giant security guard to help you."

"Mmm, great idea," Melanie hummed into the phone.

"I knew you'd like it."

"Anything else?"

"A few boxes of those Christmas decorations if you can spare them."

"Spare them. I haven't even opened them. Without you here spreading Christmas joy the boxes are lucky to have made it out of the closet."

"That's something."

"Yeah, but it's not the same."

"I know."

"I miss you, my friend."

"Same here, Mel.'

"Okay, enough of that. Here's the plan. Church, find giant, tree shopping, boxes, then you."

"Sounds good. See you then."

The phone clicked. Cassie hung up and went to find a tape, CD or album, anything with Christmas music. All her own Christmas tapes were still in those boxes at her old apartment. The only Christmas music she could find was an old album by the Jackson 5. It was intact and without scratches, so Cassie put it on and went back to her tracing creations. The traditional "Have Yourself a Merry Little Christmas" songs about Santa, Frosty, Rudolph, and a few originals by the Jackson 5 themselves filled the apartment and Cassie with the Christmas spirit.

Her comic drawings were slowly forming a stack of square, rectangular, and circular patterns, all filled with holiday fun.

This would be their first Christmas together. The end of an old year with hopes of the new one opening a ton of possibilities for them.

Midmorning, the phone rang. Cassie's heart jumped, hoping it was Daniel, despite knowing that he hadn't planned to call.

"Hello."

"Hello, may I speak to Cassie."

"She's right here, I mean, this is she," Cassie answered, allowing herself to feel a touch of disappointment.

"This is Ness. I'm sorry, I didn't recognize your voice."

It was Daniel's very nice, easily excited cousin.

"I wanted to call before I went to church and before we got to my mama's house where you wouldn't have heard a thing because of all the noise. I'm not bugging you, am I?"

"No, of course not," Cassie answered, not knowing what else to say. She had no intention of contacting Daniel's family, but if they called her, what could she do? Being rude wasn't in her nature. Besides, Cassie liked Daniel's cousin.

"Good. We could be phone buddies until I convince Daniel to bring you down for a visit."

"Umm, okay," Cassie answered, a bit of a frown forming on her forehead, a finger nervously tapping her temple. Daniel's cousin didn't seem to notice her hesitancy. Cassie wondered what Daniel would think of that and decided that he'd have to deal with it just as he'd had to deal with her receiving gifts from a frequent passenger. The fact that the passenger was a seventy-two-year-old cattle rancher didn't matter. Daniel needed to trust her.

"MaNessa, the babies are all buckled up in the van and makin' faces. Daddy said we had to go before they start yelling like banshees. What's a banshee?" a little voice yelled somewhere in New Orleans but was heard loud and clear in Houston.

"Megan, tell Daddy I'll be right there," Cassie heard Ness tell the little girl.

"Scott's constantly complaining that his eardrums are going to bust wide open one day. He just can't stand to hear the babies whimper, let alone cry, so I'd better get going. It's just that I had to call. When I woke up this morning, I had trouble believing Daniel was actually married."

"I promise you, he really is."

"Just what I wanted. Talk to you later, Cuz."

"Good-bye, Ness." Cuz? Cassie put the receiver down. Marrying Daniel connected her to a whole new family. A big one, if she went by the pictures she saw. And a family without the typical prejudices that still separated people by race. Those pictures gave her a promising feeling for their marriage.

Her Christmas joy rising even more, Cassie found an eight by ten sheet of paper and folded it into fourths. Without much thought, she began drawing her own characters. A frowning airline pilot resembling a stick man wearing oversized clothes appeared in one square. Zig-zag lines on his forehead, round eyes that looked downward and a teeth clenching grimace formed the face. "Come Fly with Me" Cassie wrote beneath the pilot's feet. Of course this was a caricature of Daniel. The cartoon suggested that maybe the pilot shouldn't be trusted. In truth, if Cassie had her choice of pilots, Daniel would be the person she would bet her life on. He already had her heart.

Ah, that was fun, Cassie thought as she drew an oval-faced stick woman with long braids wearing a short V neck dress. Just the kind of thing that looked gorgeous on Melanie. Cassie found herself adding a huge silver bullet to one hand and a life preserver to the other. The bubble above the character's head declared, *Bite the bullet—it could save your life.* A cartoon only Melanie would understand. Cassie chuckled, her shoulders shaking as she put away her art work.

When she got up to relieve her bladder, she filled her glass with milk and turned the album to the other side. She relaxed on the sofa as the young Michael Jackson's voice filled the apartment with the song about a little drummer boy who came to visit the baby Jesus.

The baby Jesus. Celebrating His birth was what Christmas was all about. The song brought back many memories of past Christmases with her aunt, uncle and cousin T. She missed them. Cassie hadn't been home for Christmas in three years and hadn't planned to go back this year.

Decorating the house, opening presents, going to church together, those were all good memories. Church. Both Melanie and Ness had mentioned going to church. Cassie hadn't gone to church on a regular basis since moving to Houston. She had gone with Melanie off and on, enjoying the soulful service and music, as well as the tight religious community she missed.

Realizing that she wanted the same experience for her baby, Cassie wondered how Daniel felt about it all. Just one more thing they needed to discuss.

She went in search of a tablet and a pen. Daniel had promised that they would talk when he returned, and she would be ready for him. On the top line of the very first page, Cassie wrote the first item to be discussed. LOVE. If they managed to admit the love they still had for each other, then they could move on. And there was plenty to move on to. After they made love and she'd had an hour or so to touch and explore at her leisure, of course.

Cassie savored that thought before going on with her list: religion, occupations. Hers would certainly change. Becoming a ticket agent had only been temporary. Places to live would be next. Cassie really missed her family and would love to meet Daniel's. New Orleans, she wrote with flair, adding a drawing of what was supposed to be a crawfish as lagniappe, a little something extra. Massages, frown lifts, and daily doses of laughter were the last additions to her list.

CHAPTER 7

Perfect. The tree was done. A star made of Styrofoam and sprayed gold by Melanie shone on top. Not more than four feet high, her little tree stood on a table in the corner of the living room, its bald spot facing the wall, its criss-crossed, sagging branches straightened and held steady with green thread.

Cassie had spent hours transforming it into the beautiful tree it was now. Its branches were adorned with handmade comic ornaments, the "Peanuts" gang, Marmaduke, Cathy, Beetle Bailey, and the war-crazed Viking. All gave sentiments of Christmas in one way or another.

Ornament making, Cassie discovered, was one of her hidden talents. She walked through the house turning off all the lights, pressed the play button to hear the tape she had made from the album and plugged in the tree. Now this was pure bliss. Cassie sat and took it all in, enjoying the beauty and satisfaction of a job well done. She couldn't wait for Daniel to come home. He'd been gone for almost a week, and he hadn't called, just as he'd said. Today was December twenty- third. One more day and her husband would be home.

The phone rang as one of the Jackson 5 originals played softly through the speakers.

"Hi, Cass." Ness's voice rang clear and cheerful.

Cassie smiled to herself. She enjoyed her daily chats with Ness. They had seemed to hit it off pretty well, despite Cassie's misgivings.

"Hey, Ness, got the kids asleep?"

"The boys are out. I don't know for how long, but I'm not

going to waste time wondering about it. Scott's reading the girls a bedtime story. Yesterday was my turn. How about you? That baby keeping you up at night yet?"

"No," Cassie answered, taking the cordless phone into the kitchen to get a glass of milk to build her calcium supply. "The baby's pretty active during the day, but I can sleep with no problem at night."

"Enjoy it while it lasts," Ness warned.

Cassie had spilled her guts about nearly every aspect of her relationship with Daniel. It wasn't a ploy to get Ness on her side but rather a search for an understanding ear and help in shedding some light on Daniel's attitude. There had also been an instant bond because of their choices in spouses and the challenge of raising bi-racial children in a society that still retained one form of segregation or another.

"Have you been taking it easy today? No lifting weights, no jogging in the park?"

Cassie drained her glass before answering. "I haven't lifted anything heavier than a Christmas ornament or a glass of milk. And I haven't left the house since I came home from the doctor's office today."

"What did he say?"

"My pressure's normal. Everything else checks out okay, but he wants me to come back next week."

"That's great!"

"Yeah," Cassie said, wishing she still felt the same excitement as Ness's voice pulsating through the phone lines.

"I know what you're thinking. Daniel's going to see this as evidence to continue to blame himself."

"Exactly. That's just like him. Daniel's always found it easier for some reason to take the blame for things he has no control over."

Cassie made her way back to the living room with another

full glass of milk.

"It's good to know that I'm not the only person who—Cassie!" Ness screeched.

"What?"

"That music! That song! Turn it up."

"The baby almost jumped into my throat. Don't scare me like that," Cassie told Ness, moving to turn up the volume of the song that was just ending.

"Sorry about that. Was that song on the radio?"

"No, from a tape I made. I found this old album—"

"You're kidding."

"No."

"Is it the Jackson 5? On the back cover is, '*Lots of love to my little man. Jackie*' written?"

"It is the Jackson 5. I don't know if anything's written on the cover. Let me check." Cassie rummaged through the wooden crate of old albums and found exactly what Ness had said would be there.

"I can't believe he kept it."

"What's all this about, Ness?"

"That album was the last present Daniel ever got from his mother."

"Jackie was his mother? He didn't call her Mom?"

"From what I can remember, my Aunt Jackie never acted like she wanted to be a mother. She didn't allow Daniel to call her anything but Jackie."

"Poor Daniel."

"Oh, no, Cass, he never had a problem with that. Daniel knew she was his mother. He would do anything for her. I always thought that he loved her a bit too much."

"He has never mentioned his mom. What happened to her, Ness?"

"It's pretty sad, but maybe it'll help you understand him a little better. Aunt Jackie gave Daniel that record and left him with our grandparents a few days before Christmas. She promised to come back."

"But she didn't."

"She called on Christmas Eve from goodness knows where. She said she got married and was never coming back."

"My poor Daniel. How old was he?"

"About ten, I think."

"He didn't say much of anything to anyone that day, just went into my twin brothers' bedroom and played that song over and over again all Christmas Day. And I tell you, Cass, Christmas wasn't the same that year. Daniel hasn't been the same since."

"He must have been heartbroken."

"He was hurt, but he kept it inside. He played that song again and again, and it seemed like there was a hollow sound in the whole house when it suddenly stopped."

"What happened?"

"Daniel came out of the room with the album. My grandmother asked where he was going, and he said to destroy something. We all thought he'd crushed the album. My dad said it was good, that he needed to let his anger out."

"But he didn't."

"No, that was a turning point for him. Daniel's personality changed from rambunctious to quiet and serious."

"Like he is now."

"When we were growing up, I used to get him to let loose once in a while."

"Same here, but that was almost three years ago."

The line was quiet.

"You can do it again, Cassie. You can make Danny realize that he deserves to be loved." There were tears in Ness's voice, just as there were tears in Cassie's eyes for the ten-year-old Daniel.

"But enough of this. I mailed you a holiday dessert package, mini-pecan tarts. Monica and the kids make them every year. Wait till you taste them. The crust melts in your mouth, like cotton candy."

"Thanks, Ness."

"No, I *thank you*, for being in my cousin's life. I have a feeling that you're his earth angel."

Placing the phone on the coffee table, Cassie turned the treasure over in her hand, moving it toward the sparkling white lights from the Christmas tree, inspecting the well-preserved album cover. She took the album out and flipped it over to side two. There was the title, "Christmas Won't Be the Same This Year." There wasn't a scratch on it. For a ten-year-old boy to play that song over and over again without one scratch from the needle showed just how much he treasured this last gift from his mother.

Cassie put the album away and went into the kitchen to get another glass of milk. She tried to imagine what kind of person would leave her child's life forever. Cassie was in love with her baby already and couldn't imagine leaving him or her to be raised by someone else. Her parents didn't have a choice. They didn't want to die in that plane crash, they didn't want to leave her. Daniel's mother did. And what about his dad? Cassie hadn't asked.

"Well, you'll always have both me and your father," she told her unborn baby, laying a comforting hand on her stomach.

The doorbell rang. Good. Cassie needed something to take her mind off things. She opened the door. "Melanie!"

"Hey, my friend." Melanie swooped in, carrying a huge pot of some delicious smelling food that brought back memories of home.

"Red beans, you cooked red beans?"

"Just like my mom taught me."

"That's right, she's from New Orleans. But who did you cook

all this for, an army?" Cass asked as Melanie placed the pot on the stove.

Melanie came back into the living room, flipping every light switch along the way. "I sent away for Camellia red beans."

"That's the kind I always used. What's all this about, Mel? There is no way we could possibly eat that whole pot of red beans by ourselves. And I'm not having them for Christmas. I've got a whole meal planned."

"Give me a sec. Let me look at you."

"Look at me. I'm pregnant. I told you the good news from the doctor, right?"

"Yes, the best news."

Melanie walked around the room straightening things up, picking up a magazine here, the comics there and arranging the pillows on the sofa.

"Okay, we're ready!"

"For what?"

"Sit right here on that nice comfortable chair, my friend, and you'll see."

Melanie was gone in a flash and back in less than a minute.

"Surprise!" nearly twenty people shouted as they crowded into her apartment with food, cake, balloons, and a ton of presents all wrapped in paper that shouted "Baby."

Cassie was amazed. Most of her friends from the airport were here to give her good wishes and lift her spirits. They ate red beans and rice, chicken drummettes, little sausages, and a variety of other party fare.

Later, Melanie directed a few games, a diaper changing race, men against the women. Cotton diapers with huge safety pins were used instead of the convenient disposable diapers to change the baby dolls Melanie provided. The guys lost, claiming that their fingers were not designed to handle safety pins.

The last game was an open-ended sentence in which everyone had to add a few words. Melanie began with: Cassie and Daniel's baby will be a medically trained . . ."

"…happy..."

"…flying attendant..."

Everyone laughed.

"who can double as a stand up comedian ..."

"…and help everyone ..."

"…over and above the call of duty ..."

Cassie smiled at that one. That was from her supervisor Karen.

"…but frowns when piloting a 737," Brad, a pilot who'd flown with Daniel many times, added.

"…because he wants to land the plane safely to get back to his wife," Paul concluded.

"That ends it," Melanie announced. "Who has ever heard of such a baby? Let's get to the presents.

Cassie received blankets, sleepers, socks, diapers, soft little jumpers, bibs, sheets, and even a stroller. She was overwhelmed with the generosity of her friends.

"Alright! Clean up time!" Melanie announced. "We can't invade a pregnant woman's home and expect her to clean it up herself."

Both men and women moved around her apartment, picking up, sweeping, washing dishes, and storing the presents in the extra bedroom.

"Thank you so much," Cassie told each friend as they left her apartment cleaner than it was before they arrived.

"You're a good friend, Mel."

"Don't I know it. Tell Fly Boy I said to behave when he gets in tomorrow."

Cassie closed the door to find Paul still inside completing a phone call. "Sorry about that. I needed to answer that page, and my cell phone was out. I didn't recharge the battery."

"No problem."

"And you got a phone call while I was on, but no one answered," Paul told her, draping an arm across her shoulder. Cassie didn't mind. From working with him in the past, she knew he was a touchy-feely person.

"If it was important, I'm sure they'll call back."

He hesitated in the open doorway. "It was important alright. The caller ID showed Daniel's cell phone."

"Really? He must be on his way home! I can't wait to see him!"

"It goes both ways then."

"What do you mean?" Cassie asked, wanting to know but also wanting Paul to leave so he wouldn't interfere with her reunion with her husband.

Paul laughed. "I can see you're ready to get rid of me. I just want to tell you that what I said earlier during the game is true, you know."

"What's true?"

"The part I added to the sentence. I was a flight attendant just yesterday in Daniel's crew. He announced to the whole plane that we were going to land safely because he couldn't wait to get home to his wife. You should have heard the ooooh's and ahhhh's on that plane. He loves you a lot."

"He said that? How sweet. Thanks for sharing that with me." Cassie could feel tears gathering in her eyes.

"I didn't tell you that to make you cry."

"No, these are good tears."

"I hope so. You two are going to have a good life together, okay?"

"I hope so." Cassie nodded as Paul wiped a tear from her

eye. He wrapped his other arm around her to issue a brotherly hug, stepping back to give her a kiss on the forehead.

Daniel couldn't wait to get home. He had been amazed at the constant direction of his thoughts this past week. His wife was all he could think about. Was Cassie resting? Was she bored sitting home all day? Did she drink her milk? What was she wearing today? When she took a bath, did she lather herself with that Blissful Berry soap? Did she miss him?

Daniel prayed that she did because he felt lost without her. After having her back in his life for only a week, he couldn't believe how much he needed her. Trying to survive without her once was more than enough to deal with in a lifetime.

A long, torturous week without Cassie had forced him to realize that his love for her was stronger than his anger and his pride. He'd accept her as she was, love her, and by doing so hopefully change her attitude.

Driving away from the airport, he couldn't wait to hear her voice, so he had called, but some man answered the phone. Daniel had hung up, sure that his nervous fingers had dialed the wrong number. Hearing her voice wouldn't have been enough anyway. He was dying to see her, to touch her, to be with his wife. To tell her he loved her.

He was home in a flash. He parked and was out in an instant, leather bag in hand and so focused on getting inside that he nearly flew past Melanie as she walked out into the parking lot. His mind vaguely registered that there were quite a lot of people leaving his apartment building.

"Something going on here, Melanie?"

"No, just leaving, Fly Boy." Melanie grabbed his arm.

"So we're back to that." Daniel stared down at her hand. "Look, I don't have time for this. I need to see Cassie."

"You know," she allowed him to slip out of her light grip, "I think you actually do."

Daniel took the stairs two at a time, pulling the heavy silver door open on the third floor. He stopped cold.

There, standing in the door of his apartment, was Paul. Blue-eyed, blond-haired Paul. He was one of the flight attendants working with him this past week. Paul had requested a replacement so that he could get home to see his sister. Cassie wasn't Paul's sister. She didn't have any brothers. Daniel could barely see Cassie with the way Paul's body hovered over her, but he knew she was there.

Daniel couldn't move; all he could do was watch. His eyes narrowed. Daniel could feel the furrow on his brow as it formed. He watched as Paul, his arm around his wife, leaned in closer to whisper something to Cassie, the whole exchange not entirely inappropriate, but much too cozy in the next moment as Paul leaned even closer to his wife to wipe a tear from her eye. Why was she crying?

Because he was due back and she had to say goodbye to Paul? And then right before his eyes with a smile Daniel could see from down the hall, Paul kissed Cassie. A slow, tender kiss on the forehead that showed care and concern. That type of intimacy was his job. Paul had no business touching his wife in that way. And exactly how else had he touched her?

With a silly smile still on his face, Paul stood staring at the closed door like some lovesick fool. That did it. That said it all.

Daniel tried counting to ten but had barely pushed the number three past his lips when he found himself face to face with Paul.

"Hey, Daniel. Man, you just missed—"

Daniel grabbed each of Paul's shoulders. "Keep your hands off my wife."

Paul went completely still and quiet. When he opened his mouth, he said the worst thing possible. "You saw us at the door? It's not what you think, Daniel."

Daniel pushed him and reached for the doorknob. Paul, fool that he was, tried to follow him. "Aw, don't go in like that."

Daniel ignored him.

"Let's go for a walk. Talk it out."

Daniel turned to stare at him. "Get away from me. That's all I have to say."

"Okay." Paul backed away, moving toward the elevators. "But you need to calm down. You're gonna be sorry, man."

Daniel stood in front of the door, the words giving him a second's pause. No more than a mere second because this hurt short circuited all his reasoning abilities. He knew it, he felt it, but key in hand he still planned to walk right in. One thought raced through his mind. Cassie couldn't change. He wouldn't be able to change her.

The door suddenly flew open. Out of the corner of his eye he saw Paul still waiting by the elevators. The anger inside him rose even more.

"Daniel, you're home!" Cassie threw her arms around him, her stomach with their baby rubbing against him. The baby. That's who was most important right now. Daniel sucked in a huge breath, drawing in the control he needed, forcing himself to resist the need to yell and rage. He stiffly laid his hands at the sides of her stomach, holding his child between his palms. With controlled movements, Daniel slowly backed Cassie into the apartment. His muscles wanted to relax, his arms were dying to hold her. Instead, he dropped them to his side.

"The doctor. You went today. What did he say?"

Cassie titled her head up at him. It was hard, but he looked into her eyes and saw confusion and hurt replace the excited light. He wondered what right she had to look that way. He was the one wronged.

"Wonderful news," Cassie said, her tone careful, slow.

She knew he was on to her.

"My pressure's normal. The doctor recommended a slower pace. I have another appointment next week."

"Good," was all he could say. If he said much more, Daniel knew what would come out. Everything. Every hurt, every feeling he had. He would not open himself up that way. Not for Cassie to walk all over him again.

"Daniel, tell me what's wrong. I've missed you," she told him with such a look of sweet innocence Daniel almost believed her.

"Nothing's wrong. I'm going to take a shower."

Daniel studied her face and watched as tears began to form in the corner of her eyes. He watched as she held them back. She was good. Full of disgust, he headed to the bedroom as the doorbell rang.

Daniel turned and leaned against the frame of the door, waiting to see who was there. Paul. Daniel dropped his bag and strode to the door, slamming it in Paul's face, cutting off whatever he was saying to Cassie.

"Why did you do that?" Cassie asked.

"What did he want?"

"To see if I was okay. For some reason, he was concerned."

"He should be."

"Why? What did you do to him, Daniel? What did you tell him?"

"Do to him? Tell him?" Daniel's voice rose with each word. He purposely lowered it. "I think I need to ask what have you done *for* Paul? What have you *told* him?"

"What's that supposed to mean?"

"Exactly what it sounds like, Cassie. What have you done for

Paul that would make him feel free to touch you, to kiss my wife?"

Cassie actually laughed. It was a giggle really. "Don't be ridiculous, Daniel. That was a little peck on the forehead. A kiss between friends."

"Sooooooo," Daniel dragged out, trying to contain his temper. "That's what you claim."

"What else would I say?"

"Describing what I witnessed as friendly means you can string me along a little longer. That way you can have your cake and eat it, too."

"What cake?" she asked quietly, almost as if she were actually confused.

Frustrated and tired of her games, Daniel yelled, "Alright, Cass, let's get it all out in the open."

"That's where I've always wanted it. But now, I'm almost afraid to hear what you have to say."

Afraid. That's exactly how she looked, scared to death. Nothing but an act, he reminded himself. But she seemed to muster some courage from somewhere right away.

"Okay, tell me." She folded her arms across her breast, standing firm but somehow still appearing vulnerable. Something inside of him tried to stop him, tried to tell him to keep his mouth shut, but he went on anyway.

"You are not what you pretend to be. You play games and act as if there's something between us, all to get what you want."

Tears did begin streaming down her face. The sight of them didn't matter. He no longer felt like a participant in this drama. Daniel's head felt light, as if he were watching himself and Cassie play out this scene.

"Why?" She swallowed. "Why would you say that?"

"You know why!" Daniel heard himself yell.

"No—I—do—not!" Cassie yelled right back, carefully pronouncing each word, her hands balled into fists at her sides.

Some part of Daniel was moved by her tears and her posture. He was hurting her. That much registered. But his own hurt was too intense to allow him to stop.

"Why? You wanted to win a bet. You wanted the novel experience of sleeping with a black man. But the novelty has worn off again, I see. You went back for some white meat."

Daniel stared hard, waiting for a reaction, dying inside for Cassie to deny it all.

She didn't. The tears stopped. She wiped away what was left of them with the backs of her hands and quietly left the room. Daniel didn't know where she'd gone. His gaze was frozen on the white wall before him.

She didn't deny it. His mind repeated that phrase over and over again. His legs felt heavy. He landed in the love seat, but he wasn't going to find any love there. Why was it called a love seat anyway, he wondered, feeling numb.

Daniel didn't know how long he sat staring at the wall. His next clear thought was to wonder what she was doing. Then Cassie walked past him, then again in a quick blur of red and white. The third time she passed, she was dragging a carry on luggage bag."

"What are you doing? Where are you going?"

"Home."

"You are home."

"No, I am not," Cassie told him. "Home is where your heart is. Home is a place where people love you, and talk about problems and trust you enough to share their insecurities. *This is not home.*"

Cassie had just described him and his lifelong struggle. Could it be that he was wrong? Had he been wrong for three long years?

The sound of the heavy bag rolling along the hardwood floor had him racing to the door. He should try to talk to her, but

Daniel felt so helpless. Anything he said now would be inadequate.

"What about the baby?" he asked, latching onto their one common ground.

"My baby will be loved. Black or white, this baby is mine."

He had ruined everything, he had lost it all. Cassie's hand was on the doorknob. He had to stop her, had to do something. Daniel grabbed her arm. The pillowcase she was holding crashed to the floor. Now what had he done? Daniel stooped to pick it up. It was the woodgraph he had bought for her in New Orleans. The wooden pieces lay scattered across the floor.

"It's broken. Just give it to me, Daniel. Give it to me so that I can go."

Don't go were the words resounding in his head that wouldn't reach his lips. He carefully picked up the pieces. He put them all inside the pillowcase and handed it to her.

"Daniel, I thought you knew me. You act and sound as if you know so much about me. But you don't. When you sort through that brain of yours and figure things out, you can find me at my aunt and uncle's house."

"Cass," was all he could say.

"If you can't figure it out, don't bother to come at all."

The sound of her bag rolling against the tiled floor of the hall and her angry footsteps hurrying away from him echoed in his mind for a long, long time.

Cassie stormed down the hall, the sound of the luggage rolling along the tile floor satisfying to her ears. Paul was still there, standing at the elevator. She gave him a smack on the shoulder.

"Why did you kiss me?"

"I'm sorry, Cassie."

She took a deep breath, so deep her shoulders rose past her ears. "I know, me, too. I didn't mean to hit you."

"You can do it again if it'll make you feel better."

"It won't, but thanks." It was Daniel she felt like hitting anyway.

When the elevator door opened, Paul lifted Cassie's bag onto his shoulder and held the doors open for her.

"Why are you still here?" it dawned on her to ask.

"I was worried."

"You didn't have to be. Daniel would never hurt me."

"Can I take you somewhere?"

"The airport," Cassie said, having used enough words already. If she said much more, the tears would come again.

Paul drove her to the airport, even going as far as taking her to the gate. Cassie walked beside him, a miserable silence surrounding her.

"I have to say again how sorry I am," Paul blurted all of a sudden. "It's all my fault."

"No, it wasn't," Cassie quietly assured him. "It was bound to happen."

"Daniel does love you. He told a whole plane full of people, remember."

Cassie only nodded her head. But he hadn't told *her*. The disappointment and loss she felt reached deep within her soul, but she refused to allow it to overtake her. As she waited on stand-by for a plane, then boarded and settled in for the hour long flight, Cassie systematically went through every detail of their confrontation. The saddest thought of all, the one that sent the pain rushing through her again, was the fact that Daniel didn't know her.

Daniel was jealous. That much showed he cared, but it also showed that he didn't trust her. Daniel, did not know her at all if he believed the things he'd said about her. That's why she had to get away. She could not be in the same room, apartment, city or state a minute more than she had to.

When the plane landed, Cassie took a cab to her aunt and uncle's house. The ride through Kenner and Metairie, two suburbs of New Orleans, was shadowed by thoughts of Daniel, despite her best efforts not to think about him anymore. The cab exited the interstate on Carrollton Avenue. The Christmas decorations and lights lifted her spirits as she drove past houses decked out for the holiday.

As the cab stopped in front of her childhood home, Cassie immediately felt a sense of comfort, comfort she hadn't wanted from Daniel even if he had tried to give it. Comfort she refused to take from Paul.

She paid the cab driver and walked up to the black wrought iron gate. It squeaked, as always, announcing her arrival. At least it would have if anyone was awake. The driver put her bags on the curb. Cassie hugged the pillowcase with the broken pieces of the woodgraph. She rang the bell. Minutes later, her aunt Margaret came to the door. Her aunt was a few inches taller than she, about five six. She had cut her hair, Cassie noticed. The short style was very becoming with the strands of gray streaking her black hair.

"Cassandra Marie, what are you doing here?" her aunt gasped, unlocking the iron door. Travis, Cassie's home!" Aunt Margaret pulled her into her arms, pillowcase and all, and the tears came rolling down.

"Cassie Bear's here, with her husband!" her snow-haired uncle called as he came down the stairs.

Snow-haired. Her aunt was turning gray, and her uncle had gone completely white.

Cassie shook her head and opened her mouth to explain, but her uncle pulled her close, surrounding her with love and warmth. Exactly what she needed. Cassie laid her head on her uncle's chest, listening to his heartbeat, savoring his presence. How many times had she done that as a child?

"Well, where is he?" Aunt Margaret asked, peering out the front door.

"He's not here," Cassie told them, drying her tears with a corner of the pillowcase.

"You don't mean that husband of yours let his pregnant wife travel all alone?" Uncle Travis demanded.

"He dropped you off and went to the store or something. Right?" Aunt Margaret said, still the peacemaker.

"If he's looking for a K&B or Schwegmann's, he's out of luck. Both stores went out of business. New Orleans fixtures, that's what we thought. Now they're both gone."

"Travis, please, let's not start that again." Cassie's uncle didn't get passionate about many things, but she could understand his being upset about the closing of these stores. The idea of never being able to walk into a K&B drugstore or a Schwegmann's grocery store again was one more disappointment.

"So, is your aunt right? Has he stopped off somewhere?"

"No," was all she could say. This homecoming, while being what she needed, left her feeling even more choked up than before.

Her aunt and uncle shared a look. That meant that they would talk about it later, when she wasn't around. It was so much like old times that Cassie couldn't suppress a glimmer of a smile.

"A smile, that's what I like to see on my Cassie Bear's face."

"Stand back," Aunt Margaret told her. "Let me get a good look at you."

Cassie reluctantly took a few steps away from her uncle's warm embrace. Aunt Margaret placed her hands on Cassie's stomach. "You look so much like your mom when she carried you."

"That was twenty-four years ago."

"There are some things you never forget, Cass. Especially things about your favorite sister. You're going to have a fine baby, going by the width of this stomach."

"You bet," her uncle agreed.

"Let's get you settled and into bed, Cassandra Marie. Both you and my great niece or nephew need to rest. Did you fly? Well, of course you did—"

"Aunt Margaret, Uncle Travis," Cassie called. Her aunt stopped on the stair directly above hers and her uncle looked up from the spot they had left him.

"Thanks."

"Merry Christmas, Cassie," her uncle whispered.

"Thanks for what? Don't you know I consider this a pleasure, to have you home..." Her aunt continued to talk, filling her head with the soothing sound of her voice.

When the lights were off and she lay all alone in her childhood bed, tears came down her face. Those stupid tears again. Cassie prayed that Daniel would search his heart and see her for who she really was.

CHAPTER 8

Daniel wanted to go after her, but he didn't. He had never seen Cassie look so sad, or so determined to get away from him. He had watched from a window as Paul helped Cassie into his car, storing the luggage in the back seat. Did they look like a couple?

Yes.

No.

Maybe.

Daniel wasn't sure. At this moment it didn't matter, as long as she got to her destination safely. Thankfully, it was a good, clear night for flying.

Moving away from the window, he prowled around the house, turning lights on and off, flipping the channels on the TV, playing with the mute button until he finally decided he preferred silence to the Christmas cheer coming through the speakers of the surround sound stereo system of the television.

On his third prowl around the house, he found an empty glass in the kitchen. It had a milk ring at the bottom. Cassie was drinking milk, he thought solemnly. He took the glass to the sink, rinsed it out and watched as the cloudy water drained away. His own thoughts seemed just as cloudy. His restlessness had him traveling around the house once more.

He stopped in front of the Christmas tree in the corner of the living room. It sat on top of a small, round table, barely tall enough to reach his shoulders. He had never seen a Christmas tree decorated anything like this one. It was full of handmade ornaments in every geometric shape imaginable. They were all bordered by pieces of garland, tinsel, mistletoe, holly berries, wrapping paper, anything and everything Christmas looking. The tree called to him, pulled him in to reveal the comic voice of his love. Each shape held a comic strip character extolling the joys of Christmas.

Cassie's own words, he thought as he read each and every one, a little bit of laughter seeping past his dejected mood. Another question answered. Cassie hadn't been bored. She'd spent her time bringing Christmas and laughter into their home. What had he brought? Accusations and distrust.

Daniel lifted his head in exasperation with himself and his actions, his eyes falling on the handmade golden star at the top of the tree with something written on it in fancy writing. What was that called? Calligraphy. That's right. He hadn't known Cassie knew how to do that. But that didn't matter. It was the words, not the way they were written that grabbed him:

Daniel and Cassie, Our First Christmas

Daniel landed in a chair with a solid thump and jumped up with a howl. His rear end had discovered a spiral tablet, the metal binding sticking straight up. Daniel absently read the page.

Things to discuss:

LOVE

The word grew and screamed at him. He quickly ran down the list. All were things they had never stopped to discuss because they meant a solid future he wasn't sure they had. His eyes froze on one particular line:

How to raise our baby. The challenges facing an interracial child.

As he read all of Cassie's concerns, Daniel heard her voice in his head. Her worries were the same as his. How could two people with the same thoughts and goals never meet in agreement?

Mistrust. In his heart, Daniel knew the real Cassie. Somehow, he had known for years that the conclusions he had drawn about her didn't fit. But, nevertheless, he'd let them build.

He threw the tablet to the floor and went to the stereo, pressing buttons just to have something to do. A song he hadn't heard in almost twenty years filled the room.

He stopped the tape. Jackie, his mother. Christmas hadn't been the same since she'd deserted him. He hadn't been the same. That was his problem, he realized. He had never forgiven her. Daniel needed to get past the hurt of a little boy so that he could deal with his problems like a man. His mother had left him, but he had survived. Now he needed to let love and trust back into his life. Daniel pressed the play button and forced himself to listen to the entire song, in a way, freeing himself from some of the pain and hurt that made it so easy to mistrust Cassie.

The song ended, some of his bitter feelings fading away with the voices. It was impossible to expect all the hurt to disappear at once. For the first time in three years, though, Daniel felt that he could accept Cassie's gifts of laughter, smiles, and soft touches. He was ready to reveal his love to Cassie. Then why was he standing in this apartment when his wife was flying hundreds of miles away from him?

Daniel spun and raced across the living room, nearly falling as a searing pain shot across the bottom of his foot.

The damn tablet. Why had he thrown it on the floor? Blood dripped onto the woven throw rug Cassie had brought when she moved in, too much blood. Gritting his teeth, Daniel hopped to the bathtub and stuck his foot under the faucet. The cold water stung, and a flood of blood washed away.

He couldn't tell how deep the cut was, but it definitely was bad. If he hadn't been in such a hurry… If he hadn't acted like such a fool…

"If, if ,if. Shut up man." he told himself as he grabbed a roll of gauze from the medicine cabinet and bound his foot as tight as he could, hoping it would stop the bleeding.

The door bell rang and rang again as he hobbled toward it.

He opened it to find Melanie and some woman wearing a huge hat. They were both all dressed up.

"Come in, have a seat if you want to," he growled, hobbling back to the bedroom. Melanie was the last person he needed to see. And not just Melanie, but Melanie and company.

"And a Merry Christmas to you, too, Grinch."

"Yeah!" Daniel yelled from his room.

He could hear Melanie say something to her companion before her voice got louder as she made her way down the hall to his open bedroom. "What happened to you?"

"Cut."

"That bandage is soaked. What did you cut it on?"

"A tablet. The one sitting in the middle of the living room floor."

"You might need stitches."

"I don't want stitches."

"Just like a man. If you need 'em, you need 'em. It doesn't matter what you want. Where's Cassie?"

"Not here," Daniel told her, going back into the bathroom.

With no hesitation at all, Melanie followed him. "Not here? What do you mean, not here? Where could your pregnant wife be this time of night?"

Daniel stared at Melanie. Concern for her friend spread wide across her face. Her eyes narrowed, and her braids swung from right to left as she moved around the room waiting for an answer. Why didn't he like this woman? There was something about her that rubbed him the wrong way. Something eating at the back of his mind, trying to get his attention. All he wanted to do was get to Cassie. Now his foot was cut wide open, and her best friend was standing over him demanding answers.

"She left me," Daniel told her, hoping that telling her the honest truth would get rid of her.

"And you let her go!"

"Melanie, what's going on back there?" a voice sang from down the hall.

"Some people have manners and don't invade other people's personal space," Daniel told Melanie. Then he thought to ask. "Who's that?" Not that he really cared but somehow recognizing the voice.

"My mother. She missed the shower but wanted to see Cassie."

"What shower?" Daniel absently asked as he hiked his foot on the edge of the sink and unwrapped the bandage.

"The baby shower, fly boy. Oh let me see," she told him, batting his hands away.

"I can handle it."

"Right, just like you handled keeping your wife here. I'm a pre-med student. I might know a little something about this."

Daniel surprised himself by letting her inspect his foot. Something continued to nag at the back of his head but quickly disappeared as she poured alcohol on the cut and re-bandaged it.

"You enjoyed that, didn't you?"

"Stitches and a tetnus shot," she told him, ignoring the comment. "What did you do to Cassie?"

"Not your business," he told her, hopping into the bedroom again.

"Melanie, what's going on? Where's Cassie?" A beautiful woman appeared in the doorway. The truth hit him all at once, knocking him onto the bed. She hadn't changed much in the last twenty-one years. She was still as beautiful as ever, that hat a crown pronouncing her queen of everything, except motherhood of course.

Daniel looked from her to Melanie. The resemblance was amazing, the face not the body. Now he understood his problem with Melanie. It all made sense.

"Hello, Jackie," Daniel whispered, forcing her to notice him in the dark room.

"Do I know you?"

That hurt. His voice had changed he knew, deepened to a man's voice, but still, it hurt. "Turn on the light, it's to your left."

"What's going here?" Melanie asked, an edge in her voice. "I hope it's not what I think it is."

Light flooded the room. "Daniel," Jackie gasped almost immediately. She stood there a moment then flew out of the room. Melanie was right behind her.

"Mama, how do you know Daniel? Mama, wait."

"Jackie!" Daniel yelled, rage filling him. She wasn't going anywhere. Jackie had a lot to answer for, a lot to explain. He had only begun to recognize his problem. Confronting her today could help him get Cassie back, help him keep her in his life forever.

Daniel limped out into the living room, every sense focused on the woman standing near the door. She still wore the same perfume. He could smell it in the air. Her mouth still turned completely down when she was sad. As a small boy, he could remember telling her a joke or doing something silly to make her laugh. He had hated to see her sad. She was crying now. He wondered if she still got the hiccups when she cried. Daniel could remember many nights waking up to hear soft sobs and hiccups coming from her room. He had never bothered her then, somehow knowing in his young mind that a joke wouldn't help.

Melanie was at the front door blocking Jackie's only exit. Daniel stood across the room listening to mother and daughter.

"Tell me what I'm thinking isn't true," Melanie whispered.

"I don't know what you're thinking." Hic. "We're going to be late for church. We'll miss the performance." Hic

"Then we'll be late."

"Your father won't like that."

"Since you won't tell me, I'll ask straight up. Have you had an affair with Daniel?"

"What?" Daniel shouted.

"My God, Melanie, how could you ask me something like that? He's your brother."

It was Melanie's turn to be stunned. "My brother!" she whispered, moving away from the door and finding a seat. "No wonder we always fought."

Jackie, the tears ending but the hiccups still coming at intervals, slowly made her way toward him. "You look so much like your father."

"I didn't think you knew who my father was."

"I deserve that."

"And a lot more."

"I'm sure."

"Are you going to just stand there staring at me all night? Have you got some kind of explanation for me? Something?"

"I do."

"Well."

"You're not ready to hear it, Danny Boy."

"I'm not your Danny Boy. I'm a man. Danny Boy grew up a long time ago, without his mother, and he never knew his father."

"I'm sorry."

"That's something, at least. But you know, I want to thank you, Jackie. Thanks for showing me the damage a parent can do to a child by deserting him. I'm going after my wife now."

"Cassie's a wonderful girl."

"I realize that. She needs me, and so does our baby. See yourself out."

Daniel limped back to his room.

When he came out again, Melanie was waiting for him.

"What are you still doing here?"

"You can't drive yourself to the hospital. That's your right foot."

"Humph."

"Mama's gone on ahead to church. I'll have to drive your car."

"Fine."

Melanie walked beside him and even helped him into the low slung car. Before starting the engine, she turned to him. "Why do you call Mama, Jackie?"

"That's what she wanted."

"She must have been a different person then."

"I wouldn't know. I don't have the pleasure of knowing her now." He didn't want to hear this.

"Do me a favor."

"Sure," Daniel agreed. Anything to shut her up. The pain in his foot, his head, and, he was brave enough to admit, his heart were at the limit of what he could tolerate right now.

"Let some time pass, get over being angry. Then come talk to her, hear Mama's story."

"She's not my mama, never has been." At Melanie's silent stare, he said the only thing that would shut her up and satisfy his need to avoid promising anything he couldn't deliver.

"Maybe."

That one word hung in the small car until Melanie, satisfied with his answer, started the engine, finally driving him to the hospital where at least one pain could be eased.

CHAPTER 9

Christmas Day was officially over. The clock on her nightstand confirmed it. Cassie lay in the huge canopy bed, her mind going over the worst Christmas of her life. She hadn't admitted to herself until just now that she had been waiting all day for Daniel. The baby apparently had too, moving inside her whenever the doorbell or the telephone rang.

The baby, once again, did a somersault across her stomach when the phone issued a loud ring. The sound echoed in the quiet house, everyone having gone to bed long ago. Cassie jumped out of her bed and went down the stairs as fast as was safely possible. She must have picked up the phone right after her uncle.

"When are you going to stop spouting such nonsense, Son." Cassie heard her uncle say.

"When you finally see the truth, Father."

That was her cousin's voice. It was so good to hear. Her homecoming was sad enough but had been even sadder without her cousin T's presence.

"T, is that you?"

"Cassie, you're home. Father, you should have told me. I would have found a way to visit. Maybe convince the general that I was on a mission of conversion."

"Father?" Cassie had a strange feeling that she wasn't going to like the answer to the question she was about to ask. "Why are you calling Uncle Travis Father? What happened to Dad?"

"A father creates a child. A dad directs that child in the correct beliefs. Need I say more?"

"Yes, I think you should." She laughed nervously. "Is this some kind of joke? And what general are you talking about. Did you join the army?"

There was too much mystery surrounding T's absence from the family. Cassie hadn't asked any questions. She'd been away three long years herself.

"You can say that, Cassie. An army that will grow in strength and rectify the imbalance of power in this society, bring it back to the right people."

Cassie didn't laugh this time. T was giving a good impression of an over-zealous white supremacist.

"And who should have this power?" she asked, going along with him, hoping that she was wrong.

"Pure white Americans, of course," he answered nonchalantly.

"Son, that's enough. Don't talk that trash to Cassie. She's expecting and doesn't need to be upset by this nonsense. Your mother and I have heard it too often ourselves."

"Nonsense, Father. It's far from that. You'll see."

Cassie's brain felt numb. Her mind had collected the evidence, but was having great difficulty matching it to what she knew about her cousin.

"Cassie, are you still there?"

"Yes," she heard herself whisper.

"You're having a baby?"

"That's what I told you, Son."

"Father, I'm talking to Cassie." There was a tense moment of silence. "Cassie?" T prompted.

"Yes, T, I'm here."

"You got a father to go along with that baby?"

"Yes," she said again.

"He had better be pure white. Not one of them Creole good-for-nothings passing for white."

Cassie gasped. T went on as if he hadn't heard.

"I'm going to be this baby's godfather. Raise him the right way, straight from the cradle. If you don't catch them young, they grow up with crazy ideas of equality."

Cassie slammed the phone down. The man on the other line was not her cousin. Someone had taken his mind, brainwashed him. *My God!* she thought. There were still people in this world who thought like that, and one of them was a relative of hers, and not just any relative, but her favorite relative.

Cassie blindly left the den where she had come to answer the phone and walked toward the stairs, using the rail to climb each step.

"Cassie," her uncle called from the upstairs landing.

She looked up, suddenly feeling dizzy. Her uncle looked blurry. Reaching for the railing, she only grasped air. Then she lost her balance and slid down the stairs. Though there were only a few, the impact of the fall and the knowledge of what T had become left her cowering at the bottom of the stairs, her hand protectively over her stomach.

"Cassie," her uncle called, running down the stairs. "Cassie Bear, are you okay?" His arms surrounded her.

"What's happening here?" Cassie heard her Aunt Margaret ask. "What's wrong? Cassie didn't fall, did she?"

Cassie cried silent tears as her uncle explained.

The door bell suddenly rang.

"Who could that be this time of night?" Aunt Margaret asked.

Cassie wondered the same thing and watched as Aunt Margaret opened the door a crack to peek past the wrought iron security door. "It's a man, with crutches," she whispered.

She turned back to the door without opening it a bit more than she had to and the mystery man, "Can I help you?"

"I'm looking for my wife. My name is—"

"Daniel!"

At the sound of Cassie's voice, Aunt Margaret jumped, opening the door wider.

"It's Daniel!"

"Do you want to let him in?"

"Yes, I do, Aunt Margaret, let him in."

He had never looked so good, even on crutches. Daniel hopped over to her the moment the door was opened. Uncle Travis gave Daniel a hard stare then moved to stand next to Aunt Margaret.

Even before he could set the crutches down to settle beside her, Daniel asked, "What happened, baby? Why are you sitting on the stairs?"

"I fell."

"You what?" he asked, looking up to the top of the stairway. "Did somebody call an ambulance? Why are you just sitting here?"

"Daniel, I'm okay. It was only a few stairs."

"A few? How many's a few?"

"Five at the most. I really am okay."

"Are you sure?" he asked, his voice calmer. Daniel felt her arms and legs then placed a caressing hand on their baby.

"I'm sure. What happened to you?"

"That tablet of yours cut my foot wide open."

"Sorry."

"I'm not. I deserved it. I was a jealous fool."

"You were."

"And a suspicious, distrustful, insecure jerk."

"Your point is clear, and I agree with every part of it."

"You agree too fast."

"It's the same way I forgive."

"Will you? Forgive me?"

"I already have."

"Hallelujah!" Daniel yelled, pulling her onto his lap. He traced a finger from the nape of her neck down her spine. The heat of the caress seeped through her thin gown. "There are some things we need to discuss."

"Yes, I know."

"Item number one on your list." Daniel's finger followed the same path in reverse and settled at the nape of her neck. The heat of the connection was intense, just like the look in his eyes. Cassie knew what he was going to say, what she had been dying to hear him say. Her hands reached for his face. She held and caressed each side of his jaw, wanting to feel the words as well as hear them.

"Cassie, I love you."

Her head fell forward, resting against his. "I know you do, Daniel. I felt it even when you tried to hide it from me. Love," Cassie told him, "is overflowing in my heart for you." Her fingers moved across his scalp, pulling his head down to meet her lips.

Using the railing for support, Daniel stood and lifted her into his arms. He looked around. "Where did those people go?"

"Those people are my aunt and uncle. They must have left to give us some privacy."

"Privacy, I like that idea. Where are you sleeping?"

"Upstairs, second door on the right. But you can't carry me."

"You're right," Daniel grimaced, standing her on her own two feet. Both of them frowned at his foot.

As soon as Daniel released her, a pain shot through Cassie's abdomen. It was so intense she doubled over with a moan.

"You're not alright. I knew it. Someone call 911!" Daniel had his arm around her supporting her.

"Daniel, I feel wet," Cassie whispered.

A look of confusion crossed his face before understanding dawned. Daniel lifted her nightgown.

"Noooo!" she screamed as what they both saw spun through

her head.

"We need an ambulance. Call 911!" Daniel yelled again as the sounds of hasty footsteps reached them.

"I'm calling, I'm calling right now, Son." Uncle Travis called, waving the cordless phone in the air. He had already assessed the situation. "You hang in there, Cassie Bear."

Daniel held her close, slowly rocking her in his arms. "It's gonna be alright, baby. I'm here, I'm here."

Thank goodness he was. Cassie couldn't concentrate on much else beyond Daniel's touch and his voice. In the background she heard talk about towels and remembered someone lifting her nightgown. Then the sirens.

Daniel stayed with her. She refused to release his hand. He hopped beside the stretcher, never losing contact. She had to touch him, had to feel him there beside her.

"I love you," he said to her over and over again.

Cassie had a death grip on his hand.

Death.

The word echoed in his head. *God, don't let Cassie die.* She was bleeding. Not excessively, but enough to scare him half to death. Never in his life had Daniel felt such fear. The nurse tried to take him away from Cassie. Some foolishness about filling out forms. Cassie wouldn't let him go, and he didn't want to let her go. So he limped beside her, keeping pace with the stretcher as they rolled her in, transferred her to the bed in the examining room, the two of them never losing contact. When the doctor examined Cassie, Daniel stood at the head of the bed with his arms around her. After what seemed like an eternity, the doctor's head came into view.

He looked baffled. "The bleeding has stopped on its own."

The tension in Cassie's shoulders eased. "That's a good sign, right?" Cassie asked, laying her head against Daniel's shoulder. They shared a brief moment of relief and thanksgiving.

"But—"

"Doctor, we don't like buts," Daniel growled.

"But," Cassie paused, pulling Daniel close for a gentle kiss, "we can deal with them." She stared so deeply into his eyes Daniel believed it, just because she had said so. She was making him feel better in spite of the pain she was in herself.

"I'm glad to hear you have that outlook," the doctor was saying. "I have to ask a few questions."

He began right away.

"What occurred just before the bleeding?"

Daniel explained about the stairs.

"I wouldn't have fallen if I hadn't felt dizzy."

"You were dizzy?" Daniel asked.

That's when the flood of questions came one after the other. "Swollen feet? High blood pressure? Blurred vision?" the doctor asked.

"Yes, to all of them," Cassie answered.

That news brought a frown to the doctor's face in an instant.

"Doctor," Cassie said, "I know what you're thinking. My obstetrician has been monitoring my pressure, and there hasn't been a sign of protein in my urine."

"What is he thinking, Cass?" Daniel asked, feeling as if he'd missed something. She gave a slight shake of her head.

"What are you thinking doctor?"

"Your wife may have preeclampsia, sometimes called toxemia, or pregnancy induced hypertension."

"I remember seeing something about that on the video," Daniel said, trying to bring to mind possible complications.

Unfortunately, he hadn't paid much attention to the complications of pregnancy because he hadn't expected any.

"We'll get a urine sample, check for protein, and take your pressure," the doctor said just before leaving the room.

Cassie nodded her head. As soon as they were alone, her grip loosened. She took his hand in both of hers and gently massaged it. "I think I squeezed the life out of your fingers."

"They didn't mind." Daniel planted a soft kiss on her forehead. "They'll get worse treatment during labor pains, when our baby's ready to come into this world."

"You sound positive that we're going to have this baby."

"I am, you told me yourself."

"I did, but I haven't told you everything Dr. Jay said."

"You can tell me now," Daniel suggested, feeling as if she needed to talk.

"After the exam, I sat in Dr. Jay's office, and he told me all about toxemia symptoms: high blood pressure, water retention, protein in the urine, headaches, blurred vision, nausea, vomiting," She paused for a breath. "There were more. The list was long."

"I should have called you; been there with you at the doctor's office. I'm sorry, Cass."

"You've already told me that."

"But I've got a lot to be sorry for."

"You'll make up for it, I'm sure." Cassie gave him a weak smile.

"I intend to. Cass, were you having any of those symptoms?"

"Just the high blood pressure. Tonight was the first time I was dizzy. I had blurred vision. You were right there when I needed you."

"I'm a sorry excuse for a husband."

"No. You're just sorry about a few things," she sighed. "You've already told me that, remember? I don't think I want to hear the word 'sorry' again."

Before Daniel could say anything to that, a nurse barged into the room. "Time for all husbands to clear out."

"Do you want me to stay, Cass?" Daniel asked, not wanting to leave unless she was comfortable with the idea.

"I'll be okay. Go tell my aunt and uncle what's happening. I'm sure they've made it here by now. What I'd really like for you to do is give a urine sample for me. It's a whole lot easier for you. Aim and shoot, that's all you have to do. Aim and shoot."

Daniel nodded, chuckling a little as he left. Cassie would be fine without him for a while. She was cracking jokes again, something he hadn't heard her do in a long time. He certainly hadn't given her anything to laugh about in their short marriage.

Daniel went into the waiting area and found Cassie's aunt and uncle sitting side by side, hands entwined.

"Is she going to be alright?" her aunt asked, jumping up as soon as she spotted him.

"The bleeding has stopped, and when I left, Cassie was telling jokes, Mrs.— " Daniel paused, unable to remember her last name. He knew it was different from Cassie's.

"Margaret, you can call me Aunt Margaret."

"Aunt Margaret," Daniel said easily, responding to her friendly though worried face.

"The name's Travis LaBranch, but Uncle Travis is fine. Since my niece has claimed you, we had better do the same."

Daniel nodded. "I appreciate that open attitude."

Cassie's uncle motioned toward the vinyl chairs they had just vacated. "Have a seat, Daniel, and tell us everything."

Did he mean everything about Cassie and his relationship or everything that had happened since they'd gotten to the hospital? Whichever, Daniel chose to fill them in on the possibility of Cassie having developed preeclampsia.

After he finished, a silence hung in the air. Daniel sat staring at his hands, thinking about nothing and everything. It must have shown on his face, because he felt a hand on his shoulder and a comforting voice say, "With all the progress in modern medicine, I'm sure Cassie will be okay, Son."

Daniel's gazed collided with that of Travis LaBranch. He was sincere in his comfort, but Daniel couldn't help feeling that he didn't deserve it.

"Sir."

"Uh-uh, Cassie's not feeling well, so we have to get this straight now so that she knows that we're a united front. Forget the sir."

"Uncle Travis, Aunt Margaret," he said, including the small lady sitting across from him. "You must think that your niece has chosen a loser for a husband."

"That thought did occur to me. The question is, do we now? Right, Travis dear?"

"I don't know. Let the young man talk."

Daniel was unsure of his standing at this moment. There was genuine concern for Cassie, a bit of openness toward him. What else could he do but dive right into it?

"What I mean is, Cassie shows up at your house in the middle of the night more than five months pregnant without a husband. And when I do turn up, I'm crippled, and don't tell me you weren't surprised by the fact that I'm a black man."

"Daniel, I'm not sure I'm following what you're saying," Travis responded to his outburst. "Now this crippled thing, I'm assuming that's only temporary, right?"

Daniel nodded. Was that the only part they'd heard?

"That's good. You can't fly a plane like that," Aunt Margaret added.

"Am I missing something here?" Daniel asked.

"We already knew about everything else. Our only surprise was finding Cassie on our doorstep," Travis confessed.

"And you don't mind the rest?"

"It would have been nice if you children had waited until after the marriage to start a family, but times are different. The important thing is that Cassie loves you. Margaret and I have witnessed the fact that you love her, too."

They were skirting around the issue. Cassie's uncle was pretty good at it, too. Daniel would just have to throw it at them. "Your niece fell in love with a black man."

"We couldn't help noticing, Son. Do you have a problem with that?" Travis asked, a serious expression on his face.

"Of course not."

"Good, because that would upset Cassie."

"Daniel," Margaret leaned forward, "Cassie called a few weeks ago with the news. We weren't too surprised. Cassie has always done things her way."

"Funny how that same description could fit her cousin." A hard look came into Uncle Travis's eyes, then suddenly turned into sadness. "Opposites, complete opposites. How can two people so alike grow up in the same house and move in two completely different directions?"

Daniel didn't have time to dwell on that strange comment. It didn't seem to be directed at him anyway. The same nurse that had sent him away was nudging him on the shoulder.

"Mr. Adams, husbands can return now, and Mrs. Adams would like to see her aunt and uncle."

"This way," Daniel said, ashamed to realize that while he had been keeping his marriage a secret, Cassie had shared the news right after the wedding.

"Daniel, what's wrong?" Cassie asked as soon as he walked into the room. "Why are you frowning? Have you seen the doctor? What did he say?"

"It's nothing, just some nasty thoughts in my head."

"About who?"

"Me."

The doctor came in then, preventing Cassie's questions. He preferred to do his confessions in private anyway.

The immediate crisis was over, but Cassie was admitted to the hospital for observation. An hour later, after one more visit from the nurse and a final goodbye to her aunt and uncle, Daniel had his wife all to himself. All he could do was sit next to the bed, his two hands clasping one of hers, staring and marveling at his wife, the woman with the biggest heart in the world. Had he already put too much strain on her love for him? Could she take one more disappointment?

"Out with it, Daniel."

"Out? You want me to leave?" he stalled.

"No, I want you to talk. Tell me what's wrong so we can get rid of the frown." Cassie scooted over in the bed to make room for him.

"I don't want to worry you."

"Then come hold me and tell me what's on your mind. If you don't, I won't stop worrying. I'll sit in this bed, wondering if you're hiding something about the baby from me."

"I wouldn't do that." Daniel carefully crawled in next to her, laying his injured foot as far to the right side as he could. "This bed's not made for two."

"It'll work. I put the bed rail up on my side. I can't fall out. Want me to call the nurse to do the same for you?"

"I can handle it."

Cassie leaned her head against his chest, snuggling close to him. It had to have been more than a week since he really had had her in his arms. Daniel pulled her closer and, for a long time, simply savored the feel of her body pressed against his, and the soft touches Cassie gave as she traced little circles in the open V of his shirt. He might have been comforting her, but she was doing the same for him. There was so much to say. Where to start?

"Daniel?"

"Yes."

"I'm waiting."

"The Christmas tree. It was amazing."

Her fingers stilled. "I'm glad you liked it."

"It must have taken a lot of time to decorate."

"All I had was time," she sighed.

"I know."

"Daniel, you're not going to confess to accidentally setting the tree on fire, are you?"

"No." He chuckled.

"Good. I would hate to think that I went through all that hard work for nothing."

"It wasn't for nothing, Cass. You brought Christmas into our home, back into my life." Daniel cleared his throat. "When I got home I was a bit angry. I didn't notice much of anything."

"Yes, you were angry, unreasonably so."

"I realize that, but I'm glad it happened."

"Why?" she asked, twisting to see his face. "Those accusations you made hurt, and I don't mean a little. They wounded my heart. A part of the pain is still there. But having you there for me and the baby has helped. Now, I need to know the cause, Daniel. Why did you say those things to me?"

"At the time, I actually believed what I was saying."

"I hope you have more to add to that," Cassie said when he remained silent. She pulled herself up and away from him.

"I do. Cassie, listen," he told her, grabbing both her hands, hating to see her move away from him. "Accusing you of having something going on with Paul or anybody was unforgivable, but it was necessary, Cass. Hearing myself accuse you of what I suspected and finally admitting out loud what I believed about you for three long years forced me to realize how wrong I was, how wrong I've always been. I do know you, Cassie, from the inside out. That's why my love for you couldn't die."

"Daniel, I love you, too. I always have. What I don't understand is how you could think that our relationship was nothing more than an experiment for me. That I was only interested in you because of a bet."

"I overheard a conversation."

"You overheard a conversation?" So many feelings flashed across her face, it was difficult to separate them. One thing he was certain of, though. Cassie had no idea what he was talking about. "Of course, I knew about the bet. Every flight attendant from California to New York knew, but I never had any interest in winning a bet. I was only out to win you."

"It was because of me and my own issues… and because of your conversation."

"What did I say? When? Where?" she asked.

He sat up, carefully sliding his feet over the side of the bed. "Cass, I'm sorry I started this. You should be concentrating on taking care of the baby. I don't want to upset you more. It's already my fault that you're in the hospital. "

"That's ridiculous, so ridiculous I won't even attempt to deal with that right now. We started this tonight, we need to finish this tonight. I need to know what you heard and when."

Daniel hopped to the chair he had vacated earlier then took a deep breath before he began. "It was the night of Brett's birthday party."

Cassie's eyes narrowed in concentration. "Not the one we went to three years ago?"

Daniel nodded.

"Go on."

"Do you remember introducing me to one of your new friends?"

Cassie thought a minute. "Cherry? That little bubblehead

whose goal in life was to sleep with every man from every country in the world?"

"Yeah. I overheard your conversation."

"And?"

"And it sounded as if… What I mean... You didn't say much of anything, Cass."

"Because I didn't know what to say to such stupidity. Don't tell me you took my silence as guilt."

It all sounded so unbelievable now. Daniel didn't want to admit that he had.

"You did? Without talking to me? Without discussing it?" she whispered. "You left me on an assumption?"

"I guess I did. I hope you'll forgive me." Daniel glanced toward the bed, unable to make eye contact. "The thing to do right now is give you some time alone. I'll be back in the morning. Where are my crutches?"

"In a safe place."

"You took them? Why?"

"Because you aren't going anywhere tonight. You're my husband, and I need you," she told him point blank. "I've already forgiven you, Daniel."

"That fast?"

"The moment you came for me. I just needed some explanation."

"And I gave you an explanation." Daniel leaned against the edge of the bed.

"You've told me enough for now. Somehow I think there's more. It has to do with that frown you wear so often. You had that before I even met you."

"But sometimes you make it disappear, Cass," he told her, his upper body moving even closer, reaching for and claiming her lips for a long, slow connection, one that dealt with more than lips. Before the kiss was over, Daniel's entire body was back in the bed, injured foot and all.

"Daniel," she said after a while. "This unusual power I seem to possess, the one that keeps your frowns at bay. I have a feeling that whatever started them is the same thing that caused you to make those assumptions."

Daniel was silent for a long time. Cassie knew him so well. "I can admit that much. But now, it all seems stupid."

"I need you to talk to me, Daniel. We're in this together."

Daniel nodded his head in agreement and that seemed to be enough for now. Cassie was soon breathing deeply and slowly. With one arm around his wife and the other resting on their child, Daniel felt complete. He was a man with a love of his own, a family of his own, something that had been lost to him from the minute his mother deserted him.

Jackie. That was an issue he would not deal with right now, but family, that was another thing altogether. Daniel had always had family: grandparents, aunts, uncles, cousins each with their own respective family. But he had always felt himself the odd man out. Daniel hadn't realized until now how envious he had been of them. That's why he'd stayed away. He should have embraced their love instead of wrapping himself up in misery.

There were many events Daniel wished that he could change, but there was nothing he could do about it. The past was over. Instead, he had hope for the future.

Daniel couldn't wait to tell everyone about Cassie and the baby. Tomorrow he would call Ness. She could spread the word.

CHAPTER 10

A strong chin. Their baby should have a firm chin just like Daniel's, especially if it's a boy. Cassie thought. Since awakening a few minutes earlier, she'd been studying Daniel. His eyebrows, now they would be perfect on a boy, but Cassie hoped a daughter wouldn't inherit that particular feature. His height, definitely, Cassie told herself, moving even closer to her husband and lifting the covers to study how much further Daniel's legs continued from the point where hers ended. Height, boy or girl, their child needed height.

"What are you doing?" Daniel whispered in her ear.

"Praying to the gods of gene distribution."

"For what?"

"Height, our child needs height."

"That's necessary?" He laughed.

"Of course, short people get no respect."

"But they're so cute."

"Cute, huh?" Cassie said as she pulled his head toward her lips, demanding a kiss he quickly bestowed. Soft, gentle, sweet, and over.

"Hey," Cassie complained, "I wasn't finished."

"We're in a hospital bed."

"We are, aren't we?" She giggled, burying her face into his chest. "I honestly forgot," she mumbled into the V of his half-buttoned shirt. Cassie looked up a minute later. "Still think short people are cute?"

"And sexy as hell."

"Good answer," she told him. "Especially since I'm round all over."

"What you are, is perfectly pregnant."

"I hope I stay that way for a whole lot longer."

"Where's the positive thinking? Everything's going to be fine."

"I have to believe that."

"And if it isn't," he told her, lifting her chin to look into her eyes, "if it isn't, we'll still have each other."

Their children had to have his beautiful green eyes, Cassie thought, staring into the depth she found in them. "Have I told you today that I love you?"

"You showed me. Didn't tell me once yet."

"I love you, Daniel Adams."

"Good, because I love you, Cassie Adams," he said, pulling her against him. Daniel took a deep breath and slowly let it out. Cassie could feel his lungs fill as his chest expanded, hear and feel the gush of air as it blew past her hair. Once, twice.

"Daniel. What is it?"

"There's something I want to tell you."

Cassie sat up. Daniel moved to put a pillow behind her back. They'd talked about so much last night. The most serious, most important conversation they'd ever had.

"I know I should have, but I never told my family about our marriage."

Funny, but she had forgotten that hurt. Before she could say anything, Daniel went on.

"I wasn't keeping it a secret. No, I take that back. I was keeping it a secret, but not because I was ashamed of you or anything like that. I wasn't sure we'd last as a couple, and I didn't want my family involved. "

"In a way that makes a lot of sense." And it did. Daniel had been sending mixed messages from the beginning. This revelation wasn't major. Everyone in his family already knew he was married. Daniel was the only person who hadn't been clued in.

Cassie had just opened her mouth to reassure him and give him the news that their marriage was old news when a quick knock and the sight of a tall, beautiful woman bursting through the door interrupted her. Cassie knew who it was immediately.

"Daniel, get out of that bed and give Cassie some room to breathe." Ness nearly pulled her cousin off the bed as she gave him a quick kiss on the cheek in greeting.

"Cassie, I finally get to see you in person." Ness sat on the edge of the bed in the same spot Daniel had recently occupied and pulled Cassie toward her for a hug. "Your face matches your voice perfectly. You have a beautiful wife, Daniel, and you had no business keeping her a secret. You do know that you're going to pay for that one?"

"How'd you know?" Daniel asked, a single frown line popping up on his forehead.

"The telephone. I called one day looking for you. Your wife answered. We've been phone buddies ever since. Right, Cass?" Cassie could only nod as she watched another frown line pop out on his brow.

"That answers one question, but I've got another. How did you know I was here, Ness?"

"Teresa told me."

"Our cousin Teresa?"

"Yep, she was getting off the night shift when you came in. She thought that maybe one of us was in the hospital, so she did some checking."

"And found out it was me," Cassie answered, finding her voice.

"Exactly."

"And of course she told you," Daniel surmised, his frown deepening.

"Of course."

"And now everyone has been informed."

"That's true, Cuz, but I told them to stay away until I was able to give a full report."

"Ha, a lot of good that'll do," Daniel grunted just as a succession of knocks resounded on the door, and it opened to admit an older couple.

"Daniel?"

"Come on in, Aunt Joyce, Uncle Cal," Daniel called.

"We were worried when we heard the news."

"Of course you were," he told her, the frown completely disappearing as he went to embrace his aunt.

"Is that who I think it is up there in that bed?"

"Yes it is, Uncle Cal. Come meet my wife." Daniel drew his arm around his aunt and laid his hand upon his uncle's shoulder as he carefully guided them to the bed, barely limping at all.

Cassie could sense how important these people were to him and was suddenly anxious to make a good impression.

"Don't look so nervous," he whispered to her. "There's plenty more family. You ain't seen nothin' yet," he told her with a slow New Orleans drawl.

Reaching for her hand, Daniel announced, "Aunt Joyce, Uncle Calvin, this is Cassie. Cassie, these people are the best substitute parents anyone could ever have."

"With you being our favorite nephew, what do you expect?" his uncle bellowed.

"Cal, we don't have favorites," Daniel's aunt denied in a soft, sweet voice.

"Of course not, Joycie," her husband agreed with a wink.

"Welcome to the family, Cassie," Joyce Lewis invited. "I'm just sorry we have to meet in the hospital." She laid a brown paper bag on the small table beside Cassie's bed. "I brought you some homemade gumbo, no salt. Ness told us about the high blood pressure."

"Yes, thank you, I appreciate it," Cassie told the nice woman who seemed to mean so much to her husband. It made her wonder again about his own parents. There was so much more to learn about Daniel.

"Thc introductions and the nice chit chat are over," Daniel's uncle boomed out. "Tell us why you've been hiding this wife of yours."

"Cal." Joyce elbowed him in the ribs. "It's not the time or the place," she whispered loudly.

"It's never the right time or the right place."

"For a man as old as you are, you'd think that you would have learned some tact by now."

"Tacks? What do tacks have to do with anything, Joycie?" He grinned.

Cassie looked from one to the other, unable to keep a smile off her own face. They were so different from each other in personality and looks. Aunt Joyce appeared to be a soft-spoken woman, merely an inch or so taller than Cassie with skin a very light brown, almost manila. Uncle Cal was tall and loud with a voice that bounced off every wall with an extra kick. His complexion was a deep dark brown.

Cassie peeked over at Daniel. The frown lines hadn't reappeared; a grin, instead, covered his face. Turning toward Ness, Cassie found a smile as wide as that of her father's.

"Stop it, Daddy. Cassie doesn't know a thing about your obstinate behavior or your tendency to be obtuse."

"Now where do you come from, using all those big 'O' words, Miss Teacher? As for Cassie, she'll just have to get used to me. I'm too obstinate to change."

Everyone laughed at that.

"Welcome to the family," Calvin told Cassie, giving her a peck on the cheek. "With you joining the ranks, maybe Ness's husband won't stand out so much. Scott and those two little angels look like three grains of rice in a bowl full of red beans," he laughed, winking at her again. "But don't red beans and rice go good together?"

Cassie didn't know what to say to that and wasn't given the opportunity to respond.

"We'll let you rest, give you two newlyweds some time alone," he told her.

"Wait till I tell your favorite son-in-law what you said about him." Ness kissed her dad on the cheek. "And Daddy, this is not a hotel, it's a hospital. Daniel and Cassie won't be having much time alone."

"Your father knows that, Ness. Don't any of y'all pay any attention to him. You rest now, Cassie, you too, Daniel. I'm not going to ask what happened but take care of that foot. And one more thing." Daniel's aunt lowered her voice. "You do know there's something else we need to talk about."

"Yes, ma'am," Daniel immediately answered.

Cassie had to do a double take. Was that her Daniel?

Before his aunt and uncle could reach the door, a very pregnant woman and a tall, handsome man walked into the room, after a quick knock, of course.

"Not a hotel, huh?" Calvin declared to everyone in general, and then to the newcomers, "Monica, girl, what are you doing here?"

"I couldn't stop her, Papa Cal. We had a doctor's appointment next door, and Monica insisted that it was her duty to come over and see about her cousins."

"That's exactly right. So please refrain from discussing it any further."

The room was suddenly completely quiet as Monica waddled over to the hospital bed.

"Daniel," Cassie couldn't resist asking, "why the silence?"

"We don't want Monica to explode," he whispered.

"Explode?"

"Pay no attention to them, Cassie. My family claims that when I'm angry, I become very polite. I've never noticed any change in my speech. Personally, I think they're all crazy."

"Oh, yeah, I agree."

"We're nuts!"

"She can't do a thing with us."

Every degree of acquiescence was voiced in a matter of seconds.

Monica laughed, ignoring them all to tell Cassie, "I'm glad to meet you Cousin. As my husband, Devin, or Bug as some people call him, the man standing next to my dad, said, I insisted on coming. There's no telling what these babies plan on doing or what restrictions the doctor will have for me today."

"That's right, you're having triplets," Cassie remembered from their phone conversations.

"Three more. First time around, I had them one at a time. I guess I was trying to get it over with in one shot."

"And you're doing a wonderful job, Brown Eyes," Devin said, coming up behind her.

"With your help, Dev. I couldn't have done it without you."

"No, you couldn't." He laughed. "Welcome to the family, Cassie. Be prepared for chaos, mayhem and fun."

"You mean this is only the beginning?"

"Just the tip of the iceberg," Devin warned. "Hey Daniel, what's up with the foot."

"Nothing much," Daniel said, making light of his accident. He gave Cassie's hand a squeeze, agreeing with Devin's assessment by whispering once again, "You ain't seen nothin' yet."

"Don't scare her," Ness chimed in, changing the subject. "Scott's adjusted, and Devin dove right in. The family's not as bad as they're saying. A bit overwhelming at first, but then you get used to it. Hey," Ness stopped to ask Monica, who had found the only seat in the overcrowded hospital room, "who's watching the kids?"

"Scott."

"All seven of them? By himself?"

"Hey, he volunteered when the sitter didn't show," Devin answered.

"Your three and our four. The babies alone will make him crazy."

"Oh, that reminds me." Devin unashamedly grinned. "Scott sent a message. Ready Monica?" He nodded in his wife's direction.

"Help!" they yelled together.

"How could you do this to your best friend, Devin?"

"That's exactly why I did it. It'll keep him on his toes."

At that moment, a nurse burst into the room. "How did all these people get in here? Visiting hours have not even begun today. This is a hospital, not a party house. All you people need to go."

"Bye."

"See you later."

"Take care," they called as the nurse ushered everyone out the door.

Cassie found herself alone with the fussy nurse. "How can people expect you to rest if they come barging in here early in the morning? And how the doctor can examine you with a roomful of people, I do not know."

The nurse fluffed Cassie's pillow and tucked her sheets in. "What's the matter? You look flushed, all red in the face. That was too much for you, huh? Those kinds of people are just loud."

"Some people are, but I'm not sure I know what you mean by 'those kinds.'"

"You know honey, black."

Cassie laughed loud and long. She didn't know why, but the

nurse's comment amused rather than upset her. "Thank you for your concern, but I was enjoying their company. My family might have been loud, but they were definitely welcome. I'll make sure my husband gives them the correct times for visiting."

The poor lady's face turned red. "Family?"

"Yes, and I'm afraid you got rid of my husband, along with everyone else."

"Oh, I'm so sorry. I was only taking care of my patient, you know."

"Yes, I know."

Daniel opened the door and peeked inside. "Can I come back in, or am I banned from the room, too?"

"So you're Mrs. Adams' husband?"

"Yes, that would make me, Mr. Adams."

"Now everything's clear. That was an honest mistake, if I do say so myself. Take better care of your wife," the nurse ordered as she huffed out the door.

Cassie shrugged her shoulders at his questioning look and patted the bed. Daniel skip-hopped on over.

"Sorry about the mad rush."

"I was happy to meet everyone."

"You haven't seen even half of them yet."

"I realize that. Ness has been telling me all about everyone."

"M-m-m, Ness, huh? I'm not surprised." Daniel paused, studying his foot as he made himself more comfortable on the bed. "I'm glad she called. It was Ness that gave me hope for us."

"I'm glad."

"Her husband Scott is white, but you probably knew that."

"Yes." Cassie waited to hear more.

"Well, seeing them together, a nice, happy family, I wanted that with you.""Exactly what I wanted."

"Cass," he said. "You do understand what I was trying to tell you earlier? My reasons for not telling my family about our marriage?"

Cassie nodded.

"I'm going to have to answer to my aunt for this, and Ness and probably Monica, too. Who am I kidding? My whole nosy family. But you, Cass, are the most important person in all of this. I have to know that you understand my reasons."

"I do. Couldn't you tell?"

"Thank God," he said, leaning over to kiss her.

"Stop it right there. That's how you two got in this predicament to begin with," a voice warned.

Daniel slowly drew away from Cassie, turning to face the doctor they had met last night.

"Think you could let me examine your wife right now?"

Daniel slid to the edge of the bed.

"Looks like you can use a new bandage. Have you been using that foot?"

"Somebody stole my crutches."

"Under the bed." Cassie pointed.

The doctor raised an eyebrow as he pulled one, then the other, from under the bed.

"You could bum a new bandage from one of the nurses while I make sure everything's fine with Mrs. Adams."

Daniel glanced at her for consent. Cassie smiled her agreement before he left.

The doctor chattered in the way all doctors do, especially obstetricians when examining private areas of the body. In her mind, Cassie replayed every moment of her life since she'd discovered that she was pregnant. Could two people ever have had more misunderstandings? Cassie was sure there were others who'd had rockier starts than theirs, but she and Daniel wouldn't be categorized with such a group ever again. They had started to talk and would continue to share their problems. They would have their baby and raise a family together, Cassie decided as the doctor completed the examination.

"Good news. No signs of spotting," he told her with a snap of the latex gloves he was removing. "And after studying your chart, I'd say you'll probably get to got home today after the ultrasound I've scheduled."

"She will?" Daniel asked, coming into the room at a much faster pace with the use of the crutches. "That means Cassie and the baby are alright now? They're going to be fine?"

"If you take a few precautions, Mrs. Adams should continue the pregnancy without any further complications."

Daniel reached the bed and sat in his spot next to Cassie, his hand finding hers. They both nodded, waiting expectantly for the doctor to continue.

He ran through a list of restrictions. Cassie was willing to do whatever he wanted if it kept her baby safe in her womb. He again asked a lot of questions concerning how she'd felt since being admitted.

Though blurry vision and the dizziness had disappeared, he warned that they could return of she didn't follow the doctor's orders.

By that evening, Cassie had been released and found herself tucked into her childhood bed, her husband beside her, and a healthy dinner provided by Aunt Margaret before her.

Daniel had provided her with comfort and support from the moment they left the hospital. Their relationship was evolving. Cassie could feel it in her bones. There was a new kind of tension, sexual but tender, wanting but giving.

They ate in silence, sharing the tray on her lap. The air between them became loaded with yearning. Their hands grazed as Daniel lifted the glass in offering.

"Milk?" he asked in a low tone.

Cassie nodded. "Strong bones."

Daniel watched her as she drained the glass. The look they

shared as he took it away was a hot wave of acknowledgment confirming their deeper feelings.

Cassie listened to the deep sound of his breathing and felt his warm breath breeze past her ear. He was that close.

"Are you done eating?"

Cassie stared at the last strip of chicken tenderloin and baby carrots on her plate and nodded. Daniel's plate was nearly full. He lifted the tray, placing it on the bedside table.

"I'll take that down later," he told her, getting up and slowly moving to the other side of the room without his crutches.

"Where are you going?"

"To take a shower," Daniel answered, as if it was the last thing he wanted to do.

"What about your foot?"

"There are ways." He shrugged with a tight smile.

I guess there are ways, Cassie thought as she watched him leave to take a shower he obviously didn't want. "Daniel, wait," she called.

He turned toward her once again, the strain of longing reflected on his handsome face.

"We can't, Cass."

"I know, but," she paused, "there are ways."

Understanding and agreement shone immediately in his eyes. He was back by her side in a second.

Cassie lifted the covers, and welcomed the feel of him as he crawled in beside her.

"Aw, Cass, you have to know this. I don't just love you, I *love* you."

"I know exactly what you mean," she told him, moving a hand between them to reach the skin beneath his sweatshirt. Her fingers spread wide in an attempt to tactically claim him. Daniel took her hand and gently stilled it.

"Let me."

Daniel raised himself and rested his head on the palm of a hand and looked down at her, his love, his tenderness shining in his light green eyes.

He loved her with caresses starting at her chin. He pressed a spot on her skin with the pad of his finger, then followed up with the tip of his tongue and the press of his lips.

Daniel took his time. Each spot he kissed was no farther than an inch from the spot that he'd just grazed with his soft, sweet touch. Cassie savored the heat as it spread down her neck and across her shoulders. Daniel continued the rhythmic press, taste, kiss, press, taste, kiss.

Snap. He released the top snap on her shirt. Cassie's whole body jumped from the unexpected sound in the quiet room. The tingle in the skin he had just exposed spread to her breast. She was heavy with wanting, couldn't wait for him to move, to act. Her hands found his chest again. She rotated her palm, her fingers flat against him.

"No, Cass." He stilled her hand and dove straight for her collar bone and moved slowly upward with tiny kisses until they were face to face, eye to eye.

"Let me love you, Cass. I owe you."

No less achy than before, Cassie withdrew her hand.

Daniel unsnapped more of her shirt, caressed, marked, tasted, and kissed a line straight to her navel. He teased her senses, doubling the intensity as he moved downward, spreading the heat within her until it reached the very tips of her fingers.

Her fingers could no longer hold back. There was no sane reason to allow the need to touch him to go unrelieved when he was so close. Cassie's fingertips managed to brush across his hard warmth. No, she corrected herself, smooth, silky, heat. Her fingers stroked once, twice...

His fingers brushed the curly hair beneath her panties. She gasped, releasing a huge rush of air, tensed and then relaxed as

Daniel's tender caresses sent shivers of pure bliss throughout her body.

Cassie opened her eyes. She found herself nestled against Daniel's chest. The hand that had barely brushed him and still ached to touch him was entwined in one of his. He had shown her so much love and such intense pleasure, and she had given him none.

"I'm so sorry, Daniel."

"For what?"

"I started this. You gave me so much, but..."

"But what?"

Cassie could hear the smile in his voice, feel it in his body. She moved away, just far enough to stare at him face to face, and lifted their entwined hands. "You stopped me."

"No, I moved your hand out of harm's way."

She grinned. "So you did."

"I did. At the time I didn't care, but now I find myself in a sticky situation."

"Daniel," she laughed, "I am so sorry."

"It was worth it."

He kissed her long and hard before hopping back to the bathroom. "Cassie?" he called.

"M-m-m-m?'

"While I'm in the shower, I'll be thinking up more of those 'other ways.' "

CHAPTER 11

"Well, a ho-ho-ho to you, big brother!"

"Melanie, what are you doing here?" Daniel hissed. "I asked you to mail the tree, not to bring it in person." He leaned against the closed door and peered down the hall. Cassie's uncle had handed him a tray full of food right before Melanie appeared.

"Well, it's nice to see you too, Fly Boy," she answered, standing on tiptoe to peer at the tray in his hands. "What do you have there? A nice nutritious breakfast for my sister-in-law. All to keep my niece or nephew healthy."

"Stop it with that kind of talk," Daniel demanded, eyeing her attire. Melanie had to be the skinniest Santa Claus he had ever seen. She was wearing an interesting version of a Santa suit. It was some kind of red outfit with white trim at her ankles and wrists. She even wore a Santa hat and carried a red sack.

"What am I doing but speaking the truth, Brother Boy?"

Daniel frowned down at her. "Cassie's not dressed. You can wait for her downstairs. I'll tell her you're here."

"Not dressed? We were roomies forever. I've even seen her in her undies."

He wasn't going to get rid of her. "Why did you come here? Couldn't you have just called?"

"Why you ungrateful… I've got a good mind to step on your foot. But lucky for you, I'm into healing. I'll let it go, this time around."

"Daniel? Is that Melanie's voice I hear?" Cassie called from inside the bedroom.

Daniel felt his frown deepen. Despite that, Melanie stared up at him, challenging him to deny it.

"Why haven't you told Cassie yet?" Melanie demanded.

Daniel couldn't pretend he didn't know what she was talking about, so he just told her the truth. "I haven't had a chance to."

"Haven't had a chance—"

Daniel, tray in hand, advanced, putting weight on his already overused foot, and slowly backed Melanie in a corner. She stopped with a soft thud. "Cassie was released from the hospital yesterday. She almost lost our baby. Don't come in here upsetting my wife. What happened the other day was not a momentous moment in my life. The last thing on my mind right now is Jackie," he hissed in a whisper, continuing to frown down at her. Melanie could be so annoying and so unpredictable. An expression he had never seen crossed her face with the speed of lightning. She looked frightened. Daniel suddenly felt guilty.

"Look, Melanie, I didn't mean to…"

"Don't worry about it, Fly Boy." She pushed past him, rattling the tray.

"Daniel, that is Melanie. You two get in here or I'm coming out."

The Melanie he was used to stared back at him a moment before bursting into the room ahead of him. "Merry Christmas, Cass. What's the idea of running out before I could tell you that?"

Daniel came in right behind her, putting the tray on a desk in one corner. He watched as Cassie was reunited with her best friend.

There had been so much to tell Cassie, so much happening, that finding Jackie had completely left his mind. He should have known Melanie would bring it back.

Daniel sat at the desk chair taking note of his newfound sister. She looked a lot like Jackie. It wasn't blatantly obvious, but it was there, especially since he knew. Melanie even had Jackie's flamboyant, sassy ways. But Melanie was different. Right smack in the middle of the holiday, she had traveled to New Orleans to see about her friend. She'd even brought Christmas presents and her own brand of cheer. Jackie and Melanie were different: one selfish, the other selfless.

Daniel grinned, shaking his head, as Melanie entertained Cassie by strutting her skinny body around the room, showing off a pair of new earrings, making Cassie laugh, taking her mind off the baby for just a little while. A new respect for Melanie began at that moment.

"Mel, you had better stop all that. Daniel's not used to seeing your glamour walk. He's liable to kick you out of here for trying to scare me to death."

"You don't mind, do you, Fly Boy?"

"That's Daniel."

"So you say."

"You two won't ever stop arguing, will you? My best friend and my husband, you get along like brother and sister. I can remember when T and I ..."

Cassie went on with her story about her cousin T, but Daniel didn't hear a word. Melanie probably didn't either. A silent acknowledgment passed between them.

"Time for breakfast." He placed a tray on her lap as Cassie finished her tale.

"I'm going to see about finding us a place to live," he whispered.

"There's no rush. Aunt Margaret and Uncle Travis aren't in a hurry for us to leave."

"I want my wife under my roof."

"I understand, sir," Cassie answered, saluting him.

Daniel gave her a quick goodbye kiss. He made eye contact

with Melanie and found himself mouthing, "Later, Sis."

Melanie smiled at that, mimicking Cassie's actions by saluting him.

"Alright, Mel, why are you hitting on my husband?"

"My friend, you've got to be kidding. Fly Boy? You got it right when you accused us of acting like brother and sister."

"I know you, Melanie. There's something going on. Maybe you two are discovering that you really don't hate each other." Cassie tilted her head to study her friend. "Don't worry, I'll find out from Daniel. I have ways."

Melanie rushed over. "I believe you do. Confess, and remember, I'm your best friend."

"Not this time, Mel. Daniel and I have come a long way."

Melanie gave a grunt of disappointment and was about to protest when Aunt Margaret came in carrying a mug of hot chocolate.

"Here's a little something for you, Melanie dear. Cassie, you haven't eaten your breakfast."

"My fault, Mrs. LaBranch. I'll make sure she eats every bite. We have to keep Cassie strong."

"That's true," Aunt Margaret agreed, a worried frown covering her face. She patted Cassie's hand. "You have a good friend, Cass, and she's so cheerful," the older woman added before closing the door.

Cassie finally took a bite out of her muffin.

"She's worried about you."

"I know. It's probably a good idea that Daniel and I get our own place. Looks like we'll be staying in good old N'awlins for a while."

Melanie nodded, sipping her chocolate, a serious expression on her face. "Daniel tells me you were released from the hospital yesterday."

Cassie's eyes watered at the thought of her near loss.

Melanie's face changed instantly. "I let you out of my sight for one day and what do you do? Run off and cause trouble."

"Is that what I did?" Cassie laughed.

"That's exactly what you did. You forced me to come to New Orleans, a place I've been dying to visit, but you know Mama, she never wanted me to come."

"That's right, she didn't."

"So here I am, defying my mother's wishes and having to tote Christmas and baby shower gifts across the entire state of Texas. All because you couldn't keep still."

"I had a fight with Daniel."

"And you made up, thank goodness."

"We did, and thanks."

"For what, my friend?"

"For not asking for details."

"That's not what I'm here for. See this hand?" Melanie waved her neatly polished hand before her. "It's here for helping. Now where do you want the rest of the presents?"

"You brought them all?"

"Had them shipped overnight the day before I left. They got here just after I did." Melanie left, returning with a big box full of the gifts Cassie had bought Daniel for Christmas. Uncle Travis followed with an even bigger box.

"What's in that one?"

"I'm not supposed to tell."

"I knew you and Daniel were up to something."

Cassie finished her breakfast, enjoying Mel's company. Then Melanie did Cassie's nails and French braided her shoulder length hair.

"You do that so quickly."

Melanie secured Cassie's hair with a barrette. "It's a gift."

"You've done so much for me, Mel, but I need to ask for one more favor."

"Let it out!"

"Could you pick up some crazy glue at K&B?"

"There is no K&B, Cassie." Uncle Travis returned with a few more boxes. "Don't you remember, they sold out on us?"

"You're right, Uncle Travis, I forgot. Go wherever you want to as long as you come back with the glue."

"You don't plan on sniffing it, do you?"

"Please, I need it for a repair job." Cassie reached inside the drawer of the nightstand and pulled out a pillowcase. She removed the pieces of what was once the woodgraph she had come to cherish in such a short time.

"Aw, Cass, how did it break?" Her tone showed how much she knew Cassie treasured the gift from Daniel.

"It only needs a little glue here and there. Then it'll be as good as new. Could you get me the glue?"

"Santa's helper."

No sooner was Melanie out the door than it was filled again with another face.

"Knock, knock."

"Ness, come in. I'm full of company today. I thought I'd be bored silly with nothing to do."

"I won't stay long. I came to drop off a sanity basket: two puzzles, one with cute little kittens, the other one of the Eiffel Tower; a giant book of crosswords and word searches to keep your brain busy; a book of comics all about New Orleans. Being a native, I figured you'd appreciate it."

"Perfect. Thanks, Ness."

"That's what I'm here for. When you run out, call for more.

Better yet, send Daniel out, keep him busy."

"Good idea."

"Who was the Santa I saw in the hall."

"My best friend Melanie."

"She looks familiar. I've probably seen her around somewhere. In New Orleans everybody seems to know everybody else."

"True, but not this time. This is Mel's first trip here."

"She must have a twin. If she wants any help getting around, call me. I've gotta run. You rest now.

"Will do," Cassie promised, waving her off.

Cassie spent the rest of the morning gluing together the pieces of the woodgraph. It reminded her of one of those wooden 3-D puzzles designed for little kids, except the pieces weren't perfectly matched. A piece of the little girl's dress was chipped at the bottom, and the streetcar looked a little worn. All in all, the pieces fit back together almost perfectly. She glued the frame together last, tracing the edges of the raised carving. It was so full of life you could almost feel it and it had been broken to pieces because of carelessness. She couldn't help seeing the similarity between what happened to the woodgraph and to her and Daniel. Fortunately it seemed their marriage would be made whole as well.

Cassie placed the woodgraph on the nightstand to dry and found herself staring at the big box Melanie had brought from Houston. Her last thought as she fell asleep was to wonder what was inside.

Cassie woke up to a darkened room with the soft melody of

one of the Jackson 5 Christmas originals floating to her ears. She didn't remember leaving the tape on. Turning her head, she saw her little tree sitting in the corner.

"Hello there," Daniel whispered.

"Daniel, you're home—" It all came back. "We're in New Orleans, aren't we?"

"Yes, we are."

"The tree?"

"I love it," he said matter-of-factly. "I sent for it. Christmas isn't over yet, you know."

"No, it isn't," she answered, trying to hold back tears, tears that built and overflowed, along with her emotions. Frustrated, she swiped at them with her hand. She was tired of tears, but there was nothing she could do but give in to them.

"Hey, baby, why are you crying?"

"Everything," was all she could say.

Daniel wrapped his arms around her, lifted her out of the bed, blanket, sheets and all, to sit on the small balcony overlooking her aunt's garden.

Cassie didn't see the poinsettias, red and white softly glowing in the moonlight, but she knew they were there as they had always been every Christmas since she was a little girl. Her aunt would order huge pots of them to decorate the patio. Daniel's chest, his scent, his arms were all she could focus on. He held her until the tears stopped.

"Finding you, losing you, almost losing the baby." Cassie paused to catch her breath.

"Sounds like we need a lost and found."

"A found, just a found," she sniffed, ending the tear explosion.

"Okay, just a found. And that's because. . ."

"Finding is better than losing. We found each other again."

"And I found out what a fool I'd been."

"It has to be better than finding that when you're pregnant you cry for *anything.*"

"Not a big deal, because I find that I don't care if you cry all night. You'd still be my beautiful wife."

"We're lucky to be finding out all this stuff, don't you think?"

"Like that music that's playing."

"Yeah," Cassie answered, peering up to find evidence of frown lines, something to indicate his reaction to those particular songs. "Ness told me about your mother."

"She did, huh?" Cassie felt his body relax as he shifted her into a more comfortable position. "Ness talks too much."

"She's a good cousin, she loves you."

"You should have seen the love she surrounded me with today."

"What happened?" Cassie sat up straighter, the covers falling off her shoulder. Daniel pulled them up again, his warm hand lingering on that spot.

"I stopped by Aunt Joyce's house today. Monica and Ness were there."

"Did they give you a hard time?"

"The hardest. Besides not informing them of my married state, my aunt assured me, in as nice a way as possible, that I was going to burn in hell if we don't get married by a priest."

Cassie shrugged her shoulder. "I'm Catholic, so are you."

"That point was made."

"And?"

"I'm happy with the way things are. We're married, and as far as I'm concerned, we're going to stay that way. Whether or not we get married again is up to you, Cass. After all, I may have rushed you a little before."

"Just a little?" Cassie asked, eyebrows raised.

"Just a tiny little bit," he admitted, nudging his head against hers. He found a small patch of skin exposed at her neck and caressed it with a gentle, warm breath.

Cassie shivered.

"Did you know that my brain has been working overtime creating dozens of 'other ways?'"

"Only dozens? I'm sure I came up with a least a hundred."

"Nice to see that our minds are on the same track." Daniel stood, carrying her inside.

"Daniel," she said, her tone forcing him to stop. "You are going to bust your foot wide open again."

"I'm fine. I got some extra padding added to the bandage. I'm almost as good as new."

"Almost is not good enough. Put me down. I think I might be able to make it from the balcony to the bed. The doctor said small trips were okay. You know, to do those important little things like go to the bathroom, get a breath of fresh air," she teased.

"I realize that. I was simply living out one of my fantasies."

"To hold and carry an emotional, short beach ball?"

"To feel the warmth, softness, and love of my wife in my arms and know that it's for no one else but me." As he finished, the phone rang.

He stopped at the bathroom door, putting Cassie on her own two feet. "Go take care of some of those important things. I need to answer to the phone. We're the only ones here."

Inside the bathroom, Cassie could hear Daniel's voice in the bedroom. Cassie took her time brushing her teeth and washing her face. Although the braid Melanie had put in her hair was still intact, tiny spirals of hair framed her face. Pregnancy might have made her emotional and fat, but it also did wonders for her complexion, Cassie noticed, staring at herself in the mirror.

"Cass, the phone's for you," Daniel called through the door.

"Who is it? It has to be Ness or Monica because I know you haven't been talking to Melanie all that time." She opened the door.

"Neither one." He looked down at her in the open doorway. "It's your cousin T."

"Oh."

"Something wrong?" Daniel asked, lifting her chin.

"No, not really." Cassie forced a smile. At this moment, she would like to forget that she had a cousin T.

"If you don't feel like talking, I'll tell him to call back later."

"No." Later, now, it didn't matter. Cassie wasn't going to like whatever it was T had to say. Her life, her husband, their child, none of these things could she discuss with him.

"Cass, you want me to carry you into the bedroom?"

"I can make it." A genuine smile touched her lips, just for Daniel.

"Then I'm going to go warm some dinner."

Cassie was relieved when he left. She needed to understand what she had heard T say to her before.

"Hello."

"It's about time, Cass. Why did you keep me waiting so long?"

That voice. This was the gentle voice of her favorite, her only cousin. Maybe she had misunderstood him before. "I was in the bathroom."

"How are you doing?"

"Fine."

"I called you earlier today. Mother wouldn't let me talk to you."

"Mother? First it's 'father' for Uncle Travis, now you're calling Aunt Margaret 'mother?'"

"M-m-m," was his only answer.

"Why?"

"Same reason. Do we need to get into that?"

Not her old cousin Cassie decided, not the same person.

"Uncle Travis was right. You have changed."

"True, but for the better. However, that's not what I called to talk to you about."

"Then what?"

"Mother told me that you almost lost your baby." His voice was soft, without the edge it had held before, luring her into continuing the conversation.

"Yes, but I'm in good shape even though I've been on bed rest."

"Why would such a near tragedy happen to you, my good cousin?" Was that sarcasm she heard slip into his voice? Cassie decided to take the comment at face value.

"I don't know, T. The doctor says sometimes women develop complications for no apparent reason."

"No, that's not it. I know why. I've done some checking. Even if I hadn't, just talking to that so-called husband of yours would have proven it."

"Daniel is not my so-called husband. He is my husband."

"Not truly."

"How's that."

"He isn't white. He doesn't even sound white. A husband that is truly yours has to be purely white. I can't allow this marriage to go on."

"That's not for you to decide, T. You have *no* right to tell me what I can and cannot do with my life."

"You're a blood relative. A pure white blood relative. I have a right to save my race."

"From what?"

"The inferior races. Now out with it. Confess. I want to hear it from your own mouth. What is your husband?"

"A man."

"What kind?"

"A good man."

"Your shame has been noted though your reluctance to give a direct reply. Which, of course, means you are not married to a good pure white man."

"I haven't answered a thing. Don't call or don't ask for me unless you're ready to apologize."

"Apologize? I don't think so. I'll say goodbye for now, Cass, but let me leave you with a thought. You almost lost that mixed up baby of yours, but not for the reason the doctor gave. It was simply a sign, a confirmation that this child of mixed races isn't meant to be. It's impure. Nature tried to correct this mistake by ending its life."

Cassie slammed the phone down.

"What was that for?" Daniel asked, coming into the room. Frown lines that she hadn't seen in a long time reappeared. She should tell him. But what would it do except add more frown lines? Later, she decided, she'd tell him later, when she wasn't so upset.

"I guess I put the phone down harder than I thought."

"Relatives will make you do that. That's why we aren't going to think about any of them. No T, no Ness, no Monica, no aunts and uncles. Instead, we're going to feed our baby."

"Good, she's starved."

"She, huh?"

"She."

"You sound sure of yourself."

"I even thought of some names."

"Too sure of yourself," he told her, taking a giant spoon of something from the plate and offering it to her.

"This is delicious," Cassie mumbled, savoring the pasta crawfish and spices. She swallowed. "Who made this?"

"Me, it's Crawfish Monica."

"So, you can cook."

"Looks like it."

"I didn't know you could cook."

"Now you do. Give me a taste of that."

"Get your own. This is mine."

"That's a huge plate of food." Daniel shook his head as she took another spoonful. "You've turned into a greedy little something. Hand the spoon over."

Cassie shook her head. "I slept through lunch, and I'm eating for two. You can't expect me to surrender this spoon to you. I know how much you eat, Daniel Adams. You've got all those muscles that you need to supply with energy. Like this firm arm." Cassie reached over with one hand to massage it with her finger. "Now this feels good."

With that, Cassie dropped the spoon to the tray where it landed with a clatter. Next, she carefully placed the tray on the nightstand out of Daniel's reach. She then claimed both of Daniel's muscled arms, pulling him toward her.

"You *are* a greedy little something."

"Those 'other ways,' Daniel. Remember the ways."

"I remember alright," he told her, putting his thoughts into action.

Sometime later, coming back from putting away the dishes, Daniel reached for the remote. Since all their appetites had been satisfied, he thought they might watch television. He sat next to Cassie on the edge of the bed, attuned to her pensive mood. He waited a moment for her to say what was on her mind. She didn't seem to be ready, but as soon as he pointed the remote toward the television, Cassie reached for his hand.

"Marry me, Daniel. Marry me again."

"When?"

"As soon as we can. I want to be married before God and our families. I want every blessing we can get."

"That can be arranged."

"I want our baby born with blessings. You know that life is going to be harder for her than for most kids. She might meet people that hate her for being both white and black or maybe looking white and being black or the other way around."

"Hold on, Cass." He saw tears forming in her eyes again. "Calm down, baby." All this crying couldn't be good for her. "Slow down, tell me what all this is about."

"T!" she shouted. "He hates you! He hates our baby, and she hasn't even been born yet. That's plain—" the word she wanted took a long time in coming, but when she said it, the way she said it spoke volumes—"evil."

"Yes, it is," Daniel answered. He moved toward the headboard, positioning her between his outstretched legs. He laid Cassie's hands on her stomach and rested both of his atop hers.

"We have to have our marriage blessed."

Daniel couldn't remember Cassie ever being a very religious person before, but now her voice held a strong conviction. If she believed blessings from God would help them, then Daniel would make sure that they had them.

"We will. Leave everything to me."

"Before the New Year. No, on New Years's Eve, at the stroke of midnight."

"I can make that happen, but Cass, you have to remember that you're still on bed rest. Do you plan on getting married in your nightgown, in this bed?"

Cassie turned her head to smile up at him. Good. That was what he wanted to see.

"Don't be ridiculous." She swatted at him. "We could do it here, though."

"I've got a better idea. Let's get married at our own house."

"We've got a house?"

"Since it looks as if we'll be staying in New Orleans, I leased a house on the bayou near City Park, on Moss Street."

"I love those houses. They're beautiful. Perfect. We have a day and a place to get married."

"Sounds like it."

Cassie was quiet for a moment. Daniel could feel the calm come over her like the eye of a hurricane in the middle of the storm. Still, he knew there was more to come.

"We need a priest."

"Father Brett. Aunt Joyce will make sure he's available."

"A small reception would be nice, so everyone could get to know each other."

"Ness, Monica, Melanie, your Aunt Margaret and again, Aunt Joyce."

"A cake."

"My cousin Warren, or Gambino's, or maybe Lawerence's Bakery. It doesn't matter."

"You can handle all this?"

"I'll have enough help. More than I need."

"Then everything's set."

Daniel held her for awhile, the warmth of his hand protecting his wife and his child. "Everything will be fine, Cass."

"I hope so."

Daniel waited a few minutes before quietly inviting. "Tell me more about T."

Cassie talked for hours, sharing childhood memories of her favorite cousin, her slight worry when he seemed to break away from the family, and the recent revelation of hatred he might have secretly harbored for years.

"He has to have been brainwashed, Daniel. T has never talked like that. He has never been prejudiced. How could he with a dad like Uncle Travis who has always recruited young students from the local high schools who were willing to learn. Their race or background never mattered. Uncle Travis helped those who wanted it. This is all so unreal."

"I know, Cassie," he told her, his hands moving downward with slow careful strokes, his touch seeming to keep her calm. The mood in the room had slowly softened. Their shared communication, understanding, and willingness to help each other drew them closer as a couple. An unseen power made them stronger.

Trust.

It was here between them now, and it gave him the strength to broach a subject he had never discussed with her before.

"Cass, I've got something to tell you." Daniel paused a second, his hand motionless on her stomach. He then rushed on to get it out in the open.

"My mother deserted me when I was a kid. I saw her again for the first time a few days ago. She's Melanie's mother. Lucky me, huh? I've got Melanie for a sister, half sister I mean."

Daniel paused. "Cass?"

He leaned to the left to get a look at her face. Her eyelids were closed. He put a hand on her chest. She was breathing deeply. He had never seen her sleep so much before. She probably needed it.

"We'll talk about it later," he told her, drifting off to sleep himself.

CHAPTER 12

"Nice house, brother dear," Melanie called, walking through the open front door with a smirk on her face and a huge flower box in her hands.

Daniel looked down at her. She was not going to let up. "Cassie's right outside, and no, she doesn't know yet. So keep your sassy mouth closed. I'm telling her after the wedding."

"Can you be more specific than that, Fly Boy?"

Daniel's eyes narrowed. He could feel the frown lines Cassie teased him about forming on his brow.

"I guess you can't," Melanie answered with a click of her tongue. "I'll go keep Cassie company and keep myself out of your way," she said, moving her skinny legs as slow as possible.

Daniel shook his head. Melanie had been enough to deal with when she was just Cassie's friend, but now she was related to him—by blood. Flamboyant, sassy, persistent, Melanie was Jackie all over again. Daniel walked over to the side door Melanie had just passed through. She was walking up and down the paved patio waving something in the air. Probably something for the wedding. Whatever it was, Cassie was having a good time. Melanie was a loyal friend, that's what she was. He couldn't remember Jackie being loyal to anyone—friend, sister, son.

Daniel went back to clearing boxes out of the huge den where the wedding would take place at midnight.

"The flowers are beautiful, Mel. Poinsettia and holly for the Christmas holiday. I love it."

"The flower shop will deliver everything later today."

"It'll be beautiful. Now tell me what you two were arguing about this time."

"Same old, same old."

"M-m-m, I bet I'll get it out of you, sooner or later."

"Later. For everything." Melanie paused to listen. "Now it's time to try on that dress I helped you pick out of the catalog the other day. Some rush delivery. It should have been here yesterday."

Cassie turned and peered through the French doors and saw Daniel signing for a large package.

"Come on, Mel, this should be fun. At least now I'll feel like I'm doing something for my own wedding."

Cassie went down the hall to the bedroom, pausing to give Daniel a kiss as Melanie grabbed the package. The long-sleeved ivory dress with its empire style waist was a perfect fit.

"This material, Mel, it's pure bliss. Feel."

"It looks good and it feels good. I'd say we did a wonderful job on such short notice."

"I'd have to agree."

"Daniel, you know you're not supposed to see me until tonight," Cassie told him, not bothering to cover what he wasn't supposed to see.

"But we're already married."

"Tradition, bro—Fly Boy," Melanie stumbled out. "It's tradition."

"She's right, Daniel. And it wouldn't hurt for us to have all the good luck we can get. We can take that good luck and add it to those blessings that we're going to get tonight," Cassie answered, not missing the slight verbal blunder from Melanie or Daniel's momentary frown. Cassie was going to figure out what was going on. They had a secret. Something they were hiding. It couldn't have anything to do with the baby. She laid a hand on her stomach. The wide skirt and style nearly concealed her pregnancy. No, they wouldn't hide news like that. It was something else.

Daniel's hands wrapped around her. "Blessings will be enough. Luck, good or bad, won't matter. We have each other."

"You're right. Go ahead and get an eyeful, Daniel Adams."

With that, he turned her around, his green eyes moving up, then down, then slowly traveling up again. "Amazing."

"The dress."

"You, Cass. You are, amazingly, mine." He kissed her, pulling back a second later. "Go take a nice long nap. We've got a midnight wedding to attend."

"All I do is rest."

"True," he agreed without apology. "That's your job."

Before Cassie could tell him how she felt about that, Melanie burst into the room. Cassie hadn't even realized that she had gone.

"You two aren't finished yet? Let her go for a minute, Daniel. You're going to wrinkle the dress. You've already ruined tradition. Think you could stop at ruining the dress, too?"

"It's okay, Mel," Cassie told her, laying her head in the crook of his arm.

"I can see that it is, my friend. I'm starting to realize exactly how okay everything's going to be. Fly Boy is not as bad as I thought."

"Not at all," Daniel agreed. "I can say the same about somebody else in this room."

"I bet you can," Mel answered, "but I don't have time for that. I've got things to do. You want to stare at Cassie in that dress, then you can help her out of it. I'll see you two tonight." And she was gone.

Daniel ran his fingers up, then down, then up once more along the trail of pearl buttons down the back of the dress.

"What are you doing?"

"Taking Melanie's advice, I think."

"Big change," Cassie couldn't help commenting.

"I'm going to need practice if there's any chance of me getting you out of this dress tonight."

"It's possible." Cassie looked into the mirror behind her, tiny tittering noises escaping her lips at the sight of the deep concentration on Daniel's face as he studied the back of the dress.

"Where do you start?" he asked, running a finger down the line of buttons again.

"Top button," she suggested with a burst of laughter.

"So this is funny?"

"Hilarious," she answered, feeling a slight breeze on her back as the dress opened.

A few minutes and a few dozen feathery caresses later, Cassie found herself completely undressed, covered only by Daniel's gentle embrace. Her feelings of love and security were exactly what she needed. Satisfaction for her body's complete state of arousal was exactly what she wanted but was not forthcoming. She was surprised and disappointed when Daniel tucked her into bed.

"Rest, Cass." he whispered to her.

"That's not likely to happen now."

"Sorry, baby," he told her, a look of complete sincerity on his face. "I'll make it up to you tonight. I've got some new 'ways' that will take that look off your face."

"Do you?"

"You had better believe it."

"I hope the anticipation doesn't kill me."

It didn't. Cassie actually fell into a deep sleep, despite her frustration. She was roused from that sound sleep by Melanie and

Ness.

"Wake up, Cass. It's time to get married."

"Again." Melanie added, causing everyone to break out laughing, setting the mood for wedding preparations.

They giggled, joked and succeeded in getting the bride dressed and her hair styled, despite the fits of laughter that interrupted the process.

"Enough, Melanie, Cass, let's take a look at the finished product."

"Not yet." Melanie lifted a headpiece that looked like a wreath made of tiny ivory and rose colored flowers. A long strip of ivory satin ribbon hung down the back.

"Beautiful," Cassie told her friend.

"Put the icing on the cake, Melanie," Ness encouraged.

"No, wait a minute," Cassie said just as there was a knock on the door.

"Cassie, I'm sorry that I'm so late. I wanted to be here to help you get dressed. Oh, but you're beautiful, dear." Cassie's aunt stopped to study her. "If only your parents were here."

Sitting at the vanity, Cassie smiled at her aunt in the mirror, the love she felt for her clearly written all over her face.

"Here, Aunt Margaret," Melanie said. She'd claimed Cassie's aunt as one of her own from the moment she met her. "We saved the best for last. I believe Cassie wants you to put the icing on the cake, but wait until I get my camera."

"It'll be my pleasure." The older woman beamed.

"And mine, too," Cassie said, just loud enough for her aunt to hear.

"You made it just in time, Margaret," Ness told her.

"I'm back," Melanie yelled, waving the camera back and forth. Melanie snapped more than a half dozen pictures before Ness pulled her out of the room. "We'll be ready to start in a few minutes. We'll send for you," Ness said, closing the door just after Melanie snapped one last picture.

"I'm glad Margaret made it before Cassie was completely dressed. I'd forgotten that she was raised by her aunt and uncle," Ness murmured.

"Is she ready?" Travis asked, making his way down the hall.

"She looked ready," Melanie glanced at her watch, "and we had better get started if they still want to be married by midnight."

"Melanie, you remind me so much of someone I know," Ness told her. "You know, I had an aunt who always said that she wanted to be called Melanie."

"Isn't that something? Let's get this show started."

Daniel was coming down the hall with the same thought when he overheard Ness's remark, and Melanie's entire conversation. He stored the flash of memory that supported Ness's comment. At the moment, Daniel had more important things to deal with. Finding the priest in the crowed den was one. There, he spotted him standing at the makeshift altar where the ceremony would take place.

"You still have some holy water left, right, Father?" Daniel asked for the third time. "If not, I can get some water from the faucet and you can bless it before we start."

"It's all taken care of, Son," the tall priest reassured Daniel, placing a hand on his shoulder.

"Then you have enough? Cassie wants everything blessed."

"I guessed as much after being convinced to bless every corner, every closet in this house."

"It's important to Cassie."

"And that makes it important to you?"

"It does, Father Brett."

"I'm happy for you, Daniel, my boy." The priest, an old family friend, slapped a hand across Daniel's shoulders.

"Father, Daniel, Cassie's ready to get married. How about

you?" Ness asked.

"Ready, Son?"

"More than ready, Father." Daniel glanced at his watch. "Remember, we rehearsed this, we've got it perfectly timed. At exactly twelve midnight you pronounce us man and wife."

"It's all under control."

"Hey, Ness, Cuz." Daniel's twin cousins, on break from college, came over toward them. "We set the old grandfather clock back ten minutes, exactly like you told us to."

"You did what?"

"Calm down, Daniel. They're teasing you. Don't be so uptight. Cassie's going to think something's wrong."

"Yeah, we were just kidding," Josh, the more outrageous of the two, interjected. "Twelve midnight, ten to twelve. What's the difference? You're still going to be married."

"Twelve midnight and ten seconds doesn't sound too bad," John, the other twin, added.

"Get out of here you two. Daniel's nervous enough."

"But he's already married." Josh shrugged. "What's the big deal?"

"The basketball court next week," he warned his two mischievous cousins.

"Deal," they said as Ness pulled them away.

"Yeah, deal." This wedding *was* a big deal. For him, even more so for Cassie. The blessings of God and the church meant so much to her. He would do anything to remove the fear he saw in her eyes and heard in her voice when she spoke of her cousin T. If the man came near her, he would be toast. Nope, too lenient. Daniel would heat him to a crisp, charring him like a blackened Cajun dish.

The wedding march began and the ceremony was under way. *Time for more pleasant thoughts.* As he decided to take his own advice, Cassie appeared at the end of the hall on the arm of her uncle and wearing the beautiful dress he had helped her remove a few hours ago. Daniel's whole world was wrapped up in this small package full of spirit and love. Cassie walked along the narrow aisle sprinkled with flower petals then took her place at his side.

"I love you," he told her.

Cassie tilted her head sideways and looked up at him, a grin on her face. "Of course, because I love you, too."

Omitting the mass but proceeding with the prayer service, Father Brett blessed the rings; the guests; Melanie, the maid of honor; and Scott, the best man; before blessing the newly wedded couple who had just exchanged vows.

Father Brett, in a unique ceremony, glanced at his watch and said, "I now pronounce you—countdown please."

All the guests, Daniel and Cassie's relatives and friends, choused together, "Ten, nine, eight, seven, six, five, four, three, two, one!"

"Man and wife!" Father Brett shouted above the loud voices.

The newly married couple were showered with rice and confetti. Horns and whistles sounded as children and adults shouted, "Happy New Year! Happy wedding!" over and over again until the food was uncovered and everyone began to enjoy the delicious buffet.

"Is everybody gone?" Cassie asked as she came in from the sparkling clean kitchen.

"I just helped carry some of the kids to their cars. I think I put them with the right parents."

"I'm surprised they lasted so long. It must have been the naps

I heard them talking about. Monica and Ness mentioned that their kids wanted to make sure they were up for the wedding."

"You mean the lively Vicki, Megan, and Jasmine trio stood still long enough to take a nap? And those two rambunctious boys, Mark and Tony?"

"I'm sure they figured it was worth it. We had a pretty strange wedding, didn't we?" Cassie stretched her arms, molding the form fitting bodice of the wedding dress to her upper body.

"Not strange, blessed. And not only by the priest—our friends and relatives were happy for us, too."

"Thank you for making all this happen so beautifully."

"I had a lot of help. Our second wedding ended up meaning a lot to me. A New Year, a new beginning for us."

"I feel it, too. Everything's going to be fine," Cassie confided. "The baby's going to be born just as healthy as Scott and Ness's boys, and we're going settle here in New Orleans, our home."

"Perfect."

"I agree."

"No, I mean your head's at the perfect angle for me to do this. . ."

A long finger made its way down the nape of her neck to her shoulder blades.

"Ah-h-h Daniel."

"M-m-m-m?" he asked, repeating the slow sensuous caress.

"You mentioned something earlier about…"

"About?" he asked, his fingers moving up and down without a break, without a second to catch her breath. "I'm waiting, Cass. About?"

"Ways," she gasped. "Those other ways."

"It took you long enough to ask," he said before bending to allow his tongue to trace the same path his finger had followed.

"Daniel."

"No more?" he asked.

"No. More." she begged.

And he complied, removing the dress faster than he'd done earlier. Right there in the now clean den, thanks to all his relatives, in the place of their wedding, they began to discover new territory. Using the sense of touch, they explored and found sensitive areas they'd never known existed.

After Daniel had stirred her body to multiple eruptions, they made their way into the bedroom. Cassie lay on the bed, expecting him to join her. She was surprised to see him disappear into the bathroom, only to return with a bag of marbles and a bucket of ice, his arousal more than evident. Guilt washed over her.

"Daniel, you've done so much. I'm sorry I haven't been able to."

"But you have, Cass. Don't worry about me. I can handle it."

He held a blue toothbrush in one hand and the netted bath sponge in the other.

"What are those for? Are we going to practice personal hygiene, now?"

"It's personal alright, but hygiene has nothing to do with it." With that, he crawled into bed bringing with him almost more bliss than she could stand.

CHAPTER 13

The first week of the New Year went by very quickly with many quiet hours alone together, a few in the company of her family, both old and new.

"Don't get up, I'll get the door," was a refrain Daniel had said all week. One relative or another was stopping by to feed them, assuming that Daniel had no talent in the cooking department.

"Thanks, Aunt Joyce, but you didn't have to make that big old pot of gumbo." Cassie heard Daniel protest.

"It's my specialty, and you both have to eat."

"You're right, but I can take care of that. I know how to cook."

Both Daniel and his aunt stood in the open doorway of the bedroom where Cassie was busy constructing the puzzle of the Eiffel Tower Ness had given her.

"Cassie, can Daniel really cook? Tell me the truth."

Cassie dropped her puzzle piece. "Well, Aunt Joyce, I've truly enjoyed your cooking, but to be a good wife, I have to tell you the truth. Daniel *can* cook," she emphasized with gusto.

"Must have been all those years watching my favorite aunt."

That pretty much ended the influx of food once the word got out. Family visits were less frequent, but Melanie, who was still on winter break, was sure to pop in once in awhile, full of news about her discoveries in the Quarter. Last night, she had told them about the haunted tour she had gone on, but most evenings and nights were their own.

"What are we having for dinner tonight? Some of Aunt Joyce's gumbo?"

"If that's what you want. We've still got tons of it left, even after I froze half of it."

Daniel warmed dinner, bringing a tray into the den where they settled in to play a game of Scrabble, using their own unique rules.

"Marion. That's not a boy's name, Daniel," Cassie insisted in the middle of the game.

"It's unisex."

"You would name our son Marion? That's asking for trouble."

"No," he admitted. "But you had me cornered, blocking the x so I couldn't make Max. I missed out on a triple word score. And what kind of name is Jax for a girl."

"A traditional one."

"Traditional how?"

"Jax Brewery, a New Orleans tradition."

"You would name our daughter after beer?"

"Of course not," Cassie laughed as the doorbell rang. "Let's call this game a draw. Everyone will be here soon anyway for the unwrapping party."

"Don't get up, I'll get the door." He stood. Daniel's soft green gaze moved up her arm to her face and back down again as she reached to begin picking up the small square tiles they hadn't used.

"I thought you were getting the door." Cassie stopped to glance up at him. "Daniel, they're going to think no one's here."

He leaned over to give her a quick kiss on the lips. "Remind me to show you the new makeup brush I bought today."

Cassie blushed. This week had been full of surprises and happiness. She had no worries. Her visit with the doctor had gone great, and she hadn't heard a word from T. She'd simply rested and enjoyed her husband and family.

"It's Melanie, with more food."

"Red beans. High protein, low fat."

"That depends. What did you put into it?"

"Turkey smoked sausage."

"You've altered a New Orleans tradition."

"Come on in, Mel. Don't pay any attention to Daniel."

"I stopped doing that a long time ago."

"No Fly Boy?" Cassie asked in surprise.

"Naw, he's been grounded and taking excellent care of my best friend. I'll stick to Daniel for now."

"Whatever change has happened, I won't question it. I'll just shout, 'Hallelujah!'" Cassie declared, arms raised to the ceiling.

"You've been to too many of our Baptist services, my friend." Melanie shook her head. "Don't tell me you two are playing Scrabble again."

"That's right," Cassie said. "Care to take a peek? I haven't removed a tile from the board yet."

"Still names only?"

"Girls for me, boys for Daniel. We came up with some good ones today."

"Jax, like the brewery? Who came up with that?"

"Your best friend here," Daniel came from the kitchen just in time to say.

"I'm sorry, but I can't have my niece or nephew called Jax for the rest of his or her life." Right after the words left her mouth, Melanie froze, a stricken expression on her face.

Daniel looked just as upset by the blunder Melanie had just made. In her mind, Cassie went over the words her friend had said, finding nothing wrong with them. They were like sisters. Cassie saw nothing wrong with the baby calling Mel auntie. It had to be that little secret they had.

"Okay, you two, I've had enough of this. Out with it."

"Out with what?" Melanie asked, finding her voice first.

"Whatever little tidbit you've been hiding."

"Tidbit. That's funny, Cass," Daniel said, sitting on the sofa and attempting to pull her down to join him.

"Daniel, I'm serious. You can't think I don't know something's going on," she told them, turning direct eyes to both of them, her short stature in no way lessening her demand.

"What do you think's been going on?"

"I don't know, Daniel. It's the way you've changed toward each other," Cassie accused, making the situation sound worse than it was.

"How? What?" Melanie asked, almost speechless. Never had Cassie heard fewer words come out of her lips.

"You don't argue anymore, you actually look at each other, and have even found a way to communicate."

"Now, what are you trying to say, Cass?" her husband asked.

"That you actually like each other."

"We do not," Melanie denied. "You're my best friend. How could you accuse me of something like that?"

Daniel laughed. "Calm down, Mel. Cassie doesn't think that at all, do you, baby?"

Cassie raised both brows and concentrated on forming a frown line, hoping one or two would pop out to intimidate them both.

They laughed at her. Cassie joined in, unable to hold steady the ridiculous notion of Melanie and Daniel together as a couple.

"Okay, my friend, I should have known I couldn't keep anything from you. A first try and I wasn't successful. It's all your husband's fault."

"Daniel?" Cassie asked expectantly.

"I tried to tell you, Cass, but you fell asleep on me. Then we had too much to deal with. It wasn't the most important thing on my mind."

"That's very sweet, Daniel, but it still leaves me in the dark. What's going on? It would be nice if I found out before everyone else gets here."

"Here, it goes. Melanie's my half sister."

"What's that?" It was Cassie's turn to be stunned. She carefully lowered herself to the sofa.

"Oh, Cass, I wish I had my camera." Melanie searched the room as if she would have used any she set her eyes on.

Daniel sat next to his wife and placed a hand in hers. Cassie listened to him tell her all that happened the night she left Houston. It seemed like months instead of a few weeks ago.

"Daniel, this is wonderful. You found your mother. You've got sisters and brothers."

"There's more of you?" Daniel turned to ask Melanie.

"I'm afraid so. I'm the oldest. You've got one more sister and two brothers."

"Half brothers and another half sister. People I don't know."

"But they're your relatives."

"*I* don't have anything to do with that. Jackie left and chose to have nothing to do with me or the rest of my family."

"Are you sure it was like that, Daniel?" Cassie squeezed his hand, seeing the hurt in his eyes. He didn't turn away. Daniel allowed her to stare deep into his eyes, sharing the hurt, trusting Cassie by sharing his feelings with her.

He suddenly turned to Melanie as if he had remembered something. "My family, my aunt, uncles, cousin, nieces and nephews, Jackie kept them all from you, too. See what kind of woman she is? Selfish."

"That's enough, Daniel. You don't know a thing about my mother. When I came here, I realized that I had a whole group of relatives I didn't know, but you can't judge Mama like that. You don't know the whole truth."

A grunt of disbelief rose from his throat.

Cass could do nothing but look from one to another. The closeness that had developed between two people she loved the most seemed to have dissolved. Hot, steamy anger filled the room. They had been laughing together only a second before.

"Daniel," she called, reaching for the hand she'd lost some time ago. "Mel." Cassie turned to her friend. "You both started something good. Don't ruin it. No matter what else is going on, you've found each other. You're brother and sister."

"Half," Daniel mumbled.

Cassie ignored that. "Daniel, Melanie's leaving today. Please, for me, try to find some common ground. It would make me and the baby happy."

Both their gazes moved from her face to her stomach. She'd known that would get them.

"Looks like we don't have a choice but to agree to disagree on this for now, Melanie."

"No, we don't."

"Well, how about a hug?" Cassie prompted, knowing she was pushing it.

"Half brother?" Melanie said, her eyes looking down at him, the sass returning.

They laughed. The doorbell rang. Daniel reached for his sister and gave her a brief hug. "Don't get up, I'll answer the door," he ordered before leaving the room to do just that.

Melanie let out a long, slow breath. "You have to help me make him see, Cass. He has to know what Mama's like now. Not what she used to be."

"I agree. Who knows your mama better than I? The woman who fixes baskets for the poor."

"And visits sick and old people from our church," Melanie added.

"And during your exams, comes over to cook and—"

"—makes pots of coffee so that I can study, sometimes cram. Mama knows me well."

"But not Daniel, not anymore. We have to give him time,

Mel."

Melanie sadly nodded her head in agreement.

"Does anyone else in the family know?"

"I think Ness suspects and maybe Aunt Joyce. I've found her staring at me sometimes. Aunt Joyce is Mama's sister, you know. Should I tell them before I go?"

"That's up to Daniel, don't you think?"

"Then they're not going to find out."

The ringing of the doorbell announced the beginning of tons of relatives coming over with more food and their normal rambunctiousness. Cassie was waited on hand and foot, not allowed to do any more than lift the fork from her plate or a cup to her lips. Monica sat beside her, allowed to do no more than Cassie. Poor Monica. She probably didn't want to do anything more than sit. A few months from now, Cassie was sure that was all she would want to do.

She and Monica moaned and shared pregnancy gripes. Ness joined her, as well as her sister-in-law Wendy, with stories of their own pregnancies. Cassie enjoyed talking with her new relatives, getting to know them better, but her eyes kept searching the large den for Daniel. She couldn't forget the deep hurt in his eyes. What was he thinking? What was he feeling? Cassie knew he needed her right now.

Melanie would be alright. She had had a mother's love through childhood, still felt it now and knew it would be there always. Daniel didn't have that. As much as Cassie had come to love her new family, she wished that they would all go so that she could comfort the hurt little boy still deep inside her husband.

Cassie's eyes finally zoomed in on him near the French doors leading to the patio. He was talking to Scott, Devin, and Jack, the husbands of Ness, Monica and Wendy. When he caught her eye, a slow smile spread across his face, and he immediately came over, followed by the other men.

"Cass," he whispered, sitting on the arm of the sofa. "Ready to open presents?" he asked, a long finger finding its way to the nape of her neck.

Cass nodded her head, the movement creating tingles down her spine.

"What were you ladies talking about?" Cassie heard Scott ask, as if from a distance.

"Pregnancy in all its glory," Ness responded

"Then change the subject. Quick," Devin demanded.

Cassie leaned her head against Daniel's chest, giving him better access.

"Excuse me, please, Mr. Father-to-Be," Monica stated. "If you were responsible for carrying three babies for over seven months you'd—"

"Time to open the presents," Scott announced.

Daniel's finger stilled, leaving her wanting.

"Scott's right. Even if she has every reason to, let's not get Monica started," Daniel whispered in Cassie's ear. "Besides, the sooner we open the gifts, the sooner they all go home. Then we can be—"

"—alone," Cassie finished for him.

"Brown Eyes, I know it hasn't been easy," Devin was telling Monica, trying to save himself. "I'll tell you what I'll do to make it up to you. I'll start having some of those sympathy pains we were reading about the other day. In fact, I feel something coming on right now. My ankles, I think they're swelling."

Cassie and Daniel shared a look before laughing out loud. Exactly that had been happening to Daniel. His foot was almost completely healed, but he felt every ache, every pain she had.

Daniel held up the first gift, both of them in hysterics.

"A crock pot, what's so funny about a crock pot?" one of the kids asked.

They continued to open every gift, laughing nonstop. If they didn't laugh, they would cry, Daniel from the deep hurt in his heart and Cassie because she felt it, too.

Within the hour nearly everyone was gone, the house once again cleaner than before.

Daniel's Uncle Cal and Aunt Joyce, as well as her aunt and uncle, came out of the kitchen together.

"We realize you know how to cook, but there's still a mountain of food left in the fridge," Aunt Joyce told her nephew.

"We'll be seeing you later, Cassie Bear." Uncle Travis gave her a hug.

"Call if you need us," Aunt Margaret told her.

"We'll be fine."

Uncle Cal, strangely quiet, gave her a peck on the cheek and absently shook Daniel's hand.

Just then Melanie, who had been quieter than Cassie had ever seen her, came in with a box. "Here you are, my friend, sealed and delivered."

"Thanks, Mel. Can you put it in my bedroom?"

"Will do," Mel said, going to the back of the house.

As soon as she left the room, Cassie went over to Daniel, pulling him away from his aunt and uncle for a minute.

"Go talk to your sister."

"My half sister."

"Just tell her goodbye. She's leaving, remember?"

"For you, Cass."

Melanie came back into the den. "Goodbye all," she said to everyone in general.

"You're not getting away with leaving like that, my friend," Cassie said, giving her a heartfelt hug. "Call, write, send an e-mail."

"You can count on it."

Melanie paused before the four older members of the family. "It's been wonderful meeting you all." She gave each one a hug, starting with Cassie's aunt and uncle.

"You've made me feel welcomed," she said, hugging Aunt Margaret.

"Thanks for putting up with me barging into your home so often," she said to Uncle Travis. "You make me laugh, Uncle Cal, and you, Aunt Joyce, make me feel at home, as if I'm with my very own family." She hugged her long and hard.

Uncle Cal nodded at that. "Of course you are," was all Aunt Joyce said.

Melanie hadn't said a word to Daniel. She hadn't even looked at him.

"I'll walk you to the rental car, Mel."

"That's not necessary, Daniel."

"I'm doing it anyway."

Daniel walked his sister outside, coming back a few minutes later to do the same for their aunts and uncles. If Cassie went by the expression on his face, all went well.

Taking advantage of his absence, Cassie ambled into their bedroom and headed straight to the bathroom. Daniel would look for her and follow her there.

She filled the tub with water as warm as she could stand it and quickly undressed.

"Cassie, what do you think you're doing?" Daniel demanded, just as she slipped the red sweater over her head. "Look at all that steam rising from that water. You know you can't get in a tub like that. Doctor's orders. It'll make you dizzy."

"You make me dizzy," Cassie told him, unbuttoning his shirt.

"Then I'd better stay here to catch you."

Cassie had seen so much of this side of Daniel's personality emerge, she hoped it wouldn't disappear with worries about his mother.

"I might even need to get in that tub of water with you. Just to make sure you're safe."

"It might not be big enough." Cassie unbuttoned his pants, lowering the zipper.

Daniel eyed the tub behind them. "We'll manage."

Considering the fact that the oval tub was big enough to hold two couples, Cassie just shrugged her shoulders.

Completely naked, Daniel decided to test the water. "O-o-oh, this feels so good," he said as he lowered himself in.

"Mind if I come in now?"

"Sure, baby." He stood again, water dripping down every long, sturdy body part. "Careful, now. Don't trip, sit down real slow." He stayed behind her, supporting her the whole way.

He didn't relax until she was settled comfortably between his solid brown thighs.

"O-o-oh, this does feel good," Cassie mimicked

"You little—"

"A-a-ah."

"What's wrong?"

"The baby's moving around like crazy. It must be the warm water."

"I told you this wasn't a good idea, Cassie. Let's get out."

"Daniel, it's okay. Warm water won't hurt the baby. Relax, stay with me until the water cools. Then we could make it hot again."

"Think we can find another way. That makeup brush. I forgot all about it."

"Later, Daniel. Hold me please."

"Can do."

Cassie laid her head against his chest, her fingers gently grazing his thighs and trickling tiny streams of water there over and over again. The caresses created a hypnotic rhythm that enclosed them in their own private world. Cassie knew it wouldn't stay that way. She wanted Daniel relaxed enough for her to feel comfortable in broaching a touchy subject, his mother's desertion. To help him, she had no choice but to shatter the peace she'd helped to create.

"Daniel," she whispered. "Daniel," she said again, her hand pausing at his knee when he didn't answer.

"Don't stop. I love when you touch me. It makes me feel so—"

"Loved," Cassie finished for him. "I do love you, but if I stop touching you, that doesn't mean I stop loving you," she teased.

"Don't be silly, Cass. You are in a goofy mood, aren't you?"

"And you like it that way."

"Yes, I do. You make me laugh and enjoy life again. You're my world."

"I bet a long, long time ago you could have said that about someone else."

All was silent. There were no more trickles of water. The steam barely rose from the water anymore. Nothing moved for an eternity. Then Daniel's chin rested on the top of her head. His body shifted slightly, making tiny waves in the water, reminding her of the emotional waves she had made just now. *Please*, she thought, *let them produce some kind of emotion other than anger.*

"Jackie *was* my world," he said with a touch of sadness. "I would have done anything for my beautiful mother. I loved her so much, and she left me." His voice held a deep hollow sound, echoing the ache he felt in his soul. "I've never told anyone exactly how much it hurt."

He stood, droplets of water falling everywhere. "Your hair's getting wet," he told her, stepping out of the tub.

"It doesn't matter," Cassie responded. She watched as a single tear formed a path down his cheek. "What matters is how you feel right now."

"How I feel?" he said, holding a robe open for her. "Unsure. Not confused and uncertain as that nine-year-old boy that Christmas Day."

Cassie turned in his arms. "It's okay to cry."

"I'm not crying…"

"Did that little boy cry?"

"No. You didn't let me finish, Cass. I'm not crying for me. I'm crying for that nine-year-old boy who played a sad song all day long one Christmas, praying for his mother to come back home."

As the silent tears fell, Cassie held her husband tight, thanking God for blessing her with the ability to say the right things.

"Enough," he said a minute later, grabbing his robe and giving his eyes a swipe. "That's the first and only time I'll cry for that woman. It's more than enough."

"Enough to forgive her?"

"I don't know if I can."

"Maybe if you talked to her, understood her reasons for leaving you."

"There are no good reasons to cut your own child out of your life."

"I agree."

"Then why are we arguing?"

"We aren't." Cassie smiled at the confused look on his face.

"The makeup brush," he whispered, changing the subject. Come to bed with me, baby. I've got something to show you." Daniel led her through the bathroom door.

Cassie followed, knowing she had done her best to heal some of Daniel's hurt. Little by little it would wear away. At least that's what she hoped.

Daniel lay awake but refused to open his eyes. He felt that

opening his eyes would force him to think about things he didn't want to. Instead, he took a deep breath, inhaling the scent of Cassie, at the same time pulling her closer toward him. Feeling her beside him and touching her smooth belly where their child safely grew, reassured him of his good fortune.

"So," Cassie sleepily murmured. "Are you done measuring? How much would you say I've grown?"

"At least ten inches overnight." He did open his eyes then, propping on an elbow to gaze down at her.

"If that were true, I'd be bigger that Monica by the time I deliver."

"I hope not! I'd have to sleep on the sofa."

Cassie laughed at that. "Look," she tilted her head toward the window, "it's a beautiful day. Why don't we eat on the patio?"

"Oh yes, why don't we?" he agreed in a snooty voice.

"If that's too high class, why don't we call it 'the yard,'" she suggested.

"Better." Daniel threw the covers off the bed. "Up and at 'em. Get your daily workout started. From the bed to the bathroom, come on, get moving."

"You're pushy this morning."

"Just happy."

"Me, too," Cassie said, stretching her arms straight up and her toes down as far as they would go. The stretch pulled her full breasts higher, begging for his touch.

"Now where did I put that brush?"

"Daniel, no more. I can't take that kind of torture on an empty stomach. Cassie slowly sat up, kissed him on the cheek and whispered, "Maybe later I can provide a little more of what we enjoyed last night."

Daniel watched as she ambled to the bathroom. She really was getting bigger. But that didn't do a thing to cool the excitement he felt whenever he looked at her. Daniel had never thought the sight of a pregnant woman would arouse him, but Cassie did. She was incredible.

He had been suffering in silence, holding back because it wasn't safe for them to make love. But then last night she'd loved him as she'd never done before, using her tongue and lips to give him more than the world. What she had given him was a universal explosion. Surprised and satisfied, he had fallen asleep immediately. And now she was promising him more.

Daniel couldn't expect it of her. She was getting too big, her stomach making it awkward for her to worry about pleasing him. He just had to be a man, grin and bear it. He could take it.

The bathroom door opened and Cassie came out still completely naked. His groin lurched to attention. He hoped he could take it.

"Still in bed? I guess I'll have to get breakfast myself. Either that or my baby and I will have to starve."

"Think again. I was on my way to the kitchen. Blueberry muffins sound good?"

"Real men don't make muffins."

"Wait till you see these he-man muffins."

As Daniel slipped on a pair of pajama bottoms, he caught sight of a gift-wrapped box. "Is this a present we missed?"

Putting her arms through a robe, Cassie stood behind him. "Yes, it's from me. A belated wedding gift."

"When did you get this?"

"I have ways. Go on, open it."

Daniel lifted the top of the box, which was decorated with white and silver bells. Inside was the woodgraph he had bought for her.

"I thought I destroyed it."

"The wooden pieces broke apart. I put them back together, like a puzzle."

"I'm glad you were able to. When I bought this gift, that's

when I first realized how much I loved you."

"I knew that even before you told me. The woodgraph said it all. Look inside. There's something else."

Daniel moved aside the white tissue paper. Under it was the portrait he had admired in the airport shop, *When the Saints*. Once again, the jazz band jumped out at him. The audience swayed and clapped before his eyes. It was so real he could almost hear them.

"How did you do this?"

"Melanie."

"Your best friend."

"Your sister," Cassie went on, "described each portrait on the phone. I just picked out the one that reminded me of you. It's full of action and fun, don't you think?"

"I'm—"

"Full of action and fun. There are more words I could use to describe you. I'll make a list for you later." Cassie reached up to softly lay a kiss on his lips. "Find a good place to hang them," she suggested before going back into the bathroom.

Daniel stood stunned. She saw all that in him? Even after all he had done? Hearing the sound of water, Daniel went to the bathroom door. "Don't make the water too hot."

At her nod, he told her, "I love you."

She smiled up at him. "I love you and the fact that you're going to make me some he-man blueberry muffins."

Daniel grinned and closed the door, taking in the joy and pleasure of being a husband.

CHAPTER 14

"That's it. I don't like this. I'm staying."

Cassie took a deep breath. "Daniel I'll be okay. A day in my own company will not kill me."

"Last time I left you alone, I hated every minute of it." He scowled, the frown lines appearing all at once. Daniel was returning to work after a four week emergency leave, this time officially based in New Orleans.

"That was different. You thought it was the best thing to do. Things were different between us then. Besides, one of us has to go back to work. I'm in no condition, so that leaves you."

"I've got enough time. I should stay home with you until the baby's born."

"Unnecessary. Anyway, you've only got ground duty. You'll be home by six o'clock every day this week."

He looked into her eyes long and hard before finally deciding. "I'm going, but call if you need me. If you can't get me, there's always Ness, or your aunt and uncle. Then there's Aunt Joyce and Uncle Cal, Monica, and, well, everyone's available."

"I know, Daniel. Kiss me goodbye."

He kissed her long and hard, patted her stomach and kissed her there, too.

Cassie closed and locked the door, releasing a long breath. How would she convince him to leave when he had an overnight flight next week? Dealing with Daniel was not going to be easy.

Leaning against the door, she heard the car leave the driveway. Before she could move away, the doorbell rang, and she turned to look through one of the narrow windows set on each side of the door. It was a UPS man. Cassie let the curtain fall. She wasn't expecting any deliveries and didn't remember Daniel mentioning anything about ordering something, but maybe it was another wedding gift.

"Can I help you?" Cassie asked through the door.

"UPS, ma'am," came the gruff, impatient reply.

This was strange. It was pretty early for a delivery, particularly one made almost as soon as her husband left the house. Cassie paused to think. Was it a coincidence or was she being too cautious?

"Ma'am, I don't have all day."

"Just leave it there."

"You'll have to sign."

A thought suddenly struck her. "Who exactly is the package for?"

"An Angelle Austin."

Angelle Austin? She didn't know anyone by that name. Cassie peeked through the side curtain again. Although the man on the other side of the door was dressed in the brown uniform and cap, he somehow didn't look like a UPS man. Where was his truck? A UPS driver was never far from his truck. Cassie wasn't opening her door for this guy.

There was an annoyed, "Miss?"

"No angels here. Why don't you try knocking on heaven's door?"

There was a muttered curse and the sound of heavy footsteps pounding down the stairs.

Her joke wasn't that bad. The whole incident was strange. She should have heard him coming up the stairs earlier, but she hadn't.

The more she thought, the more relieved she was that she hadn't opened the door. That guy hadn't looked like the UPS type. He was huge with bulging muscles and dark glasses. And the UPS cap had been pulled down over his forehead, almost as if he didn't want his face to be seen. This was definitely something that Cassie would not mention to Daniel. He'd never leave the house again.

Cassie settled into the bedroom with a glass of milk and a how-to-crochet kit, ready to start her new hobby. If she caught on, she would crochet a few outfits and booties for the baby, maybe even something for Monica and Devin's triplets. She definitely had the time. Daniel wouldn't let her lift a finger.

She took her supplies—five different colors of yarn, a variety of needles, and a book full of step-by-step illustrations of a least a hundred stitches—to the window seat. For the next three hours, Cassie enjoyed the view of Bayou St. John as she practiced stitch after stitch until she could form neat little rows. She tried to visualize a nice blanket for the baby made from all the practice squares.

When the phone rang, she nearly jumped out of the window seat. The phone was attached to her waist, correction, what used to be her waist, so that she didn't have to rush around the house to answer it.

"Hello."

"Hey, Cass, I miss you, baby."

"We do, too."

"Both you and little Jax, huh?"

"We are not naming our baby Jax, Daniel."

"If you say so. Everything's okay over there, right? You're not lonely without me?"

"I'm trying to survive," Cassie joked. "I started my new hobby."

"Good, I'll come home right now. You can show me what you're up to."

She quickly cut him off. "No, I'll see you at six. I love you," she added and hung up. She knew that if she prolonged the conversation, it would evolve into a drive home to check on her.

Glancing at her watch, she saw that it was lunch time. She passed the rest of the day with lunch, a nap, more crocheting, and chats on the phone with Melanie and Ness. Although Cassie missed having him home with her all day, she refused to let Daniel in on that fact.

That first day marked a routine. Every evening they would talk about his day at work and her day of crocheting, but not a word about the unresolved problem that was eating away at him. Although Daniel was open and loving toward her, Cassie sometimes caught him staring at nothing, frown lines etched deep in his brow. It was simple for Cassie to pull him away from those dark thoughts. A touch, a kiss and the frown was gone. But one night, Cassie had another plan. She would once again try to pull him away from those thoughts altogether. Daniel wouldn't feel better until he confronted them and made a decision on how he was going to deal with the discovery of a whole new family. On that Thursday night, Cassie sat at the kitchen table as Daniel unloaded the dishwasher.

"So, after I crocheted the fifth leg on the sweater for our baby octopus—" Cassie stopped. She had just confirmed that he wasn't listening. Lost in his thoughts, Daniel was standing completely still, a plate in his hand. He glared at it a full minute before putting it in the dishwasher. More dishes got similar treatment.

"Daniel, you weren't listening."

"What was that?"

"You have stared your last dish down, sheriff, saving the kitchen from danger."

"Cassie, what are you talking about? I knew staying home all day by yourself was going to make you crazy. It hasn't even been a whole week, but listen to you."

"Oh, no. Watching you strike fear into the heart of those dishes until they gave up peacefully is what's causing me to worry about you."

Daniel laughed. "You come up with some weird ideas sometimes. But you always did make me laugh, baby." He kissed her on the forehead. "All finished here. Let's head to the den."

"Good, because I have a challenge for you."

"Trying to excite my evening?"

"Since that's exactly what you do for me, I decided to reciprocate."

Daniel pulled her to him. "That is very sweet." His green eyes stared into her eyes.

That look normally began a round of inventive ways of making love, but this time he only laid a quick kiss on her lips.

"What's the challenge?"

"Scrabble."

"Again?"

"We haven't played all week. Not since the party." Cassie got comfortable in her favorite corner of the sofa.

"You mean not since we found the perfect name for the baby. I realized today that Jax is actually a unisex name. If we have a boy or a girl, it won't matter."

"No daughter or son of mine will be named Jax."

"We'll see," he said, settling next to her. Cassie threw a pillow at him. He retaliated by pulling her entire bulky frame into his lap, noisily nuzzling her neck.

At the same moment, his finger found the nape of her neck, Cassie discovered his hardness against her thighs. Daniel growled, "Enough of this. Let the challenge begin."

Cassie's hand lingered on his thigh, and slowly inched upward. "We can save the challenge for later."

"Scrabble now, later for everything else.

"Later sounds good." She was a little disappointed, but there was always a "later" for them. "The rules are, we are going to play a normal game of Scrabble."

"You've eliminated the challenge."

"It's still there, especially when you haven't played that way in weeks."

"Alright then, pick first."

They played with Cassie taking the lead. Unfortunately, she lost points when she found an opportunity to put her plan in motion. "M-o-m, mom."

"Short, but sweet. I can see your connection to that particular word. His hand reached over to pat her stomach.

"Seven points." She added them to the pad where they kept score, happy with her addition.

"Zoology, triple word. That's sixty. I've passed you, Cass."

"Taking advantage of a poor, defenseless pregnant woman."

"Never," he told her smugly, adding his score.

Cassie waited patiently for her next opening and a few moves later laid out m-o-t-h-e-r.

"That maternal instinct of yours is coming out tonight," he smiled.

"Could be." She grinned right back.

Five minutes later, she found the chance to spell the word sister and, amazingly, *brother* for her next move. Daniel gave her a strange look.

"I'm still ahead by thirty points. You're making some lousy words tonight."

"Not these. They are exactly the right words, especially this one." Cassie carefully laid down each tile to spell the word *mama*.

Daniel narrowed his eyes at her, his green gaze full of accusation. "I knew you were up to something," he quietly told her.

Cassie turned an innocent face up to him and used her finger to trace a line from the tip of his nose upward, erasing the frown lines. "Don't frown down on me like that Daniel Adams."

He unexpectedly laughed. "You little cheater. Look at all those m's on the board. Let's see." Daniel read the side of the game board. "Letter frequency. The game came with two m's! Where did you get all those extras?"

"Ness," Cassie gladly admitted.

"My cousin again, huh?" The grin left his face quicker than it would have taken to spell the word *no* on the board. "Is she conspiring against me, too? Does Ness know about Jackie?"

"Not unless you told her. I wouldn't." Cassie laid a hand on his cheek. "I know this situation with your mom isn't easy."

"Not my mom, not mama, not even mother. I had a Jackie," he said, not shouting but delivering each word a littler louder and more forcefully than the one before it as he removed the words from the board, scattering the tiles all over the wooden chest that doubled as a coffee table.

"I realize that." Cassie tried to take his hand, but it was balled into a fist, closed as tightly as his mind about opening communication with his mother.

"What did you think you were doing with that little game, Cass?"

"Trying to get you to think—"

"Trying to get me to think about her. Oh, I have. I try not to. I have you and the baby. Those are good things to fill my head, but Jackie's been there too many times. I don't need you to remind me about her."

With that he left the den, frown in place, and headed straight out the front door.

Cassie slowly picked up the pieces of the game. She separated the extra tiles to return to Ness. She hadn't thought this was going to be easy. Daniel had a lot of anger and resentment stored up inside, more than he probably knew.

Going into the bedroom, she sat on the window seat. Since she hadn't heard the car engine, she knew he hadn't gone far. And she was right. She watched him jog past their house, cross the small wood and iron bridge that stretched across Bayou St. John and go around again. Two, three, four, five times he ran that circular path before coming back into the house.

"Cass!" he yelled even before the door slammed shut behind him.

"I'm in here."

Daniel joined her, settling on the edge of the window seat, making the space smaller, cozier. Beads of sweat instead of frown lines covered his forehead.

"You were watching me?"

"Only making sure no one came to steal you away."

"M-m-m," he smiled. "I didn't mean to get so angry. I'm not mad at you, but I've got this temper and..."

"No kidding," she leaned in closer to say.

He took a deep breath. "You've got to let me do this in my own time."

"I don't like to see you so sad sometimes. I want you to be happy."

"I am, with you. You're my life, Cass. I love you."

"I love you, too. That's exactly why I want you to deal with this now. Find some peace."

He nodded. "When I'm ready."

Cassie consented with a slight nod of her head.

"Come on. Let's take a nice, long, relaxing bath."

They took a long bath, and, afterwards, they held each other all night long.

CHAPTER 15

Not more than two minutes after Daniel left for work the next day, the phone rang. Cassie lifted the headset to her ear. It reminded her of a smaller version of the earphones used in elementary school with those Think and Listen tapes. As she answered, she went into the kitchen for a second glass of milk.

"Hello."

"Hello, Cass. I bet you just saw your husband off to work."

"T?" she asked cautiously, surprised to hear his voice.

"Miss me, Cousin?"

"Not at all," she answered in a rush. "Are you calling to apologize?" Cassie couldn't help asking. At the same time, a voice in her head whispered urgently, "Hang up the phone, hang it up now." But Cassie didn't listen. Some other force demanded that she stay on the line.

"Now what would I have to apologize for?" He immediately continued, not giving her time for a reply. "Your so-called husband leaves mighty early every morning. Tell me, what kind of man leaves his wife home alone to sit in a window all day waiting for him?"

"How did—T, are you in town? Are you watching me?"

"No to both questions, but I have friends."

"Friends? What do these friends do?"

"Whatever I ask them to."

"Are they as obsessed with my husband's work schedule as you seem to be?"

"If it will help to save a sister in need of salvation, then yes."

Sister in need of salvation. How ironic. A white supremacist making a stereotypical black statement. Cassie wasn't going to point that out to him.

"... and when the time's right, we'll take you under our wing of pure white love to save you from yourself." Hearing the comforting tone in the voice that used to be her cousin's, she almost believed that he had her best interest at heart. He obviously thought he did. Maybe if she reasoned with him, let him know she didn't need saving. Maybe then she could get in touch with the old T.

"T, I'm okay. I don't need any help or protection. I've got Aunt Margaret and Uncle Travis."

"Two misguided fools."

"A wonderful husband."

"A contamination taking advantage of you, ruining your soul and infecting your uterus."

His categorizing her husband as a disease and their child as an infection immobilized Cassie for a moment. Then she pulled the headset from her ears and flung it across the room, exactly what she'd like to do to T. How could anyone respond to such hatred and evil?

Although she was determined not to let a phone call upset her, it did just the same. Despite the blessings, the holy water, the priest marrying them, evil was reaching out in the form of her own cousin.

Cassie finally poured a glass of milk and drained it in one huge gulp. Then she slowly sank onto one of the wooden kitchen chairs, the same chair she'd sat in yesterday as Daniel loaded the dishwasher. Her problem then had been convincing Daniel to face his mother. That seemed an easy worry now compared to the dread that was sweeping through her bones, absorbing her strength, leaving her feeling weak and helpless. This was a feeling she didn't like at all.

Cassie replayed the phone conversation in her head. T knew

too much about her for someone who was tucked away in some unknown part of the country. Friends, T said he had friends. Friends that did what? Watch her every move, Daniel's too?

Who was watching them?

Cassie slowly stood and walked through the den to her bedroom, pausing right outside the door. Overcoming her fear, she went into the room, moving straight to the window seat. She pushed the curtain aside and peered out. What she saw frightened her.

Everything looked normal.

There was no menacing evil force she could detect lurking around outside. A middle-aged woman was walking her dog. Two girls in plaid skirts were talking as they crossed the pedestrian bridge. A rounded roof with a tall steeple stood where it always had. Everything looked the same, yet different, because now she knew that there was something out there threatening her happiness.

Cassie scanned the area once, twice, not caring if the unknown friends of T discovered that she was on to them. Her third sweep of the area made her freeze. A van, a plain white van, was parked on the other side of Bayou St. John. Hadn't it been there last night? Hadn't it been there all week? Of course it would be if it belonged to the owners of one of the houses across the street, way across the street on the other side of the bayou. She would wait to see if it moved. She hoped a nice family would come out of one of the houses to claim the van as their own.

All morning, she sat in the window covertly watching, knotting her crocheting as she carelessly stitched. Every few minutes, she'd pull it apart and begin again. No one came. The van stood still and alone. Cassie felt ridiculous but somehow justified in her vigil. There was someone out there watching.

T calling right after Daniel left for work was too much of a coincidence. What was his plan? He'd talked about saving her.

How? By doing something to hurt Daniel? Cassie dropped the yarn and needle. She had to warn Daniel. Although she hadn't wanted to tell him earlier, she realized now that Daniel could be in danger.

The front door slammed.

"Cass? Are you ready?"

"Daniel," she called, the sound barely leaving her throat which was dry from worry. She went into the den and leaned into him, her arm possessively wrapping around his waist. She stepped back, tilted her head to look up at him. "I love you, Daniel."

"Hey, I do, too, Cass," he whispered. She could tell he didn't know what to think about this outpouring of love. "If I had known I'd get this for coming home early, I would have done it all week."

"I missed you and—"

Looking straight into her husband's eyes, Cassie knew that she would tell him the situation. Lack of communication had been their problem before. It wouldn't be again.

"I know this is going to sound strange, but I was worried about you."

"Me? Why?" A grin eased onto his face. "I'm the worrier in this family."

Cassie took his hand, leading him to the bedroom. She stopped at the door. "The blessings didn't work. I got a call from T today."

Daniel's face changed instantly, a frown beginning at his mouth. "He did? He tracked us down? Did he upset you? Make any more threats?"

"Yes and no."

"What does that mean?"

"He made vague remarks about saving me."

"From me, of course."

Cassie nodded. Her face, she knew, reflected the anxiety she'd felt all morning.

"Baby." Daniel placed a gentle hand on her shoulders. "As long as you don't feel the need to be saved, I don't see what his threats can do."

"Hurt you."

"How? With words? I'm a stronger man than that."

"No. T said he had friends in New Orleans. I think they've been watching us."

"Cass, you've been cooped up in the house too long. It's a good thing you have a doctor's appointment today. It'll give you a chance to get out for awhile."

"It's true, Daniel, and I'm almost sure I know where they are."

"Almost sure?"

"Come see." Cassie guided him into the bedroom. She sat at the window and motioned for Daniel to join her when he didn't move. He stood towering over her, his presence with her at the window already diminishing her fears.

"Look out straight across the bayou. Don't look too hard; they might notice you staring."

"What am I looking for?" he asked in a gentle, indulgent tone.

"A white van."

Cassie watched Daniel's face, not needing to look outside. She had done that all morning. He scanned the area. His eyes shifted left, then right, his head barely moving.

"There's no white van, Cass," he said in a firm, careful tone.

"There's no white van? It's gone? But it was there all morning. All week, I'm sure of it. I can't remember it not being there." Cassie's eyes first pleaded, then she demanded, "Don't raise your eyebrows at me, Daniel. It has always been there, never moving."

"It's moved now."

"I can't explain that. I only know that it has been there. I somehow ignored it all week, like the steeple or the bridge, because it was always there."

Daniel tried to erase the look of disbelief from his face, tried to form his face into the mask he'd worn for so many years, but found that it wouldn't cooperate. It seemed his emotions could no longer stay in hiding, at least, not from Cassie.

He tried to reason with her, genuinely worried. "Like I said, staying inside this house all day, all alone, is not a good idea."

"I can tell you don't believe me. This is real, Daniel."

"I'm sure you think it is."

"Because it is. T called. That was real. The van out there everyday, that was real."

"Then where is it now?"

"It probably left when you came."

"Why? If the people in the van were watching us, why would they leave when I came home? According to what you said, they were here when I was jogging. They didn't leave then."

Daniel tried to keep an even tone. His pregnant wife already had enough to deal with. More stress was not needed.

"I don't know what they're thinking. Maybe you surprised them. I don't know why they left."

"Cassie, who exactly is *they* anyway?"

"T's friends. He said they were watching us."

"Today? Those were his exact words?"

Cassie nodded.

The idea of someone watching them seemed so farfetched Daniel didn't want to believe it. But Cassie wasn't the kind of person to go into hysterics or simply make things up because she was bored.

"What more did he say. Cass?"

"He called Aunt Margaret and Uncle Travis fools. His own parents! And there was some more trash about pure white love and contamination. He sounded so zealous and sick. He was just—full of hatred."

"And you believe that he's full of enough hatred to hurt someone?"

"To hurt you or the baby, all because he has this misguided idea of saving me."

Worry etched his brow. "I knew I shouldn't have gone back to work."

"Daniel, don't be ridiculous. Don't make me sorry I told you."

"You wouldn't have kept this from me."

"No. We've had enough of that..."

Cassie's voice trailed off. Daniel pulled her toward him. He rested his chin on the top of her head, caressed her belly, and took a deep breath, hoping to hold back his anger and fear. The anger inside him was directed at Cassie's cousin. The fear came from not knowing what to expect. He needed to protect his wife and baby. They were both so small and vulnerable. His worry tipped the scale in the direction of fear as his most immediate concern.

He would have preferred to be angry. He dealt with that emotion better. It was anger that had helped him deal with the loss of Jackie. Daniel shook his head. Jackie was not who he wanted to think about.

"Daniel?"

"It's okay." He kissed Cassie on the top of her head. "We're going to deal with this."

He felt her nod.

"We'll start by sitting here for," Daniel glanced at his watch, "for the next twenty minutes. We'll wait to see if the van comes back. Then we'll head for the doctor's office."

"Does that mean you believe me?"

"I believe that if your cousin said he had friends watching us, then he does. We'll see if they happen to drive a white van."

"Okay." Cassie sighed loud and long.

"While we wait, tell me more about this telephone call. Every detail."

Cassie told him everything. "I think I broke the headset."

"I'll get you another one."

"I'm sorry, Daniel."

"Sorry? Sorry for what?" he asked, twisting his body to look directly at her.

"My cousin. I thought we would have to deal with outsiders giving us a hard time, not my own cousin."

"Cassie, we can't control him any more than we can control other ignorant people we've dealt with before. Scott and Ness deal with it, and we can handle it, too."

"We haven't come across too many ignorant people lately."

"Because you've been stuck at home on bed rest."

"Partial bed rest."

"Right, but there was that nurse."

"She was okay. She wasn't out and out rude."

"I'm sure you haven't forgotten how to put the bold, ill-mannered ones back in their place."

"I remember, but I'm out of practice."

Daniel laughed, giving her waist a little squeeze. The baby moved beneath his widespread hands. "Little Jax likes what you said."

"She will probably like a lot of things, but not that awful name."

Though Cassie had relaxed a little more against him, concentration stiffened her shoulders when her head turned toward the window. Trying to distract her as he kept watch, Daniel asked, "Remember those two nosy women at the airport? The loud one and her fuzzy headed friend?"

"The ones that were such a pain during a flight from Chicago to Houston?"

"I wouldn't know. I was too busy flying the plane."

"I spent the entire flight making their drinks with the exact amount of ice, finding fluffy pillows and blankets that didn't smell like other people."

"You remember all that?"

"Who could forget the worst passengers in history?"

"That bad, huh? I hadn't realized," Daniel commented as a white van pulled into the exact spot Cassie had pointed out earlier. "What I remember is what happened after the flight."

"You mean the way they almost fainted when I ran up to give you a kiss?"

"Go on," Daniel encouraged, waiting to see who would come out of the van.

Cassie continued, "Why they were still hanging around so long after the flight, I can't imagine, but it was the loud one who stared, remember?" Talking through her nose, Cassie impersonated the woman she'd met over three years earlier, "'Did you see that? What an outrage!' I can still see them marching toward us, suitcases in hand, having the nerve to say and I quote, 'You two don't look right together.' Wasn't that something else? I didn't know what to expect, but it wasn't that."

"Me either," Daniel answered, training his eyes outside and willing someone to get out of the van.

"Then the fuzzy-headed one put her nose in the air and said, 'Looks can be deceiving. That might not be why they're together,' as if that made sense."

"No sense, none at all," Daniel agreed, trying to think up reasons for the lack of movement in the white van across the bayou.

"And then, the loudmouthed one in a voice everyone standing at the gate could hear said to her friend, 'There can be other things that keep a monstrously unfit couple together. She's doing it for attention.' Daniel, do you remember how mad you got?"

"That's why I left it up to you. I don't hit women." Faces. He wanted to see the faces of the occupants of the van. How many people were inside? Men or women? The doors remained closed.

"Then," Cassie continued, "she had the gall to talk to me. 'Tell me honestly, were you neglected as a child?' I wanted to laugh right in her face."

"But you did something better," Daniel answered, more distracted and alarmed by the minute. How long had it been? Five, ten minutes?

"The insult backfired. I sent it directly back to them." Cassie visibly relaxed with the telling of the story. "I looked them both straight into the eye and said, 'Not at all, in fact, I was taught manners, respect, and the right to make intelligent choices.' They were set on embarrassing us, but we did it to them, right, Daniel?"

"Yes, indeed."

Cassie snuggled further into him, only to jerk up again, nearly falling out of the seat. Daniel's arms steadied her. "That's the van."

"I know."

"You saw it and didn't tell me."

"I was listening to the story, and I didn't want to distract you."

"You were more likely distracting me with the story."

Daniel shrugged his shoulders. She knew him well.

"No one got out."

"No, and we have a doctor's appointment to keep."

"But we can't just leave."

"Yes we can. If they are T's friends, the van will probably follow us."

"That makes sense, but I don't want to be followed."

"Neither do I. Let's look at this as a test."

Cassie nodded. She went into the bathroom then slipped on her shoes and jacket as Daniel kept a careful watch on the van from the front door.

Cassie stood behind him. A rumbling sound came from her stomach. He turned to her. "You didn't eat lunch."

"I had a glass of milk."

"You never miss a meal."

"Is that an insult?" she tried to joke before her face fell. "What kind of mother am I? I forgot to feed my poor baby. I was so worried and..."

"It's okay. It's not your fault. If I ever get my hands on this cousin of yours, Cass…" Daniel couldn't finish. Cassie looked as if she were going to cry. She hadn't cried in a while, so long he had almost forgotten the continuous flood of tears that had fallen throughout the first part of their marriage.

"Don't cry. I'll get you something. You can eat on the way to the doctor's office."

Cassie sniffed. "I'm okay. I'll keep watch. I'm through crying."

Daniel grabbed a box of crackers, some carrot sticks, and a scoop of fresh chicken salad he had made that morning. He put everything into a container then went back to his wife.

"At the rate you eat these carrots, Jax is going to be able to see in complete darkness," he told her to keep her mind off crying.

"Our daughter will not be named Jax, you hardheaded man." There wasn't a tear in sight.

"Anybody come out yet?" he asked, ignoring her denial. As far as he was concerned, their baby, boy or girl, was going to be named Jax.

"Nobody."

"Let's go. Be casual, act natural and don't look in that direction."

"I was going to say that."

"And I beat you to it."

Cassie laughed, which was exactly what he wanted.

Daniel drove past the van on his way to the doctor's office.

"Tinted windows," Cassie whispered. "T's friends have some intelligence."

"If they really are T's friends."

During the twenty minute ride, Cassie and Daniel kept watch for the white van. She couldn't remember tasting any of the food Daniel had fixed for her, but she soon discovered an empty container in her lap.

The trip was uneventful, causing Cassie to feel idiotic and completely paranoid. Daniel said not a word as he helped her out of the car and said only two words when they returned from the doctor's visit.

"Good visit."

"It was," Cassie agreed. Her pressure was normal, and she hadn't had any recurrence of the symptoms she'd had right after Christmas. The baby's heartbeat was loud, strong, and clear. Despite the good news, Cassie felt terrible. Her worry and paranoia had upset her so much it had affected Daniel. They were both actually looking for spies. But thank goodness it hadn't affected baby Jax. Cassie couldn't help but giggle.

"Something funny?"

"I was thinking about the baby."

"Who is perfectly healthy. That's a blessing, Cass."

"A good one," she laughed, "but I think the baby's going to be cursed with a horrible name for the rest of her life. I'm starting to think of her as Jax."

"That's not so bad."

"Oh, yes, it is."

"I think you could admit that it's not as bad as the fact that a white van with tinted windows has been following us since we left the doctor's office."

Cassie froze, not daring to look back, taking Daniel's word for it. "I wasn't being paranoid," she muttered.

"I never said you were."

"You thought it."

"For a minute or two, no more. And this might be crazy to say right now, with possible bigots trailing us and all, but realizing just how well you know me gives me one of the most satisfying feelings inside."

Cassie gripped his hand. Daniel had uncovered so much of his true inner self since she'd known him. From out of nowhere, she was reminded of how alike people in the world really were. Everyone gave support to those they loved, just as they were doing for each other. It made no difference that the hand holding hers was a few shades darker than hers. It was the hand of her love, her husband. And the mere fact that they were together as man and wife was threatening to her cousin and his friends.

Daniel gave her hand one more squeeze before releasing it. "Let's see if we can get a look at our admirers."

He swung into a gas station.

"We don't need gas," Cassie whispered, a covert atmosphere filling the car.

"Let's call this fuel for T's fire." He kissed her long and hard. "Keep a lookout, Cass. You're becoming an expert at it."

Daniel leaned against the car, looking as if he were searching for a credit card. As Cassie watched, the white van pulled next to a pump almost diagonal to them. She rested her head on the palm of her hand, feigning tiredness, all the while alert and watchful.

It seemed as if a million seconds passed as Daniel intentionally fumbled with his wallet. Cassie maintained her vigil, her eyes trained on the side view mirror. When the passenger door of the van suddenly opened, her eyes grew wide. With a will she didn't know she possessed, Cassie remained calm and still as the man ignored them and went straight into the store. She tilted her head toward Daniel, giving him a weak smile. He gave her one in return. He replaced the nozzle after pumping $2.15 worth of gas and slid behind the wheel.

"Get a piece of paper, Cass."

Unable to say a word, Cassie dug into the glove compartment and retrieved a small pad and pencil. As Daniel ticked off a description of the man, Cassie jotted down each bit of information. When he started the engine, they both looked up to see the man passing in front of their car. He stopped a second, nodded then moved on.

"Arrogant—" Daniel muttered and pulled into traffic. "Let's see what happens now."

He had squeezed into a narrow space in traffic before their trailing buddy made his way back to the white van, and now he casually dodged in and out of traffic, taking a circular route home.

Cassie searched but couldn't spot the white van. Her gaze went back to the pad in her hand, automatically reading the description Daniel had called out to her:

Tall, about 6' 3"
White
Big, muscular
Dark brown hair
Military stance

She could have given the description a week ago. It was the UPS man. Cassie read and reread it, not looking up until they were home.

When Daniel muttered a curse, Cassie turned in the direction of his gaze. Across the bayou, the white van was just parking. "Come on, Cass, let's get you inside."

Refusing to look at the van again, Cassie went into the house with Daniel, appreciating the support of his arm around her waist.

Once inside, Daniel released Cassie and went straight for the phone. So much had gone through his head in the last few hours. Worry over Cassie's possible paranoia, fear for her when it turned out to be real, and then feelings of total inadequacy. If he called the police and they came to investigate, their watchers would know Daniel and Cassie were on to them and go deeper. He would do the next best thing, call a cop he knew, his cousin Randy.

Daniel punched in some numbers. "Sonya, this is Daniel. Randy there?" Daniel listened to her chit chat a few seconds, barely able to contain his frustration.

"Sonya, I know we have a lot to catch up on, but is Randy there?" He paused to listen to the long explanation on the other end of the line.

"I realize that he must be tired with court and working all night, but this is very important."

"Hey, man, what's up?" Randy's voice, gravelly with sleep, came across the line.

Daniel laid out the situation for Randy and made arrangements to go to Randy's house later in the day.

"Come on in, Cuz, but don't make a sound. Sonya got the monster to sleep only five minutes ago. How's it going, Cass? Not too great right now, huh?" Randy continued to talk in a low voice. When they got to the back of the house, he used a normal tone. "We made it. My wife would have had a fit if we woke Tierra. I never saw a child who hated to go to sleep so much. Guess she's scared that she's going to miss something. Being the baby and all is probably what does it." Randy motioned with his hand. "Have a seat, get comfortable," he offered. "Everybody's been giving Tierra her way. At two years old, that's dangerous."

"But she's adorable," Cassie said, sitting on the plush love seat. Daniel joined her a second later, perching on the very edge, hunched over, frown lines etched in place as he stared at his cousin.

"That's another part of the problem," Cassie heard Randy say as she watched her husband's tense features. His hands that a second ago covered his knees were now balled into fists. Daniel's body language reflected her own feelings.

Cassie was scared, terrified of what might happen. What could they do? She and Daniel shouldn't have to be worrying about anything like this. After all, it wasn't the 60's.

"Enough about Tierra. My cousin's gonna bust wide open if we don't get right down to the reason for this nighttime visit."

Randy dragged a footstool over and sat, placing a firm hand on Daniel's shoulder and taking one of Cassie's hands in his own. "Give it to me long and slow. Don't leave anything out."

"That's what we came here for." The irritation in Daniel's voice came through loud and clear.

"I know the dissection of Tierra's personality wasn't what you came here to discuss, but the both of you looked too tense to get right into it. It helped Cassie, but I see it didn't do a thing for you. So let's hear it."

He sat back, crossed his arms and waited expectantly. Cassie gave a half smile in thanks to the cousin she had seen only occasionally because of the long, odd hours he worked. She let Daniel do most of the talking while she sat with both hands resting on her stomach, her shoulder pressed against Daniel's, listening but then again, not listening. That explained why it took her awhile to realize that the room was as still and quiet as the morning after Mardi Gras and that both men were staring at her. Daniel wore a worried frown, and Randy looked as if he knew what she was thinking.

"Cass?" Daniel asked, laying a warm hand on one of hers.

"Tell us what you're holding back," Randy requested in a laid back manner, never taking his eyes off her face.

"She's not—"

"She is," Randy insisted quietly

Daniel gently turned her face to his and a hurt look slowly rose into his eyes. "You are holding something back. There's something more about this you haven't told me?"

Cassie nodded. What she had to say had seemed unimportant at the time, and she hadn't wanted to worry him unnecessarily. Now it looked as if she had been hiding something. "I've seen that man before."

"You what?" Daniel almost shouted.

"Calm down, man, don't go flying off," Randy cautioned.

Daniel clamped his mouth shut then opened it again to ask, "Where?"

"At our front door."

"At our house?" Daniel shouted even louder as he jumped up and away from her to pace the room.

"If Tierra wakes up, you're putting her back to sleep before you leave here tonight," Randy said.

Daniel made a low growling sound then nodded.

"Control that famous temper of yours, Cuz. Have a seat and listen to what your wife has to say."

Daniel paused to stare at his older cousin, obviously trying to control himself, but he remained standing.

"Getting you to listen halfway is better than no way." Randy shrugged his shoulders good-naturedly.

"It's not as bad as you're thinking, Daniel," Cassie said from across the room, hoping to somehow counter that look of accusation with some explanation. "I had no idea that it was something I needed to worry about."

"A strange man coming to our door?"

"He said he was the UPS man."

"And you believed him?"

"I had no real reason not to, but for some reason, I didn't. Something inside wouldn't let me open the door. It was so strange."

"Thank God," Daniel muttered, coming back to sit next to her. "You scared me, Cass. I know you're right here in front of me safe and sound, but the idea of that man standing on the other side of our front door waiting for you to open it and do... whatever his bigoted brain had in mind..." He shook his head.

Cassie let out a huge breath when Daniel put his arm around her.

"How was it strange?" Randy asked.

Cassie heard Randy ask something, but at the moment she was soaking up the comfort Daniel was unselfconsciously offering.

"Alright, newlyweds, don't make me take my gun out to fire a warning shot."

"That would wake Tierra," Daniel reminded, turning to face Randy, his arms still wrapped around Cassie.

"Definitely not worth it. Y'all go ahead and finish the smooching, and then Cassie can tell me the details about the UPS incident."

Cassie explained that the encounter had lasted no more than a few minutes and had completely left her mind as anything important until she recognized the man as her mysterious UPS visitor. She couldn't really say why she'd felt strange at the time.

"Good judgment, Cass. Too many people get robbed or killed opening doors when they shouldn't."

"He's right, but you still should have told me about this," Daniel whispered.

Randy laid out a plan for filing a report without going to the police station and thereby tipping off their friends in the white van before evidence was gathered.

As Cassie and Daniel were leaving, Randy suggested, "You might want to talk to Scott and Ness and definitely Monica and Devin, too."

"Why?" they both asked.

"You don't know? I guess not if you're asking me why. I hate to be the one to tell you, Cassie, but your cousin T, known as T.J., or Travis LaBranch, Jr., tried to break up Scott and Ness. A couple of years later, he got the idea to ruin Prestway, Scott and Devin's construction firm."

"He didn't," Cassie gasped.

"Not for lack of trying. But that's not the worst of it. T.J. also attempted to kidnap Vicki and Megan, Scott's girls from a previous marriage. Your cousin claimed that he was rescuing two pure little girls from an unnatural environment.

It couldn't be true. The refrain ran through Cassie's head like the steady hum of the car's engine all the way home. But it *was* true. T had done *all* those horrible things. He had become a dangerous man.

CHAPTER 16

"Cass, are you ready to go?" Daniel walked into the bedroom to find her searching for something.

"Almost, I can't find my shoe."

"Sit down," he told her, stooping to look under the bed. Finding the loafer, he slipped it onto her foot, absently caressing her ankle, then moving a hand slowly upward. It was a mistake, he realized, as the effect reached his groin fast and hard. He quietly transferred his hand to the bed and stood.

Cassie looked up at him, a playful, sexy smile on her face. "When do we have to leave?"

"Now," he muttered gruffly. Way too gruffly, he realized when her face fell. "We'll be late if we don't go now," he explained, attempting to make amends for his short answer.

"You're right." Cassie stood, the sadness that had smothered her normally cheerful personality gone for the moment. "I haven't been to church since before Christmas, and that was with Melanie in Houston," she chattered on. "Her dad preached a sermon that moved the entire congregation."

Daniel stopped cold at the front door. "Melanie's father is a preacher?"

"Yes," Cassie nodded. "I thought I'd told you that."

"Never," he laughed harshly. He couldn't remember Jackie ever setting foot in any church. His grandmother or Aunt Joyce had taken him every Sunday. "Jackie's married to a preacher? Unbelievable."

"It is believable. You should see the way she helps Reverend Jordan organize—"

"Cass, I don't want to know," Daniel said firmly.

"I'll be here when you do," she told him right back, her sweet face full of understanding but firm with resolution. All that she'd been through, all that they were going through had not changed her one bit.

As Cassie and Daniel drove to church, the white van trailed them, a reminder, as if they could forget, of their present problems. The night before, they had come to the conclusion that they needed support from God, family, and friends. The doctor allowing Cassie more freedom coincided with their need for spiritual and familial fortification. A Sunday visit with aunts, uncles and cousins was necessary. Daniel could barely contain his need to talk to Ness, Monica and their husbands.

His self-imposed separation from his family had kept him out of touch and uninformed. What a self-absorbed jerk he'd become. He hadn't known a thing about their trouble with Travis LaBranch, Jr. Daniel slammed a hand on the steering wheel. Almost immediately, Cassie reached over to caress that same hand, unfurling each finger and gently lifting his hand off the steering wheel to place a kiss in the center of his palm.

A red light, right on time. If he was going to be dwelling on any self-imposed tendencies, this complete abstinence was one that he needed to worry about because it was going to do him in.

Cassie's gentle breath directed to the center of his palm fanned out, spreading across his entire hand. Her soft lips pressed against his sensitive skin produced misery and pain in other more sensitive parts of his body. Forcing himself not to snatch his hand away took more control and fortitude than his first solo flight years ago.

Cassie laid his hand against her cheek. "With so much going on, we haven't found time to experiment with some of those 'other ways' you mentioned before. Do you think you might be up to finding some time to experiment with those 'other ways?'"

In his mind, Daniel blew a breath of relief that her lips and breath were no longer teasing him. He took his foot off the brake and concentrated on driving to the next corner, where St. Ann's church was located.

"Daniel, did you hear me? Is the fact that the white van is still following us bothering you? Don't let it. I'm ignoring it. I think they want us to know that they're there. Randy's going to help us take care of all this."

Daniel parked. "I heard you, Cass." He didn't want to answer her. He loved finding other ways to make love to his wife beyond the traditional method. Sexual intercourse had been out of the question for so long that they had had to become inventive. The hours they spent loving each other with their hands and lips were sometimes more satisfying. She was right about the men trailing them, but they didn't worry him right now as much as responding to her question. Did he want to experiment with more ways of loving her? Of course, but then, she'd want to do the same for him. At the rate she was growing, that was becoming too awkward to accomplish. Satisfying her was enough, but Cassie would insist on doing the same for him.

Her cheek still rested in the palm of his hand. He moved his fingers in a gentle massage. Cassie's skin was so smooth. "I've been wanting to talk to you about the 'other ways,' but later, okay?"

"What's there to talk about?"

"A lot."

"You've got to do better than 'a lot,' Daniel. That's a bit more than I can handle along with everything else." Silent tears flowed down her face. "I didn't want to do this again."

"It's okay, Cass."

"Nothing's okay," Cassie yelled. For the second time in her life, Cassie had yelled at him.

"I'm the one with the temper," he reminded her.

"I've got one, too. And it's rising because the one thing I need right now is you, and you're trying to tell me we have to discuss whether or not I can show you how much I love you. We're already limited to kisses and caresses. And now you're saying we have to *discuss* sharing those."

"Maybe not discuss them. More or less talk about it."

"It's the same thing."

She actually laughed a little, giving him hope that she would understand his reasoning.

"You have me, Cass. I'm here for you always. But right now, not for..."

"Not for?"

Were her eyes narrowing? Daniel shook his head. "Not for making love."

"In any way?"

"It's not safe. For you or the baby."

This time he was sure Cassie's eyes were drawn together and directly focused on him.

"What makes you say that?"

Daniel couldn't answer right away. His attention was drawn to the narrow line that had appeared out of nowhere on Cassie's forehead. He brushed his finger above her eyebrows, smoothing it away then gently closed her eyes with the wide tips of his fingers. "Don't do that, baby."

"It wasn't working anyway."

"No, it wasn't."

"It's fine. I understand why you don't want to make love to me anymore."

"Do you?"

"Yes, let's go to mass."

Daniel hesitated to accept Cassie's quick explanation.

"Everyone will be surprised to see us," she went on, interrupting his thoughts. "Who knows, Mr. Tough Guy and his friend might join us. A sprinkle of holy water, a few prayers and a miracle might happen. Maybe then they'd leave us alone."

That sounded more like his Cassie. Daniel went around to open the door. They made it inside the church just as the bells chimed the hour and the processional hymn began. They found a place near a few members of Daniel's family. Correction, most of *their* family. They got smiles and nods from everyone. Aunt Joyce, who was in the pew in front of them, turned to give Daniel and Cassie a welcoming pat. Uncle Cal stared pointedly at his watch, giving Daniel the "How dare you be late for church?" look that he'd seen many times as a teenager.

"I'm on time," Daniel mouthed before Uncle Cal turned back around.

As he sat in the middle of the three pews that made up the family, feelings of belonging, of having a shared history emerged. All on its own, an image of Jackie popped into his head.

An unwanted image.

Daniel cleared his head. There was no room for Jackie. Instead, he concentrated on the solemn tradition and responses of the mass.

The ease in which he joined in the prayers felt like putting on a familiar shoe which had been lost. The mixture of new and traditional hymns was a spark to his soul. He had to believe they'd get through their trouble with help from God and family. He had to have faith; otherwise, there was no way he would follow Randy's plan.

An hour later, they settled on a couch at Aunt Joyce and Uncle Cal's house. Daniel and Cassie each ended up with a baby in their arms.

"Which one do you have?" Daniel asked.

"I think I'm holding Kyle."

"Then I must have Kacey."

"That's Kacey, Cousin Daniel," Jasmine, Monica's only

daughter informed him.

"Oh he's making that face again," Vicki, Kacey's big sister said, a note of dread in her voice.

"The stinky face that comes before the stinky smell," Megan, Kacey's other big sister, stated matter-of-factly before yelling, "Let's get out of here!"

The three girls raced off just as Kacey's little face twisted up, then suddenly relaxed.

"Did you see that?" Daniel asked.

Cassie could barely contain her laugh.

"You smell that?"

"Oh yeah."

"Wanna trade?"

"No way. Mine is falling asleep."

Daniel stood, holding the baby securely but as far away from his upper body as possible. "I need to find Ness or Scott or somebody."

"Ness is helping Aunt Joyce in the kitchen, and Scott went with Devin to pick up some French bread."

"It takes two men to get bread?"

"Maybe it does, but I bet it only takes one to change a diaper."

"I don't know how to do that."

"It's a good time to learn." Cassie patted her belly.

"This isn't funny." Daniel stood a minute, staring at the baby's diaper. "So you won't trade?"

"Nope."

"Ah-h-h, Monica," he remembered.

"She's outside resting and watching the other children."

"Uncle Cal?"

"You *are* desperate." She laughed.

"You're enjoying this."

"He's starting to squirm," Cassie warned. "You had better do something, Daniel."

His face full of panic, Daniel grabbed a diaper bag from a nearby chair and headed in the direction of the bathroom.

Cassie quietly waited five, ten, then fifteen minutes for Daniel to come back with a freshly diapered baby. It couldn't be too hard. There weren't any pins involved.

Knowing she was probably spoiling him rotten by continuing to hold the sleeping baby in her arms, Cassie stood. She nuzzled his soft little cheek. He was such a perfect mix of his mother and father. Cassie wondered what their baby would look like and how people would view the child. One more worry, but at least that one wasn't as threatening as the people in the white van supposedly hidden down the street.

When Cassie walked into the room at the back of the house, smells of a New Orleans kitchen hit both her and the baby. He squirmed in her arms. "Ness?"

Both Vanessa and Joyce looked up.

"Shouldn't you be resting?" the older woman asked.

"Is Kyle giving you trouble?"

"No, Ness, I'm fine. It's Daniel."

"What's wrong with that boy?" Uncle Cal asked, stomping into the kitchen.

"Nothing much. He's spent the last fifteen minutes in the bathroom changing Kacey's diaper.

"Oh, Kacey gave his present to Daniel."

"That must be some present. Glad it's not me," Cal commented.

"I'll see what's going on. Scott's not back yet?" Ness asked as she went to Daniel's rescue.

"No," Cassie answered.

"That must be some special French bread they're buying."

"That was only an excuse, Daddy." Monica slowly walked into the kitchen. "You know as well as I do that they went to check out that property near the parish line."

"I'm not surprised." Joyce dipped a spoon into the huge gumbo pot. "They've got another project cooking."

"Of course. They'll be here soon enough."

"Without that bread, I bet," Calvin Lewis boomed out with laughter.

Kyle woke with a cry.

"Come here, little man. You should be used to your paw-paw's big mouth by now." Calvin lifted Kyle out of Cassie's arms.

"Come on, Cass. Let us pregnant people get a load off. I've got less than a week left of privilege to sponge off my family," Monica said.

"Do it while you still can, ladies," Joyce advised.

"A nice cold glass of water and..." Monica paused, glancing at Cassie.

"A tall glass of milk."

"...and a tall glass of milk. We'll be waiting in the den, Daddy."

Calvin's laughter was cut short. "Oh, no, Joycie! He's making that face."

"That's nice, Cal."

Monica and Cassie made a retreat as quickly as their heavy loads would allow.

Devin and Scott walked through the front door just as they settled down on the sofa.

"Hey, Brown Eyes." Devin leaned over to kiss Monica.

Before Scott could open his mouth to greet anyone, Calvin burst into the room along with a nasty odor.

"Ah, there's your daddy. This boy needs changing, and you're the man to do it."

"Gee, thanks, Paw-paw Cal." Scott grimaced. "Come on, Kyle, let's get you cleaned up."

Cassie watched as Scott stopped and turned at the sound of

a snort coming from the middle of the room. "Not one word, Dev. Five days, that's all I have to say. Five days, and it's your turn."

Ness and Daniel breezed in, passing Scott along the way. Ness plopped the freshly diapered baby in her father's arms.

"This one smells clean."

"I heard that, Cal," Joyce called through the kitchen. "The way you act, everyone would think you never changed a dirty diaper."

"Haven't done it in twenty years, and don't want to do it ever again."

Daniel slowly rolled into the empty spot next to Cassie. "What a mess."

"It was that bad?"

"That stuff was all over the place. I was trying to get to it a little at a time. Ness breezed in, stripped the little fella, washed, diapered, and dressed him again in less than two minutes."

"Don't worry, Daniel, you'll break that record in no time." Cassie patted his leg in comfort.

Before he could counter that purposely misunderstood comment, other family members began to arrive.

Warren, his wife, and kids came in carrying individual homemade king cakes, a traditional Mardi Gras treat. The tiny circular rolls were decorated with purple, green, and gold-colored sugar and were sold in every bakery and grocery store from King's Day in January until Mardi Gras Day.

Josh and John, Aunt Joyce and Uncle Calvin's youngest twin sons, came in with a softball and bat, promising their nieces and nephews a game. Sonya crept in, finger to her lips in a plea for quiet as she carried in a sleeping Tierra. Her two boys came in right behind.

"Looks like we're all here," Calvin announced, his voice lower than usual.

"I don't think so," Randy called as he entered.

"Randy? What are you doing here?" Monica asked.

"Hasn't Mardi Gras season started?" someone else interjected.

"Aren't you supposed to be on parade route keeping the streets safe."

"Or resting before you go on duty tonight?" another family member questioned.

"Well, thank you for that welcome, family," Randy said in way of an answer.

"You know we don't mean it that way." Joyce was the first to make her way over to him. "We never see you during Mardi Gras season, and isn't it a little more than a week away?"

"You're gonna have to use an armored truck to take all that overtime home, right, Randy."

"Almost, Daddy. And yes, Mama, you're right about Mardi Gras. I'm here because we've got some business to discuss."

"We do?"

"What's going on?"

"Something wrong?"

Questions filled the room.

"Sounds serious," Calvin said, handing the baby back to Ness.

"It is." Daniel stood, one hand clasping Cassie's.

Scott came into the room with the other baby. "Where's all the noise? Did something happen while I was gone?"

"We're waiting to see," Devin answered, serious and calm.

"And you will see, in a minute. Cassie and I need your help and support right now."

"You've got that, Daniel." A gentle hand touched his shoulder. "We're always here for you and Cassie."

"I know, Aunt Joyce."

The doorbell rang.

"I thought everyone was here." Calvin opened the door wide.

"Margaret, Travis, come on in," Joyce said as different reactions spread across the room. Cassie could feel them all. It wasn't, she thought, so much the unexpected guests as the reason for her aunt and uncle's visit. There were many quietly murmured welcomes. It didn't take long for realization to dawn.

"I s-e-e-e-e-e-e," Devin dragged out long and slow.

"T.J.," Scott muttered with disgust.

"Oh my, what has he done now?" Margaret asked, obvious strain pulling her face tight.

"Not much, Aunt Margaret."

"Not yet anyway," Daniel added.

"Forgive us. Travis, Margaret, have a seat," Joyce offered. "Would you like a drink?"

"Yes, please, anything you have. Tea, water." Margaret sat next to Cassie.

"Hello, sweetheart."

"How are things going, Cassie Bear?"

"Not too good," she answered, holding back a tear. She wasn't going to cry. "We've got some bad news about T."

"Not much of a surprise. I didn't think T.J. would let your marriage to Daniel go," Travis Sr. sighed, sitting next to his wife.

"Travis, do you know where he is?"

"No, Devin, but I'm sure you want that information. I know my son has caused this family a lot of grief, and as I've said before, I apologize for T.J."

"You aren't responsible for T. J.'s actions. We don't blame you," Ness said.

"You're part of the family now," Monica added.

Joyce came back from the kitchen carrying drinks for the couple. "We didn't mean to be rude earlier. Right before you walked in, Cassie and Daniel alluded to a problem."

"I understand, Joyce." Margaret accepted the tall glass of iced tea. "Thank you."

"Please continue with what you were going to say, Daniel, Cassie." Travis waited expectantly.

Daniel cleared his throat. He explained what had been going on, giving complete details of T.J.'s sudden interference in their lives.

"They've been following and watching you for how long?" Aunt Margaret asked.

"At least a week, we think."

"That's terrible, Cass." Ness shifted the baby in her arms, moving closer to Scott. Other voices joined hers in agreement.

"Are you certain? Has T.J. actually claimed responsibility?"

"Yes, he has, Aunt Margaret. With pride."

"He called to harass Cassie. The conversation wasn't a pleasant one."

"We've had the experience, Daniel. Too often, wouldn't you say, Margaret?"

Uncle Travis's face looked weary and old. He wasn't old in years, not yet. But T was making him age much sooner than he should. For how many years had his behavior worried her aunt and uncle? Well, they were doing something about it now. "Daniel installed a recorder on the phone, and Randy's looking into a tracer."

"We'll be ready for the next call," Randy interjected.

"I just realized something. If they've been following you all this time, then they're somewhere around here right now," Sonya surmised.

"The kids?" Monica called.

"Will be okay," Randy assured everyone. "You're thinking like a cop, Sonya."

"I married one. It rubs off."

"I bet it does," Daniel said before attempting to reassure the worried faces of his family. "Randy's got everything under control."

"Exactly."

"After Cassie and I visited him last night, we decided to fill you in, warn you, and get as much help as we can."

"You've got that," Uncle Cal repeated.

"Without question. But do you realize exactly how dangerous this situation can be?" Scott asked.

"Or how twisted T.J. has become?" Devin added.

"I found out for myself, firsthand. Those calls weren't friendly little chats."

"Oh, Cassie, what did he say to you?"

"Enough to know that T was not the cousin I grew up with, Aunt Margaret. He's not the same person you raised."

The room became completely still and silent. The babies lay quietly in their parents' arms, sensing the mood in the quiet room.

"Hey, is this a funeral or what?" Josh burst into the room with John right behind him.

"No," Randy answered for everyone, "family meeting."

"Sounds serious."

"It is. Can you and John continue to keep an eye on the kids outside? We'll fill you in later."

"Sure thing."

"What's going on in there, man?" John asked his brother.

"I have absolutely no idea. It's the curse."

"The curse of being the youngest," John said, immediately understanding.

"Do everything, know nothing," they both announced, slamming the back door behind them.

The comment released some of the tension in the room.

Some laughter worked its way past many of the anxious frowns when Vicki's usual proposal of marriage to her Uncle John was heard from outside.

"That puts things back into perspective," Ness said.

"How?" Scott wanted to know.

"We've had trouble with T.J. before."

"Too much," Devin growled.

"But things have always gotten back to normal."

"Ness is right. We can't let T.J. and his attempts to upset this family ruin our time together," Monica added.

"True, Brown Eyes, no one can. Randy, lay down your plan. Then I'll tell you what I know."

"What do you know?" Daniel exclaimed.

"His possible location."

"You do?" Scott turned with a look of surprise.

"No way, the man's disappeared. The police can't find him," Randy explained.

"That's the pitiful truth."

"Than how can you know where he might be?" Travis Sr. asked.

"Yes, Devin, please explain how you acquired that information."

Cassie was amazed to notice a flash of worry cross Devin's face as he turned toward his wife. This big man, who oozed confidence, seemed extremely concerned about his wife's reaction.

"I hired someone to find him."

"You didn't." Monica folded her arms and clamped her mouth shut.

In a firm but quiet voice Devin stated, "I did. I couldn't let T.J. get away with harming anyone in my family. He hurt Jasmine, tried to kidnap Vicki and Megan, threatened both Scott and me. I know you didn't expect me to let this be."

"No, you wouldn't."

A wave of depression fell on Cassie as the discussion continued. The same wave obviously engulfed both her aunt and uncle. A member of their family had caused a tremendous amount of grief to Cassie's new extended family. She should be spending time with them, getting to know them, not bringing grief to them.

"I realize you didn't know all this, Cassie Bear," Uncle Travis leaned toward her to softly say.

"We knew you'd find out eventually," Margaret whispered, "but we didn't want to be the ones to tell you."

Cassie strained to listen to her aunt and uncle, tuning out the voices discussing T and all the havoc he had caused.

"And we thought we'd instilled enough common sense and morals into T.J. that he wouldn't threaten his own cousin," Uncle Travis added.

"He's not himself," Cassie whispered. "T needs help. He's like someone else."

"I want him found and put behind bars." Devin's voice rose above everyone else's.

Cassie suddenly couldn't stand any more. Everyone in this room had a right to want justice. T had done terrible things, he'd said terrible things to her and was probably planning so much more, but… She stood. "T—needs—help. He is not himself. He's somebody else!"

Cassie had gotten everyone's attention. Why had she said that? She didn't want to alienate her new family. Daniel's strong arm eased across her shoulder and held her close to him.

"It's okay, Cass."

"Why did I say that?" she whispered to him.

"Because, despite what T has done, you still love your cousin. Your memory of him is clashing with what you know about him now."

"Daniel's right," Ness told her.

"We can understand that what you, Margaret, and Travis are going through must be hard," Joyce added.

Cassie slowly looked around the room. The faces staring back at her were full of compassion.

"Thank you," Cassie said before sitting back down with her husband.

A sense of calm had returned to the room.

"Now back to business," Randy began. "Cassie and Daniel have twenty-four hour protection."

"The police are providing the protection?" Scott asked.

"Private security," Daniel answered.

"I see. You hired off duty police officers as security." Devin nodded. "That's why you weren't worried about the kids in the yard."

"Exactly, and we'll have our friends in jail in a matter of days."

"On what charge?"

"One will come," Randy said mysteriously. "In the meantime, I suggest that we do everything exactly as if we have no idea what's going on."

"But Daniel and Cassie came here today. Not that they're not welcome anytime, but that's not part of their usual routine," Monica stated.

"The watchers don't necessarily know that since they seemed to have been following us for only about a week," Daniel explained. "Cassie just got the okay from the doctor to go on short outings, which they probably know by now, which would explain why we haven't come before. I'm sure they somehow know that I'm scheduled to fly out Tuesday for the first time since before Christmas." Daniel paused to take a deep breath. "The last thing I want to do is leave Cassie right now, but I know I can depend on everyone in this room to us get through this."

Echoes of affirmation filled the room once again.

"That's the way it's going to be," Uncle Cal agreed.

"How can we help?"

"Be there for Cassie. I don't want her alone for a minute."

"I'll be staying with Aunt Margaret and Uncle Travis when

Daniel's away. I don't want to change anyone's schedule or put anyone out."

"No, we don't, but I'll be better able to concentrate on landings and takeoffs knowing Cassie has so many people to turn to, to trust in an emergency.

The doorbell rang. A nonverbal question hung in the air as Devin went to answer it. He cracked the door open, turned his back to the room and shrugged. "What can I do for you?"

"I think the kids in your yard lost this," a deep voice rumbled through the door. A second later Devin caught a softball.

"Thanks," he said, closing the door.

"That was him," Cassie announced. "That voice, I remember it."

"Big white guy, Rambo type?"

"Yes." Cassie shouted.

At once the room was full of activity.

Randy and Daniel raced for the front door. Randy had a radio in his hand, Daniel nothing at all. The other men ran straight to the back door, the children's safety on everyone's mind.

Cassie sank further into the sofa, her aunt beside her, offering comfort. Joyce held the baby Scott had handed to her before dashing out.

Daniel walked back into the house. "He's gone."

"But not without a trace," Randy said, hooking his radio to his belt. "As soon as he moved, our protection decided to take his dog for a walk."

"A police dog?"

"You got it, Cuz."

Devin strode in. "Everyone's okay in the backyard. The kids are coming in to wash up for dinner."

Cassie looked up. "Sorry, we didn't mean to put everyone in danger."

"We've been a part of this from the beginning, Cass." Scott patted her shoulder.

"Why do you think he came to the door? Josh or John could have gotten the ball," Daniel muttered to Randy.

"Who knows, some kind of sick joke maybe."

"Time to eat," Calvin bellowed. "Let's forget this mess for a while."

"That means we still don't get to know what's going on," Josh complained to his brother as they came in.

"You'd think we'd be entitled to a little information," John agreed.

"Later."

"How much later, Dad? When we turn into two decaying corpses?"

The family settled at the huge dining room table.

Worry, fright, and relief created a tension in the air. That feeling was shattered by a little voice heard from somewhere in the house.

"I'm up and I took a l-l-l-l-long nap, Mommie. Come get me."

"That's Tierra," Randy sighed.

Everyone laughed as Sonya went to get her daughter.

The laughter was cut short when a loud series of knocks resounded in the suddenly quiet house.

CHAPTER 18

Cassie stood in front of the bathroom mirror, dreading the time when Daniel would have to leave. The last thing in the world she wanted was for her husband to go. Although she would have family who would be there for her, they weren't Daniel. She thought about how protective he'd been at Aunt Joyce's with the unexpected knock on the door so soon after their scare. He'd been the one who answered the door, but not before he barricaded her body with his chair. Fortunately, there'd been no danger this time around. To everyone's relief, it had been Scott's sister, Wendy, and her family.

Unzipping the red maternity dress, she let it fall to her ankles. She peeled off the white blouse she wore underneath. Her panties and bra came next.

Yes, she was bigger and rounder and completely unattractive to her husband.

Cassie went to the shower stall and turned the water on full blast.

"Exactly what are you doing?" Daniel's voice cut into her thoughts. He stood at the bathroom door.

"Taking a shower."

"Ah-ah."

Was that a spark of desire in his eyes? "Ah-ah as in no?"

"Ah-ah, as in you're not taking a shower without me."

He was directly behind her now, and the familiar caress began at the nape of her neck and moved down her spine.

"Why?"

Cassie wasn't sure if she was asking why he was doing this to her or why she wasn't supposed to take a shower without him. With the gentle pressure of his finger he was arousing her passion.

"Because," he breathed into her ear, placing a finger in the erotic spot, trailing it down as he spoke. "Because it's not safe for you or the baby. You could slip and fall." He replaced his fingertip with his lips, kissing his way down her back, stopping right above her bottom.

"Safer than making love in *any way*?"

Daniel froze. He slowly turned her to face him. "Throwing my words back at me?" he asked before guiding her into the stall.

"That's right."

"I deserve it. I don't know why I thought I could keep my hands off you." Daniel spread the suds he had just lathered between his hands across her shoulders, reaching behind her neck to make the journey once again, building up her passion.

"If you really mean that, I suggest that you take off those clothes. They are soaking wet and in my way."

Daniel didn't want to leave. The last thing he wanted to do was to walk away from his wife and leave someone else to protect her. But that's what he had to do. What he was going to do in a matter of hours. "Five hours and ten minutes," he whispered.

"What?" Cassie asked sleepily, burrowing her head into his chest.

"Five hours and ten minutes before I take off."

"That's not much longer."

"No, it isn't."

All was quiet for awhile, but neither of them wanted to sleep away their time together. Daniel held her tighter, closer. "Everything will be fine."

"I know it will be."

His hand moved down to cover her stomach. "You and baby Jax will be fine."

"Did you feel her move?"

"She's saying hi to daddy," he proudly said.

"You're finally ready to admit that our baby's a girl?"

"Since you finally realized that we were naming the baby Jax, I had to concede."

"M-m-m-m."

"I don't know if I like the sound of that."

"I was actually agreeing."

"Good, then the name question is settled."

"Ah, m-m-m-m."

"What was that for?"

"I need to ask you something."

"Go ahead, Cass."

"Did you mean what you said about not being able to keep your hands off me?"

"I had good intentions, but I'm a weak man."

"For what reason would you even consider keeping your hands to yourself? Did you want both of us to suffer?"

"I *have* been suffering, but I can handle it. Cass, you're seven months pregnant, and we almost lost the baby. Your needs come before my desires."

"What about mine?"

"Yours?"

"I have desires, too."

"I realize that, but I don't want you to feel obligated to satisfy my needs with all those amazing 'other ways' you had of making love to me without actually making love. I didn't want you to do that for me in your condition just because I satisfied you."

"Now I understand."

"I thought you did before."

"No, I put the blame on my round figure.

"Cass."

"I know. Call it low self-esteem pregnantitus. I thought my extremely full figure was what was keeping you away. I needed your touch, even if we couldn't make love. I enjoyed making loved to you without actually making love. And what I did for you was just as much for me."

"I'm glad you told me this. I've never seen you as anything but sexy and desirable. Especially since you've been carrying my baby."

"I needed to hear that."

"Then I'll say it all the time. And I meant what I said about you worrying about satisfying me."

"What if I choose to?" Cassie slowly turned to her side, resting her head on her palm.

"I wouldn't feel comfortable."

"But what if I had an urge that left me completely uncomfortable, the kind of urge that led me to seduce you with my hands, my voice, and warm cocoa butter lotion?"

"Tempting."

"What if I didn't give you a chance to deny me that desire?"

"Then I might have to give in."

"I wouldn't give you a choice."

This was laughable. His wife was as big as a house, but she was determined to seduce him. If they could keep their passion and their humor alive through all this mess, they could definitely keep it forever. "What am I going to do with you?"

"Let me make love to you the any way I want to?"

"Whenever you want," Daniel agreed.

"How about now?" Cassie sat up and grabbed something from the nightstand. She waved the light brown bottle of lotion before him.

Now is good, the bottom half of Daniel said. The other half was laying the guilt on already. A serious dilemma. "Now is good," he decided, "but I get to use the lotion first. Hand it over so I can warm it up."

Thirty minutes later, Cassie lay on her side sound asleep as Daniel rubbed the lotion into her back. He once again snuggled her close to him, dreading the moment he would have to leave.

Uneventful. The last two days had been completely full of nothing exciting or dangerous. *And I'm thankful for that,* Cassie thought as she continued to look out the front window of her childhood home. There was not a white van in sight.

"No, that wasn't Daniel," Cassie muttered to herself as the second cab in the last five minutes passed by.

It had been over half an hour since Daniel had called to say that he was on his way.

The phone rang, but Cassie didn't leave her post at the door. She might miss Daniel.

The ringing stopped and Cassie could hear her uncle's voice. He must have caught the phone in his study down the hall.

"T.J.?" she heard him question.

She turned away from the window. They hadn't heard from T in days. It couldn't be anything good.

Determined to keep her focus on Daniel's return, Cassie turned back to the window, but couldn't help hearing Uncle Travis's side of the conversation.

"No, I have no idea where Cassie can be." A pause. "You say she's disappeared? Well, how can you know that, Son? Where are you living now?"

There was another pause, long and silent.

"It's a secret? Well, then, I guess I've got a few of my own."

Cassie cracked a smile. Her uncle was the strong silent type, but he got his point across.

A minute later, she heard him say, "No sign of that husband of yours yet, Cassie Bear?"

"Not yet." She peeked over her shoulder to give him the smile she'd been wearing. "But soon. You know how horrible Metairie traffic is at rush hour when everybody's trying to get home."

"Unfortunately, not everybody wants to come home."

"T?"

"You heard. I knew you could."

"So, he has no idea where I am?"

"None whatsoever."

"Staying in must have helped."

A horn blew.

"There's Daniel." Cassie wobbled out the door and down the steps as fast as she could. He looked so good in that uniform. A second later, she couldn't see an inch in front of her because she was pressed against the top half of his uniform. He smelled so good. Daniel lifted her head and his green eyes studied her face. "Missed you."

"Then kiss me."

And he did. Long and gentle and full of love. Then he stooped to her belly. "Daddy's back, and I missed you, too." Daniel kissed her stomach.

"Sir, I hate to break this up, but you forgot your bag."

"Sorry about that." Daniel took his bag from the patient driver.

"That's one man that loves you," the short, burly man said. "All he could talk about was you and the baby you're expectin'."

"The feeling's mutual."

The man nodded. "Have a happy life."

"Without a doubt," Daniel told the cab driver.

With their arms around each other, Daniel and Cassie went into the house.

"Glad to see you back."

"More than glad to be back, Uncle Travis." Glancing down at Cassie, Daniel asked, "How have the last two days been for you?"

"Long, boring, and without any sighting of our shadows."

"No white van."

"No anything. They have no idea where I am."

"How do you know that?"

"T called Uncle Travis."

"He was trying to get information on Cassie's whereabouts, but he didn't have much luck," her uncle confirmed.

"So leaving in the wee hours of the night and taking a cab here must have worked."

"T's friends were probably asleep on the job."

"I wonder when they figured out that no one was home."

"Judging by his call, today."

"Daniel, welcome back," Aunt Margaret greeted. "Dinner's ready."

Cassie enjoyed the peaceful meal. They ate, spoke quietly and, by mutual consent, had no more discussion of T.

"I can't wait to hold a baby in my arms again," Aunt Margaret said after dinner was done.

"I can't wait to bounce him around again. I haven't done that since Cassie Bear was little," Uncle Travis added.

"Her," both Cassie and Daniel corrected, then laughed.

"Oh, you've had an ultra sound. They told you what the baby is, didn't they?"

"No, Aunt Margaret."

"No ultrasound, after all you've been through?"

"What Cassie means," Daniel explained, "is that we've had

ultrasounds but never wanted to know the sex of the baby."

"We just happen to know that baby Jax is a girl," Cassie finished.

"Jax? You're not naming the baby Jax."

"Calm down, Margaret, they wouldn't name the baby after a brewery turned tourist attraction. Would you?" Travis asked, turning to them.

"The name has pretty much grown on us, hasn't it, Cass?"

"It has," Cassie said, not wasting a second to answer.

"But, Cassie, Daniel," Aunt Margaret looked from one to the other.

"Yes, what is it?"

"This baby. Your baby. Our niece. Don't you think she'll have enough to contend with just being born in this world with so many people like..."

"T?"

"Not only T.J."

The conversation had been so nice without T's presence and Cassie had had to bring him up herself.

"I think your aunt means closed-minded people," Uncle Travis answered.

"Please don't give her a name that would cause another problem."

Aunt Margaret's pleading eyes went to Cassie and Daniel once again. "I don't want to tell you what to do, but I'm worried about people treating my niece badly because she's different. People can be cruel."

"We realize that, Aunt Margaret." Cassie reached for her aunt's hand. "And we appreciate the fact that you have the same concerns as we do. That will make life easier for Jax."

"She'll have tons of love from you both and every member of my family. You've seen them," Daniel cocked his head to the side for emphasis, "a crazier, more lovable bunch you won't meet. Jax will be filled with confidence and love from both sides of her family, both races. And she'll learn that she cannot control what people think—"

"Only her own actions," Daniel and Cassie ended together.

Something passed between them, a deeper understanding of each other perhaps. Whatever it was, she was filled with it. Daniel, too. Cassie was certain her aunt and uncle saw it, because they had nothing else to say when Daniel announced, "That's the way we feel about it. A name won't change much about people's attitudes."

Strange, Cassie thought. She and Daniel had never discussed this issue in depth but they had come together with the same thoughts as if they had.

Smiling, Randy was waiting for them on the steps in front of their house.

"You have some good news for us, Cuz?" Daniel asked from the open car window.

"Better than good," he answered, hopping down the steps.

Daniel got out and went around the car to open the door for Cassie.

"Don't keep us waiting," Cassie insisted as Daniel helped her out of the car.

A sudden gust of wind blew, peppering them with tiny bits of debris.

"This wind is kickin'," Daniel yelled, pulling Cassie closer to his chest.

"There's a storm coming," she muttered.

"Let's hear this better-than-good news inside." Daniel headed them in that direction.

"I know you're glad not to be flying out of New Orleans tonight, Cuz." Randy remarked, closing the front door as the first heavy drops of rain began to fall.

"The news, Randy," Daniel growled.

Cassie laughed, swiping a finger down the row of ridges on her husband's forehead. "Remember, it's good news."

They both turned to Randy expectantly.

"Your shadows are now in the custody of the NOPD."

Cassie buried her head into Daniel's chest as she'd done earlier, wrapped her arms around his waist and squeezed out all her pent-up fears and frustrations with one huge sigh. Daniel's arms around her hung onto her with just as much strength.

"When? How?" they both asked at the same time.

"Not more than ten minutes ago. They were charged with loitering. We had the van towed."

"Loitering? Will that hold them?" Daniel asked.

"That along with assault on a police officer."

"He didn't. I mean, they didn't." Cassie paused. "How many were there?"

"Two."

"That's what I thought," Daniel muttered, guiding Cassie to the sofa and motioning for Randy to sit.

"Can't stay. I'm on my way to work and hung around to tell you in person. I knew you'd be in soon."

"Our guard must have been bored these last two days."

"Frank and June survived. They took shifts."

"A woman?" Daniel shook his head in disbelief.

"Yes, a woman. We can do anything." Cassie declared.

"June is my partner Frank's sister. She and her K-9 Bud make a great team. The lack of action is what gave her the idea. Since the van just sat there, June reported it as abandoned. She also reported two suspicious characters hanging around the neighborhood, just to give them some trouble."

"They were out and walking around?"

"Probably tired of sitting."

"What about the other charge, assaulting a police officer?"

"Well, Cuz, it so happened that the officers who came out on the call weren't to their liking, an African-American and an Asian-American. The van dwellers didn't take too kindly to being told what to do by these fine officers."

"I understand," Cassie nodded. "They simply dug themselves in deeper."

"Yeah, that's about right." Randy kissed her cheek. "Feel safe."

He shook Daniel's hand. "I'm here when you need me. Just call."

"Thanks, Randy. Thank June, Frank and Bud for me, too. We don't know what else to say."

"You just said all you needed to." Then Randy was out the door.

"I do feel safe," Cassie told Daniel. "So safe I want to go out to celebrate."

"Got any ideas?"

"Dinner?"

"We just ate."

"Movie? No, it's too late. I'd fall asleep. What can we do to celebrate?"

"We don't need much, Cass. Me, you, some cocoa butter lotion."

"That's what I'd call a celebration. And I won't fall asleep tonight. That's a promise."

An hour later Daniel smiled to himself as he gently rubbed the last of the warmed lotion across her belly. The baby moved beneath his hands. Jax was safe and growing strong. Without his friends around to follow through for him, T's threats had been defused. Life was looking better. Daniel relaxed beside Cassie, wrapping the covers around them both, allowing contentment to surround them as the rain fell at a steady pace.

Without conscious thought, his mind moved in the direction it had lately wandered more often then he wanted to admit.

Jackie.

Had she changed?

Had she turned into a great mother after deserting him?

If he was to believe his sister, correction, his half sister, then Jackie had. If that was the case, could he deny his baby a relationship with her grandmother and whoever else there was in this other extended family he knew nothing about? Daniel knew how important family was, even though he had distanced himself from his own for so long. Their love, their concern, had always been there.

Daniel hugged Cassie closer. As he drifted off to sleep, his last thoughts were of Jackie, a mother he knew little about, and Jax his unborn child. Daniel couldn't wait to meet Jax, to know her.

Jackie and Jax. They both start with a J. How about that? he thought as sleep overcame him.

"Hello." Cassie answered the phone groggily, then moved the receiver away from her ear and stared at it with a narrow squint. She turned the phone into the correct position.

"Cassie, are you there? Cass, it's me."

"Melanie. What's going on? Why are you calling me so early in the morning?"

"It's not early. I've been up for hours."

Cassie used her elbows to pull herself up, bumping Daniel in the process.

"Ow!"

"Sorry." She giggled. She peered at the clock. "It is late. Morning's almost over."

"Keeping late nights, huh?"

"Trying, but not succeeding. Daniel's got these hands that simply lull me to sleep before they even begin to heat my blood enough to—"

"Enough, my friend. I don't think I want to hear about your and my brother's love life."

"Since when?"

"Since Daniel started acting like a brother. Too weird, Cass."

"Tell Melanie goodbye and come back to me," Daniel growled.

"In a minute. I have to tell her the good news. She's only heard the worst."

"Good news? Tell me all," Melanie screeched into the phone.

Cassie reported the recent arrest of T's friends as Daniel nibbled on various parts of her body. Her toes, her knees, a wet kiss on her enlarged belly button.

"Daniel," Cassie couldn't help but say in a breathy sigh.

"What's he doing?"

"You don't want to know, Mel, remember?"

"Right now? At this moment? That brother of mine is too much."

"Ohhhh, you're right about that," Cassie agreed, drawing in a deep breath between clenched teeth.

"If you want to go right now, I understand."

"It's not that. I think—I just—had a contraction."

"What?" Melanie shouted into one ear.

"What?" Daniel yelled into the other.

Daniel took the phone from her hand. "We'll talk to you later." He threw the receiver at the base of the phone. "It's too soon, you're not even eight months pregnant yet."

"I know."

"Jax can't be born yet."

"She might be."

"Okay, let's not panic."

"I'm trying not to, Daniel, but you're not making this easy."

Instantly he was calm. "I'm sorry, baby. I'll get the stop-watch."

"Good thinking." Cassie held her breath as another pain hit her. She let her breath out slow and easy as it receded and continued, "It's in my bag, in the closet. Remember?"

Cassie watched as Daniel dug through the bag, scattering little crocheted booties, a sweater, and a blanket all over the floor.

"Found it!"

"In the side zippered pocket, right?"

"Yeah, I know, I could have asked. I didn't. Now tell me when it hits you again."

An uncontrollable need to giggle rose from the pit of her stomach to her throat, creating a tingling sensation in her chest and down her arms. Unable to hold it in, Cassie let loose with an incredible series of tittering noises.

"Cass, what's wrong?" Are you hurting that bad?" Daniel knelt before her on the bed, a knee on either side of her outstretched legs. "You're hysterical," Cassie heard Daniel mutter, one hand holding the watch, the other resting on her forehead, making her efforts to temper the laughter even harder.

"Yes—I mean no—I mean, I'm okay," she attempted to tell him firmly.

Daniel didn't look as if he believed her. His frowned-up face and creased forehead almost set her off again. But the soft concern in his green gaze dampened the urge.

"I'm fine, Daniel."

His steady unchanging stare looked unconvinced. "Then why all this giggling?"

"You don't want to know."

"I do."

"Ohhhh, it just hit me," Cassie yelled and giggled at the same time, but the pain immediately gained the upper hand.

Giggles and pain continued for the next half hour, allowing no time for explanation. Then, suddenly, it all stopped, the giggles, the pain. Daniel's thumb was motionless above the little red button on the stopwatch.

"No more?" Daniel rubbed his hand across her belly.

"Hopefully." Cassie laid her head back against his chest. Daniel had somehow positioned himself behind her. That's when it dawned on her. "Braxton—"

"—Hicks," Daniel finished. "I should have known. The contractions were so irregular. False labor."

"But doesn't it last longer than that?"

"You wanted more?"

"Not at all. It was just strange."

"Strange is right. I've never seen you act like that, Cass. What was going through your head?"

"Tell me when it hits you."

"Try that again?" Daniel leaned to the side to look at her.

"When you said that, all I could picture was the sight of me in the middle of labor socking you with my fist each time a pain hit me."

"And that was funny?"

"Oh yeah, I can still see the image. I could probably draw a picture of it right now."

The phone chose that moment to ring.

"Whoever that is on the other side of the phone line saved you." Daniel grabbed the phone.

"She is? She has? Isn't that something. Okay, bye."

He quietly replaced the receiver and brushed back the strands of hair that weren't plastered to her head from sweating and laughing through those Braxton-Hicks contractions. Cassie leaned her head back, feeling she could lie that way forever, savoring the feel of Daniel's warm fingers stroking the sides of her face. But Cassie was dying to know what that abrupt phone conversation was about.

"Are you going to tell me?"

"Tell you what?" he asked, his fingers making a part in her hair.

"Who was that on the phone?"

"Ness."

"And?"

"And I'll tell you about it after you promise not to immortalize the image of you punching me out in the throes of labor."

"I won't. Now what was that all about?"

"I'm holding you to that promise." Daniel sealed it with a kiss on her neck before giving her the news. "At 10:10, 10:15 and 10:23 a.m. Monica delivered three small but healthy babies."

"That's wonderful news. They're all healthy, you said?"

"According to Ness, as healthy as premie triplets can be."

"What did she have?"

"Babies, Cass, what else."

"Boys or girls, Daniel?" Cassie lifted a hand, attempting to connect it with his head.

"Had that image again, huh?" Daniel grabbed her hand and kissed it softly. "Two boys and a girl."

"We have to go see them." Cassie tried to get up, but both of Daniel's arms were wrapped beneath her breasts.

"We have to call the doctor, possibly make a visit."

"Daniel, I'm fine. They were only Braxton-Hicks contractions. That's normal. Probably the only normal thing in this pregnancy."

"Normal or not, we're calling."

Cassie knew he was right. "Jax comes first."

CHAPTER 18

Two pieces of wonderful news had the entire family buzzing with excitement. The traditional Sunday dinners for Daniels' family had always been lively, but this Sunday was elevated to party status.

"Did you see the babies?"

"They're too tiny."

"They are so cute."

"Way too tiny to hold."

"And all that hair!"

"So tiny I'd be too scared to even touch one."

"But they can holler."

"Nothing tiny about those voices."

"Those three will let Monica and Devin know what they need."

"What are their names?"

"Aaron, Blaze, and Chance."

"Think they'll fit into those names?"

"As easy as ABC. They're beautiful names."

"For three tiny babies, so tiny you're not going to catch me even trying to change those diapers."

"Calvin, we've had enough of the tiny nonsense. And no, we won't ask you to change a diaper."

"Why, thank you, Joycie." Daniel's uncle kissed his wife on the forehead as the rest of the family laughed.

"What are you crocheting there, Cassie?" Joyce asked.

"Just finishing a little gift for the triplets."

"Let me see." Joyce lifted the partially complete item for a close inspection. "Nice even stitches. You've been doing this for a long time?"

"No, in fact, it's a new hobby."

"Cassie has a natural talent for it," Daniel told his aunt. "You should see the things she made for Jax."

"Jax? Jax who?"

"Our baby. The one that hasn't been born yet."

"You're naming the baby after a brewery in the French Quarter!" Calvin bellowed.

"Not exactly."

"I hope not. I'm sure that choice was made when you two were under so much stress with that T.J. problem." Joyce patted Cassie on the leg. "You keep up the crocheting. It's good therapy. Think about some good names while you're at it."

"Speaking of T. J.," Ness sat next to Cassie, one of the twins in her arms, "have you heard any more from him?"

"We haven't heard a word for at least a week."

"That's a good sign. I hope that means he's given up whatever scheme he had in mind."

The discussion went back to the triplets. Cassie seemed more than happy to discuss the babies. All the baby talk and the excitement following the birth of Monica and Devin's triplets made Daniel anxious for his little Jax to be born. Not that he wanted her to come now. The doctor hadn't been too worried about the contractions, but he had scheduled Cassie for another visit the coming week.

"Devin. It's about time you got here," Aunt Joyce called. Tony, Jasmine, and Mark came running in behind him. "I've got everything packed and ready to go. And how are the brothers and sister of the three new babies doing?"

"Great, but the babies aren't home yet," Tony informed her.

"Just Mama," Mark clarified. "The babies have to get fatter before they come home."

"Did you know that now we have twice as many kids in our family, Maw-maw Joyce?" Jasmine asked.

"Isn't that something? How about the three of you spending the day with Maw-maw Joyce and Paw-paw Cal while your daddy takes some dinner to your mama."

"Alright!" they yelled, heading outside into the backyard.

"Thanks, Maw-maw Joyce." Devin kissed her on the cheek.

"How's Monica?"

"Fine, she just wants her babies home."

"Sounds familiar," Scott said, trading babies with Ness so that she could breast feed the other.

"Yeah, but we only had two days to wait. The doctor told Monica and Devin at least two weeks," Ness said as she left the room.

"That's not too long. They'll have them for the rest of their lives," Calvin added.

"Sounds ominous," Devin predicted.

That word decided it for Daniel. He hadn't wanted to approach Devin with the ominous thoughts about T. J that had been hanging in the back of his mind since the arrest of T's friends. Especially since Devin had so much to deal with just now. But Daniel needed to talk to both of his cousins-in-law.

He gave Cassie a quick peck on the cheek. She was playing with the baby she had taken from Scott and was preoccupied with making Kyle laugh by blowing on his belly. Good. Daniel scanned the room to see where Devin and Scott had gone. He found them coming from the kitchen.

"You'd better grow an extra pair of arms with some steady hands," Scott was saying to Devin as Daniel approached them. "We have two babies, and I know I could use an extra pair myself."

"Scott, Dev," Daniel nodded to them. "I need to talk to you both about T. J., but I don't want Cassie to hear. She might worry. The kitchen's out, Aunt Joyce and Warren are in there."

"The bedrooms, too," Scott said. "Too many possible interruptions. Sonya just put Tierra in one, Ness is feeding one of the boys in another and we change the babies in the guest bedroom. That happens often."

"The bathroom?"

"With all these people in the house? I think I've got it," Scott announced in a low voice. "The basketball court."

"A game of horse sounds good," Daniel agreed.

"Give us a minute, we'll meet you out there." As Devin headed into the kitchen, Scott went toward the bathroom and Daniel went out the front door. All unnoticed, Daniel hoped.

He stood under the basketball goal no more than two minutes before Devin threw a ball to him. "First shot's yours."

Daniel bounced the ball once, twice, then made a clear shot from the far right side of the basket.

"Good. Now tell us what you want to know about T. J.," Scott said.

"Every detail you kept out of the discussion we had over a week ago."

"There is a bit more," Devin agreed, making a perfect shot. Scott followed, doing the same.

"We don't keep much from our wives. We old married men have found out that you can get into a whole lot of trouble that way." Scott passed the ball to Daniel. "Go for it."

"I know it and I don't blame you. But you did keep something secret. Do you know where T. J. might be found?"

"We know that he's hiding somewhere in the southeast, maybe Kentucky, Virginia, or even West Virginia. My source is not sure."

"Your source."

"My detective, investigator, private eye, whatever you want to call him. T.J. and his group are semi-mobile, moving from one camp to another in the tri-state area."

"That's all he knows?"

"That's all he found out before he quit. Right, Dev?"

"He got scared. He was a lone black man trying to track a white man who was deeply involved with a white supremacist group."

"And T. J. was a member of that organization?"

"T. J. was never actually seen there, but evidence points to him being at each camp."

Daniel bounced the ball, the steady thump creating a background sound as he soaked in all the information. T. J. was still out there. His white van cronies had been taken care of, but the threat was still there.

Daniel stopped bouncing the ball. "I'd like to talk to this investigator."

"Don't know where he is or where to find him, Daniel. Sorry. The man's disappeared."

"If it helps, we know what you're going through," Scott said.

"Not quite. This is Cassie's cousin we're talking about. They were raised together."

"That makes it worse. I can give you a copy of the report," Devin offered, "and I'll do anything else you need to see that T. J. pays for what he's done."

"I'd appreciate that, Devin." Daniel took the shot. The ball went high and appeared to be true. It rolled around the rim and bounced to the ground.

"Too bad." Scott snatched the bouncing ball before it went into the street. "I'm there for you, too."

"That is some sorry basketball," Josh announced as he and John came strolling out.

"Mama sent us to tell you guys to get inside before the food is gone, but it looks like we're obligated to liven up these old men."

"Old?" Daniel asked, his eyes going from one to the other.

"We've developed a reputation with these guys," Scott explained

"They have somehow assumed that they can beat us in every game we play. In truth they can't," Devin said. "They realize this and feel the need to taunt and rib us before every game."

"Only to fuel their insecurities, of course," Scott added.

"Listen to the brothers-in-law. Didn't we win the last game, John?"

"That we did," John nodded.

"How about the two before that?" Scott inquired.

Josh ignored the question. "We'll take a handicap. Three on two. You can have Cousin Daniel."

"Handicap? Oh, little cousins, believe me, you've got that wrong."

"Devin," a voice called from inside the house, "phone."

"That's Monica. Two o'clock is our visiting time at the hospital. If I don't get my wife to those babies, there's hell to pay. Rain check," he called before jogging to the front door.

"Two on two?" John asked.

Scott raised an eyebrow in question.

After missing that easy shot, Daniel knew he wasn't up to it. "Got too much on my mind, Josh, John. Rain check for me, too."

"Where's the rain?" Josh asked, pointing to the sky.

"None today, but when it comes, it pours. Watch out for us old guys," Scott said for them all.

Daniel followed the same path Devin had just taken with Scott following behind him.

"Let's hope the rain calms down to a drizzle for this family. We have had enough of Hurricane T. J.," Scott said, voicing Daniel's own thoughts loud and clear.

CHAPTER 19

"You got everything you need? Everything all packed?"

"If I say yes one more time, will you stop asking me that question?"

"Alright." Daniel's frown immediately relaxed at Cassie's pointed look. "I want to be sure you have everything you need."

"Absolutely everything. What are you so nervous about? We're free of people following us. Try freeing yourself from worry."

Daniel couldn't help it. That report on T. J. hadn't revealed anymore than what Devin had already told him. Still, Daniel didn't feel as if the danger was over yet. He wasn't leaving Cassie home alone.

"Are you sure you want to stay with Ness and Scott? You wouldn't rather be with your family?"

"They are my family."

"You really feel that way, don't you?"

"I definitely do. Daniel, stop worrying. You're making me crazy. If you're determined to be anxious about something, try thinking about what you're going to say to your mother when you finally decide to talk to her."

"Not Jackie again. Cassie, I told you—" he paused. "Why are you smiling?"

"Got you to think about something else, didn't I?"

"You little—"

"At this moment, I'm not a little anything. Like my idea to dress up as a beach ball for Mardi Gras?"

Cassie didn't give him a chance to answer. She walked out the door ahead of him. "Let's get there before the parades do."

They were meeting the family at a little house on the parade route that Devin had bought about a month ago. At least he'd called it little. Parking in the last available spot in the driveway of the address Ness had given him changed Daniel's thinking. This wasn't a little house. It wasn't even a house. Mansion was more like it.

"Devin has got to be loaded."

Cassie deliberately misunderstood. "With three new babies I'd say he's blessed with love and family."

"That, too."

Cassie and Daniel were surrounded before they even got out of the car.

"Isn't this house great?" Ness raved. "Big and spacious."

"It's got four bathrooms," Scott added, as if it mattered. "No Port-o-lets this year."

Daniel's face broke into a grin as understanding dawned. No one relished using the portable toilets provided along the parade route.

"I was so glad when Devin bought this house last month," Ness was saying. "It's so convenient. We walk out the door and the parade is right there."

"It's a good investment. Too bad he's not here to enjoy it," Scott added.

"He's not here?" Cassie looked around the crowd of relatives on the spacious front yard.

"No, Devin and Monica dropped the kids off and went to the hospital to see the babies. "They'll be here later, hopefully with some good news. Could be that they get to bring the babies home sooner than they thought."

"What does Devin have planned for this place?" Daniel couldn't help asking as they walked inside. "Restoring and reselling is part of what you do at Prestway, right, Scott?"

"Normally, but let's not even think about selling this house."

"Bite that tongue of yours, Daniel," Ness demanded.

"I think you said something wrong," Cassie told him.

"You betcha," Josh informed them. "Ness and Scott don't want to be reduced to camping out on St. Charles Avenue at four o'clock in the morning. All to reserve a perfect spot for the family to view the parades."

"It was a tradition," John added.

"One we gladly broke and will continue to break as long as Devin owns this house." Ness waved her hands at her brothers. "Why don't you two go find something to do?"

"Josh, John, I need some strong young men over here," Joyce called.

"That's our cue." They left.

"Those two." Ness waved at their retreating backs. She turned to Cass and Daniel. So you're both dressed for Mardi Gras? Daniel, how unique, an airline pilot."

"Could be because I'm going to work."

"And Cassie's ahhh... let's see. Long, vertical strips, very colorful. You're a beach ball. Perfect."

"I thought so."

"Let me show you where to put your bags. We decided to spend the night here."

"Here?" Daniel yelled so loud everyone turned to look at him. "What I mean is," he managed to lower his voice to a semi-whisper that might as well have been a shout since it bounced off the smooth walls of the almost empty room, "what I mean is, does this place have an alarm system? Exactly who's staying here tonight? And do the windows have locks?" he ticked off in quick order.

`"Yes, family, and yes, the windows have locks," Ness answered.

"Good."

Daniel didn't notice the mix of inquiring, amused, and indulgent looks that came his way. The only face he could focus on was Cassie's, and hers looked fearful. Daniel hadn't meant to do that.

"Cassie will be safe and sound in the room next to ours," Scott told Daniel. "Down the hall, second door on your right."

"Right. Come on, Cass, let's get you settled in."

Before Daniel could put her bag down, Cassie's voice rang out. "You found out something more."

"No, Cass." Daniel dropped the bag to hold her. His chin rested on the top of her head. He ran his hand down her hair, which had grown at least two inches since they'd gotten married. Everything had grown. He'd grown, they'd grown. They'd grown together as a couple. The baby moved between them. She was growing strong and healthy, according to the doctor.

"It's just a feeling, Cass."

"No new information?"

"None at all."

"Just useless worry."

"You could put it that way."

"I am. I do. We've had enough problems. More than enough trouble, Daniel. I'm not looking for any when things are going fine."

"True, Cass." Daniel tried to agree with her. He tried to lift the feeling of doom from his face. "Forget about what I said. Have a good time today watching the parades, but don't get all mixed up in that crowd. Have fun with the gang, but don't stay up too late. If you can't—"

Cassie pulled him down by his lapels and kissed him on the lips. "Don't you have a plane to fly?"

"Yeah. I'll see you tomorrow night. I love you, and I'm gonna miss you, baby."

"I love you, too. We'll be waiting for you safe and sound in this huge *secure* house."

Daniel left, despite the feeling that he needed to be there to protect her.

"What a long day," Ness said, taking the sleeping baby from Cassie's arms.

"But it was fun. I hadn't seen a Mardi Gras parade in years."

"Missed it?"

Cassie followed Ness into the next room where Scott was busy changing Kyle.

"More than I realized," Cassie answered as Ness deftly, but carefully, laid the baby down in the portable crib. "Does it come naturally? Being a mom?"

"The instinct's there, but you also learn as you go."

"This fella's almost out," Scott whispered. "He didn't stay awake to stare at his daddy tonight, not tonight," he sang to the baby cradled in his arms.

Cassie went over to look at the droopy-eyed baby. "You two are great parents."

"Thanks, Cass," Ness answered, her expression a huge question mark. "Is there something you want to ask or say?"

"No, I'm just tired. The rest of the house is sleeping, so I'll get some rest myself."

"Get all the rest you need while you still can," Scott teased.

Just as Cassie turned to go, her eyes landed on a magazine lying on the edge of the bed. *Raising Black and Bi-racial Children.* "You two don't know it all. You're concerned, too."

"About?"

"Your boys and how the world sees them."

"Of course." They both nodded.

"Whew, what a relief. I was wondering if Daniel and I were going to handle raising one baby with as much cool as you both seem to have."

"That doesn't come naturally," Ness told her.

"You learn it," Scott added.

"Take the journal. It has some good advice, a few opinions, and some ideas you might want to keep in mind for later use."

"Thanks."

Cassie left Scott and Ness to go to her own room. The day had been filled with bands, floats and kids. Daniel's little cousins had been a wealth of information and entertainment. But now the house, no, the mansion, was completely quiet. The kids had long ago crashed in two of the upstairs bedrooms. In the stillness of the house, Cassie missed Daniel even more. Everyone else had someone to sleep with, even the twins.

Cassie went to her bag. It sat on a chair, the only other furniture besides the bed in the whole room. She searched inside the bag, but couldn't find what she was looking for. The woodgraph Daniel had given her as a wedding gift was nowhere inside. Cassie had taken it with her every time she was away from Daniel. How could she have forgotten it? Oh, well, at least it was safe and sound at home, on their bedroom wall.

Safe and sound. Suddenly, Cassie wasn't feeling much of either. Daniel's uneasiness before he left was beginning to affect her. "Silly," she whispered to herself as she slipped into bed.

Over the next two hours, Cassie read the thin journal from cover to cover. It was interesting and informative. She finished it, knowing that she wanted and needed more information and shared experiences from others in her position. She'd have to check out the bookstores. Someone certainly had to have written a book on the subject. Cassie threw the covers back and was about to make what looked like a long trip to the light switch when she heard a noise. She held her breath, her bladder, and her nerves.

There was a knock on her door and Ness's head appeared in the crack. "I didn't wake you, did I? I saw the light on."

"No, I was still up."

"I brought you some more reading material. We enjoyed this book."

Cassie read the title. "Sounds like a must read for a mixed couple."

"Not mixed, Cassie, culturally meshed for life."

"I like that."

"Try to sleep. I don't think I'll be doing much of that since Scott's been whispering sweet pleasures in my ear." Ness closed the door behind her.

Cassie, already into the book, barely registered Ness's words.

"That's a good book. My mommy and daddy's been reading it to each other," a little voice said in Cassie's ear.

She opened her eyes to find three pairs of mischievous ones staring at her.

"Megan," Vicki explained with a long exasperated sign, "Cousin Cassie's reading it because she's white and Cousin Daniel's brown."

"And their baby will be like Kacey and Kyle," Jasmine explained.

"Loud and smelly, and sometimes funny?"

"Cousin Cassie, please tell Megan about your baby coming out looking somewhere between brown and white like our brothers," Vicki said, obviously exasperated with her little sister.

Jasmine looked just as affected as she stood with her hands on her hips waiting for Cassie to set Megan straight.

"Well?" Megan demanded, "What are they besides noisy baby brothers?"

Reading about race issues and actually dealing with them were two different things, Cassie realized. She was about to scream for help, when she spotted Ness at her now open bedroom door.

"I told you they woke up Cousin Cassie," Tony reported.

"We did not, Auntie Ness. Cousin Cassie was almost awake when we got here," Jasmine said, making a face at her older brother Tony.

"Yes, Cousin Cassie was already awake, weren't you Cousin Cassie?" Vicki asked, her eyes pleading.

"Cousin Cassie is too long. Can we call you C. C.?" Megan asked.

"Sure," Cassie nodded, her head spinning with the quick change of subject.

"Well, now that Cousin Cassie—"

"C. C., MaNessa," Megan insisted.

"Now that C. C. is awake," Ness corrected herself, "she might want to relax for awhile, even go back to sleep. Everybody out."

The room cleared in seconds.

"How do you do that?" Cassie asked.

"It's a gift." Scott poked his head in long enough to answer, a baby on his shoulder. "Kacey's ready for breakfast," he told Ness.

Ness shrugged. "Sorry about that. The girls were dying to serve you breakfast in bed. I guess they were hoping you were awake."

"I would have been if I hadn't spent half the night reading."

"It's a good book, isn't it?"

"I thought so until Vicki came in demanding an explanation."

"Oh." Ness had a knowing glint in her eye.

Cassie retold the entire unexpected episode.

"Vicki stumped you too, huh?"

"Too? She's done this before?"

"Vicki's caught on to the idea that everyone's essentially the same. She's been asking as many adults as she can the difference between Kacey and Kyle and other people, black or white, red or yellow. It doesn't matter."

"But I didn't answer. Did I fail?"

"Not anymore than anyone else."

"Good, I think. But why should a simple explanation like that stump me or anyone else?"

"It's a sensitive issue, and you're new to the realm of answering questions from precocious little girls. Don't let it bother you, Cass. Rest, you don't have to get up yet."

"Surprisingly, I'm not tired anymore, but that breakfast in bed does sound good to me."

The girls served Cassie breakfast on a tray that wobbled as they entered the room. Jasmine directed as Megan and Vicki held the tray. Cassie sat and enjoyed the company of her young cousins by marriage, the momentary unease leaving her for the brief meal.

After breakfast, the family went to mass together. The day after Mardi Gras was Ash Wednesday, the first day of Lent and fasting, forty days before Easter Sunday.

As they exited the church, the children raced to steal a few minutes on the playground. Ness told her, "I'm going to meet Monica at the hospital to cheer her up a little. The babies can't come home until next Friday. Do you want to come?"

"Sure, I've only seen the triplets once, and now might be a good time to give Monica the little caps I made for them."

"Good. Scott," Ness called to her husband, "I'll be home in a couple of hours."

"It'll be my pleasure."

"What does he mean by that?" Cassie couldn't resist asking.

"Secret joke."

Satisfied with that, Cassie asked no more, knowing that she and Daniel had a few of their own. "I hope you don't mind stopping at my house, Ness." Cass said as they left the church parking lot.

"As long as you don't mind stopping for gas. Scott didn't leave enough in the tank to go all the way to the hospital."

"Not a problem."

"We'll get the caps then go to a gas station near your house."

Ness parked in the driveway. When Cassie got out of the car, a whole lot easier than she normally did from Daniel's, something fell onto the side walk with a thump.

"Don't even think of trying to bend down to get that," Ness told her, coming around to the passenger side. "I remember those days." Ness handed Cassie the book she had been reading last night.

"That's what I dropped? I didn't realize I'd taken it with me. Do you want it back?"

"Keep it as long as you like. We've read through it three times, at least."

"You know it by heart then," Cassie said, clasping the book in her hand.

She went straight to the bedroom as soon as they got inside the house. She searched for the gift she had wrapped the day before, slowly realizing that she had no idea where she had put it.

"Ness, I can't find it."

"Did you bring it with you yesterday?"

"No, I emptied my overnight bag last night. It wasn't in there."

"You keep looking while I go fill the tank. Monica's going to be wondering where I am."

"I'm sure I'll find it before you get back. I'll even be waiting for you."

The instant Ness's car zoomed off, the phone rang. "You stupid, stupid woman!" an enraged voice yelled in Cassie's ear. She hung up immediately.

The phone rang again. Dread crawled up her spine. This was it. This was why Daniel had had those feelings. When the ringing wouldn't stop, Cassie picked up the phone. She refused to stand there in the middle of her own house petrified, scared to death of a voice. A voice couldn't hurt you. Cassie knew who it was.

"Cassie." She could hear the forced calm, the tight edginess in his tone as he continued. "How could you do that? How could you incarcerate two of your own kind? You are worse off than I thought. Don't be afraid. I'll be there to help you."

"I don't need your help," Cassie screamed. Unfortunately, she heard a dial tone. T had hung up.

She hung up and turned to look around the bedroom. There on the wall was

the woodgraph she had been looking for last night. She took it off the wall and wrapped her arms around the cool hard wood, wishing for Daniel.

A knock sounded on the door.

"Ness! Thank God," she whispered to herself. With the woodgraph still in her hand, she went to the door and swung it open.

It wasn't Ness. She prayed right there on the spot that the hard-faced man at her door would transform into her husband's cousin. She prayed so hard, but it didn't happen.

CHAPTER 20

The hard-faced man was in her house walking toward her. Cassie backed away as slowly as she could manage. Her legs felt like solid sticks of ice. She wanted to run full speed anywhere, anyplace, as long as it was away, but she was too terrified to run.

Though neither said a word, Cassie knew who he was, and he knew who she was. All Cassie wanted to do was get away. He wanted to—Cassie couldn't begin to guess at what he wanted.

"What do you want?" Cassie heard herself ask, hugging the woodgraph even tighter than before.

"Don't be afraid," the intruder said in a tone he probably thought was pleasant. It was far from pleasant.

A short, wiry man with sandy colored hair stood against the door. He was holding a silver lighter in his hand, flicking it on and off. The click, click of the lighter was the only sound in the room. That sound and the strangeness of the entire scene made the whole experience feel even more surreal.

"Keep a look out," the big man said.

"She ain't back yet. I followed her to the gas station and when she went to pay I let the air out of her tires." He stared at Cass, flicking the lighter off and on and mumbling something too low for Cassie to understand though she knew it involved her.

"That's not good enough," the big man said in response. "His Eminence is already unhappy. Stay where you're supposed to."

Cassie watched as they argued with each other. Neither one of them was paying any attention to her. If she was going to act, now was the time. Cassie began to slowly edge away with careful, tiny steps. Despite her awkward movements, she avoided bumping into or tripping on some unseen object and made it into her bedroom quietly shutting the door just as the big man issued an order.

"Go! By order of all that is white and right. Go now! Where the hell are you! We don't have time for this, Miss Villiere. We're here to save you and preserve the future of our race. It's your own cousin who sent us."

What to do now? Ness, where are you? Rattled, Cassie leaned against the closed door, wishing it had a lock. The phone she thought. Just as Cassie moved for the instrument that could bring her help, the woodgraph crashed to the floor. It had slipped out of her hand. Cassie had forgotten that she was holding it.

Footsteps came running in her direction, then stopped outside the bedroom door. Cassie saw the door start to inch open. Frantically reaching blindly for something to protect herself and her baby, her hand landed on something thick and heavy. As soon as the big man's head came into view Cassie flung the makeshift weapon at him then watched as it missed, bounced off the wall and landed at his feet. He didn't so much as blink.

The big man picked the book up and read the title out loud. "You're more confused than we thought, Miss Villiere. This idea of mixing up the races…" He shook his head in complete disgust.

"*That's* pure ignorance, and the name is *Mrs. Daniel Adams!*"

"You're talking now? Good, we need some words. Sit down here," he demanded, lifting the vanity chair a few inches off the floor and slamming it back down.

Cassie shook her head.

"I don't want to hurt you, but this will get done."

Cassie wanted to stand firm, but a tick over his right eye and his cold unflinching stare frightened her into compliance. She moved forward one step, but then stopped. She didn't want to be anywhere near him.

"Either we do this nice and easy or we'll be waiting here when that boy of yours comes back tonight."

"You wouldn't hurt Daniel. T wouldn't want you to hurt Daniel."

"The General doesn't want anybody hurt. We need the mud races. But that's beside the point. We'll do whatever we have to. If you don't cooperate, we have orders to make it real hard for your black boy—"

"Man, Daniel is a man, and he's my husband."

"If that's what you want to think right now, fine." He breathed down her neck as he stood over her. "But if you want him to have two good eyes to fly those airplanes, you'll do as I say."

Cassie sank into the chair before the vanity Daniel had bought for her. "You would ruin his vision?"

"Just one eye. We'd leave him with the other one. If you don't want that to happen, then write what I tell you to write." He shoved paper and pen in front of her.

As Cassie scribbled the horrible note full of lies and impossibilities, tears ran down her face and landed on the white paper, smearing the words in spots.

When she finished, the big man grabbed her arm in a death grip. "Come on, we're saving your life."

He pulled her from the chair and out the door. In a matter of seconds, Cassie was in the back seat of a dark car that she didn't recognize and pulled against the hard frame of a man she truly hated.

"Buckle up. Our orders are to deliver you safe and sound."

"Where?" she asked but was ignored.

"Then the de-programming can begin. Right, Red?" the short man with the lighter asked, flicking the lighter and studying her through the flame. He quickly mumbled something else, then flicked off the lighter and stared at her.

"That's right, now drive."

Cassie cringed inside as the big man reached across her shoulder to buckle her in. How could a man who had taken her away from her world have the audacity to be concerned about her safety?

"Don't—touch—me," Cassie hissed as his upper body leaned over hers.

He stopped, waited a moment then moved away, keeping to his side of the car.

Cassie buckled herself in, making sure to secure the seatbelt in the safest position for her unborn child. The safety of her baby was her greatest worry now.

They rode along the bayou and turned down Esplanade Avenue. Cassie could clearly see people on the other side of the tinted glass and felt frustrated because they couldn't see her plight.

An unexpected sight came into view as the car waited at the stoplight. Ness. There she was at the gas station. Cassie saw her glancing anxiously at her watch as the attendant filled her tires.

Cassie didn't think, just acted.

She quickly pressed the button to lower the window. Even before the window began its slow crawl downward, Cassie screamed as loud as she could. "Ness! Help! Ness!"

A hand covered her mouth, the window rose, and Ness didn't hear a sound.

"My wife did not leave me."

"According to this note, that's exactly what she's done," the stern-faced police officer said. "Face it buddy. She's gone. Move on with your life."

Daniel had been going around in circles with this police officer for the last twenty minutes. "My wife has been kidnapped by bigots. If you are not going to help me, then leave my house." Daniel turned away before he could say something that would get *him* locked up. That would not help him find Cassie.

"Ness!" Daniel screamed, stomping out of the bedroom.

The officer followed him. "There is no evidence to point to kidnapping."

"What about the tear-stained note?" Daniel asked with as much control as he could muster.

"Maybe she felt sorry for you."

"The woodgraph I gave her for a wedding present is on the floor, broken."

"She had a fit and threw it to get back at you."

"You seem to have an answer for everything."

"Your wife left of her own free will."

"That I will never believe. Go—just go."

"That might be a good idea, Officer. We'll call if we need you," Scott said, directing the officer to the door.

"Daniel, we'll get some real help, and we will find Cassie," Scott said a minute later.

Daniel came out of the trance he had fallen into. "Ness, where is she?"

"I was gone for ten minutes, Daniel, no more than that. When I came back, the door was open and Cassie was gone. I'm so sorry," his cousin said, grabbing both his hands.

"I know, you told me, Ness. I don't blame you. Did you get in touch with Randy, Frank or June?"

"No, Sonya said they all went to an investigation seminar in Baton Rouge. She's having trouble contacting them."

"They're probably the only cops who are going to believe what really happened."

"We'll keep trying, Daniel."

"Thanks, Ness, Scott. You've both been here for hours. Go on home, get your kids from Aunt Joyce and go home. I'll be fine."

"But Daniel—"

"Ness, I think Daniel's right," Scott interrupted.

"Just remember, we're here for you, Ness said."

"I know that. I've always known that."

Though Daniel appreciated their help and concern, right now he needed to be alone. Cassie's abduction was all his fault. He'd felt something bad was going to happen, but, nevertheless, he'd left Cassie and their baby without his protection.

He had found his own love, his own family, and they had been taken away from him. But he was determined to get them back, alive and healthy. She had been forced to write that note, Daniel knew it. He opened it and flattened it out as much as he could and read it once again.

I don't want to be near you anymore.
I can't stand another minute in your presence.
The idea of having your child sickens me.
I'm giving it up for adoption. Don't look for it or me.
Cassie Villiere

"Lies! Lies! Lies!" Daniel balled his fists and screamed into the empty house. His anger and despair far outweighed what he'd experienced just before Christmas when Cassie had *actually* left him of her own free will. That had not placed her in danger. This actually threatened her life and their child's. He had to come up with a plan to save them.

Pushing aside all fear of what the kidnappers might do or what complications might occur from the high-risk pregnancy, he freed his mind and an idea came to him.

He picked up the phone and dialed long distance to Houston.

"Hello," a soft female voice answered. It wasn't his sister.

"I need to talk to Melanie. Now."

"Who's speaking?"

Daniel didn't have time for this, but he contained his impatience, figuring the best way to get what he wanted was to humor the person the other end of the line.

"Her brother, Daniel."

He heard a gasp.

"I need to speak to Melanie."

"Why?"

Somehow Daniel knew this voice. That fact seeped past the frustration and anger pulsing through him. "Never mind that. Put Melanie on the phone."

"You sound very upset, Daniel, and I can't let you disturb Melanie for no good reason. She's studying for a very important exam."

"Who is this?"

"Her mother." There was a slight pause. "Your mother."

"Jackie." He didn't need this.

"Yes, it's Jackie. Tell me what you want, and I'll relay the message."

Jackie had left his life when he needed her, and now she was in his way when his life had reached its lowest point.

"Daniel, I can do that much. Take it or leave it."

She was protecting Melanie. That was something. "Ask her when she last heard

from Cassie."

The line went empty, as empty as his life was at this minute. Then Jackie's voice again filled the line. Daniel didn't want it to be, but somehow, her voice was comforting.

"Cassie called a couple of days ago to tell Melanie about the false labor."

"Okay." That idea was shot.

"Why? Is something wrong with Cassie?"

"She's been kidnapped." Daniel slammed down the receiver, not interested in explaining more.

The idea that Cassie had somehow spoken to or contacted Melanie was a dead end. With no other immediate idea, Daniel grabbed his keys, went out to his car and drove through the streets of New Orleans, searching in vain.

CHAPTER 21

Daniel was Cassie's first thought when she woke up, just as he had been every morning. She'd been taken away from her husband three days earlier. For three days, Cassie had been stuck in a little back room of a shotgun house except for trips to the bathroom. There were no doors to any room other than the one she was locked in and the bathroom.

Her only glimpse of the entire house had come the first day. After spending all of Ash Wednesday driving, her captors had smuggled her in during the night. She had tried to look for landmarks so that she had some idea of where they had taken her. A hasty look at the houses and the people in the neighborhood had Cassie wondering if they had actually driven somewhere outside the city or driven all over the city to give her that impression. Could she still be in New Orleans? She had no idea. After her attempt to get Ness's attention, Cassie had been blindfolded and gagged until she had gotten out of the car. For her own protection, she had been told.

"She up?" Cassie heard the short man named Joe asks on the other side of the door.

"No," Red, the obvious leader of the two, answered.

"Heard from the General yet?"

"No," Red said again.

This morning marked her fourth day with her kidnappers. She'd heard this same conversation each day. Cassie sat up and waited for the short knock on the door that preceded a bowl of grits and a cup of juice brought in by Joe. He would play with his lighter, study her intently, and mumble some incoherent words before leaving her breakfast.

Instead of a knock on the door this morning, though, she heard Joe whining.

"Something's happened to him. This ain't right. Why are we wasting all this time on her anyway?"

"Because she is the General's blood kin and can be made to see the truth."

"I say we tie her up, dump her someplace, and head on back to headquarters."

"I say we stay and wait." Red's voice was firm.

"I ain't going back to no jail."

"You won't have to," Cassie heard Red say. Then there was the scrape of a chair and footsteps moving toward the front of the house.

A minute later, a knock sounded on her door, and instead of Joe, Red came into the room with her breakfast.

"Eat," he said then left.

At least they fed her. At first Cassie had been afraid to eat the food, more worried for Jax's well being than her own. The thoughts of poison or drugs being added to the food had been uppermost in her mind. But Red's constant references to keeping her safe had influenced her decision to eat the food. Jax needed the nourishment.

Methodically spooning the grits into her mouth, she sipped the juice between spoonfuls. She needed milk but wasn't going to bring any more attention to herself by requesting it. Her bones would just have to suffer a little calcium depletion as the baby took from her what she needed.

Finishing her breakfast, she stood and slowly walked around the small room. A large white water heater stood on the far side of the room, and she worried that its proximity to the cot seemed like a fire hazard. But what could she do? There was a back door bolted shut but no windows, a depressing room.

After walking around in circles for a few minutes, Cassie sat on the cot that was her bed, dinning table, and sofa all in one.

What must Daniel be thinking?

How was he feeling right now?

If there were only a way that she could tell her husband that she and the baby were okay. If only she could get away.

Cassie went over every piece of information she had overheard. Her kidnapers didn't seem to care that she heard everything they said. She figured they wanted her to know.

From this morning's conversation, she gathered that T was missing. That bit of information seemed like good news. Surely, that meant they wouldn't continue with their plans to take her back to headquarters, wherever that was, to de-program her and give her baby away as soon as she was born.

These things were not going to happen.

Lying down on the cot, Cassie stretched her legs as far as she could. She put her hands on her belly. "We'll be okay, Jax. We'll get through this and back to daddy."

Slowly organ music filtered through the cracks of the little room, and the harmonious sound of a gospel choir found its way to her ears. The sound was as comforting and familiar as the inside of Melanie's church in Houston. But the music was puzzling. Why would bigots hide out in what had to be a predominately black neighborhood? Strange, but then nothing had been normal since she had been taken away.

It was Sunday, Cassie realized. People were going to church. Was Daniel with Aunt Joyce and Uncle Cal, Ness, Scott and everyone? Were they helping him through it all? And what about her aunt and uncle? First their disappointment in T, now their worry for her. Cassie hoped all the stress wouldn't put a strain on their health. T's choices had already made them look older than they actually were.

Concentrating, Cassie caught the refrain, letting it flow

around and inside of her. "Through it All," that was the hymn. She remembered singing it at Reverend Jordan's church. She softly sang the refrain with the choir then intently listened to each verse in between. Each stanza gave her a message, fortifying her strength, building her courage, and escalating her resolve to get out of this room and away from these men. Her feelings of helplessness dissolved as the last notes faded away.

God was a part of her life and her marriage had His blessings. Somehow, with God's help, she would find a way out before Red decided to take Joe's advice and get rid of her.

Cassie shivered as a vision of the little man staring at her through the hot flame of a lighter came to her. Why did he do that? As far as she could tell, he didn't smoke. He must love looking at fire.

The door opened, suddenly, without the usual preliminary knock. "Bathroom," Red told her.

Other than the tub and toilet, the bathroom was nearly bare. There was a bar of soap and a small hand towel. Another towel covered the window. Could she escape through the window? In her pre-pregnant days maybe.

Red handed her a toothbrush then waited at the open door while she brushed. As required, Cassie handed the toothbrush back to him. How she could use that against him, Cassie had no idea, but he waited for it each time. Then he closed the door, giving her five minutes of privacy.

Help yourself, Cassie, she said over and over in her head as she used the facilities. The best way to do that was to keep her head clear for any opportunity to escape. Daniel was out there looking for her, she was sure.

Red didn't say another word to her. He merely locked her back into the room. Their plans seemed to be falling apart. What if they decided to just leave her here locked in this room? No, Cassie didn't think that would happen as long as they were loyal to T. Their strange protectiveness toward her and obvious respect for T meant they wouldn't desert her. Unless they never heard from him again. Would their loyalty continue then?

She had to get away from these men. If only she could find a way to get people's attention. She needed to do something that would get the neighbors' attention.

The next few hours dragged, seeming far longer than the last few days she had spent in this room. And still, she had no answer to her dilemma. She listened to the hymns that she could still hear from the nearby church. She was in need of some divine inspiration.

A knock sounded on the door. All had been quiet in the other room all morning long. What if Red had decided to go along with Joe's plan to get rid of her? Cassie let out a low breath of relief as Joe walked into the room, a paper plate of food in one hand and the lighter in the other, the keys dangling from his hand. As always, he walked right up to her and flicked the lighter directly in her face. It flamed up.

"Ain't you gonna ask why I do this every day?" he asked for the first time.

"Why do you burn that flame in my face everyday?" Cassie asked, not wanting to upset Joe in any way.

"Because you need to see the light. You need to get away from the darkness that made you to choose one of those mud people over a pure white man like myself."

"A-h-h-h," Cassie said slowly, nodding her head up and down as if she understood. She was more frightened then ever of this strange man. So frightened that there was no room for her to take offense at his insulting words. He adjusted the flame to its highest point as he continued to stare at her, chanting, "See the light. The light will guide you back to your own kind."

The keys in his hand jingled as he repeated the chant over and over and his eyes glazed over, taking on a trance-like quality.

Then without warning, he extinguished the flame and moved so close that Cassie could feel his hot breath on her face. He inched even closer, if that were possible. "Nothing more to say about that? Of course not, because none of what you been doing with your life makes sense."

Cassie gulped. Joe was losing it.

"Here, take your lunch. Let your body be nourished by this food prepared by a white man." He laid the plate on her lap. "We, as the supreme . . ."

Joe continued to rant until Red threw open the door. "Joe! Out!"

"But, Red," he began. "I was into the de-programming process."

Cassie relaxed a bit with the presence of Red. Red made her uneasy, but Joe's erratic behavior terrified her.

"That's not for you to begin," he told Joe in a hard, unrelenting tone.

Joe stood as tall as his wiry frame allowed, and obviously offended, stomped away like a two-year-old deprived of some fun he'd had his heart set on.

Cassie watched as Red stared at Joe's retreating back. Suddenly, Joe stopped and spun around. He glanced at her, then Red, the hurt look gone from his face as he said to his partner, "But I was good. Did you hear me? The General would be proud. He's got to call."

"Leave this room now, Joe."

Joe stomped away, muttering to himself.

"Eat," Red told her.

As soon as she heard the lock click into place, she did just that, the chewing motion somehow calming her. It was essential that she keep a clear head. The need to get away from these crazy people was an urgency she felt deep inside her bones. If she could get past the kitchen, then maybe she could find a way to get out.

She needed a reason to leave the room. The bathroom. When they allowed her to use the bathroom again. That would be her chance.

Cassie waited. Quietly, prayerfully, hopefully, she waited.

Instead of the return of Joe, Red came to unlock the door, allowing her to use the bathroom once again.

"Do you mind if I use some warm water to wash a bit? I haven't had a bath in almost four days."

He stared down at her without answering.

Cassie's heart skipped a beat. Her tongue, though, had no problem saying, "I don't need a bath, but I really could use a wash off."

"Fine," he grunted, leading her out of the room. He handed her a washcloth and towel before warning her, "You got ten minutes, no more."

Ten minutes to do what? She still had no plan, no idea of what to do, only that she had to do something. Knowing Red was on the other side of the door, Cassie stood at the sink and turned the hot water tap on as high as it would go. She wet the washcloth with warm water that quickly became hot. Cassie watched as the steam rise from the sink. Steam? Could it be useful? Moving to the bathtub, she turned the hot water tap as high as it would go. Steam soon filled the small room. Not having much time left, Cassie felt her opportunity to do something slipping away. She turned the water off at the tub and sat on the toilet to think, not moving until Red opened the door signaling that her time was up.

"I'm not done!" she said in what she hoped was an offended tone. Surprisingly, Red turned the color of his name and immediately closed the door, muttering an apology.

Cassie stood and paced the small confines of the bathroom. Two steps left and two steps right. With no plan in mind, she felt panic rising as perspiration from the steam and her nervousness rolled down her face. She wiped it with the towel in her hand. She hadn't perspired this much since those false contractions.

Contractions.

"Time's up now. What are you trying to do, use all the hot water?" Red shouted, opening the bathroom door and shutting off the faucet at the sink.

"Ohhh, Cassie moaned, gripping her stomach.

"What now?" He looked at her suspiciously.

She answered with another moan this time gripping the sink with both hands.

"Come on out of there. I've got other things to worry about." He looked at her with cold, hard eyes.

He wasn't buying it. Still, Cassie didn't move. Fear caused her to truly perspire, adding a bit more realism to her act.

"Red, Red, the phone's ringing. It's ringing, Red!" Joe came skipping toward them with the cell phone in his hand.

Red turned toward Joe who was dancing around the small kitchen. He firmly pulled her out of the bathroom, shut the door and hurried her into the back room. Cassie leaned against the wall and let out a loud screech, giving the performance of her life. She could feel both of their eyes on her.

"What's wrong with you?" Red asked as she stood there gasping.

"The baby, I think it's time."

"It can't be time, stop play acting and get into that room," he commanded, forgetting to lock the door as he yelled for the phone.

Cassie wanted to dance and shout, exactly as Joe was still doing on the other side of the door. But she dared not. Red hadn't believed her, but her little performance and Joe's interruption had distracted him enough to leave the door unlocked. This was her opportunity.

CHAPTER 22

Sunday morning, Daniel went into the kitchen. Why was *she* still here?

Jackie was in his kitchen where she had been every day for the last three days. She had shown up unwanted and uninvited, causing havoc in his already crazy life.

She was the prodigal sister to his Aunt Joyce, but Jackie refused the invitation to stay with her sister, declaring that she'd returned for Daniel's sake. Daniel at first didn't believe it, didn't care much, but had begun to think that maybe it was true. She cooked for him, cleaned and washed, too. Jackie had even somehow gotten media coverage on Cassie's disappearance, hoping someone would report seeing her.

Daniel had been coming home each day after useless hours spent searching to a meal he couldn't eat, and a mother he didn't want to talk to. Yet, with her there, Daniel felt a comforting presence in his home.

It had been four long days since Cassie was kidnapped. Coming in after another long, useless search, Daniel plopped onto the sofa. A few minutes later Jackie placed a plate of pancakes on the coffee table in front of him. This was crazy. Daniel didn't want Jackie here, but it made him feel better to know that she was there. He didn't want her help, but she gave it despite his anger.

"Why don't you go home to your family, Jackie?" he asked.

"I will. When you find Cassie and when you're happy again."

"Happy? As if you care about my happiness?"

"I do. I always have. That's why I left you."

"Right, that makes perfect sense."

"That's why I left you, Danny Boy. I knew you'd be taken care of. How could I have taken care of you when I couldn't even take care of myself?" She sat down next to him in the same place Cassie sat when they played Scrabble together.

"Don't you remember how things were?" Jackie was saying. "Don't you remember the drinking?"

"Maybe I do, but the thing I remember most was that I loved you and you deserted me." He wouldn't desert Cassie or his baby. Ever.

"I did, but only to get my life back together."

"And when you did, why didn't you come for me? I would have done anything to be with you."

"I know that, but your grandmother said you were doing fine. She probably thought I was still drinking, and it seemed to me that you didn't miss me."

"You came to see me?"

"Once. You looked so happy I couldn't take you away."

Daniel stood. He didn't want to hear this right now. Now was not the time. What he needed was his wife. "I'm going out to find Cassie," he said as he walked toward the door.

"I hope you do this time," Daniel heard her whisper as he left.

Daniel drove aimlessly, searching up and down little side streets he had ignored before. He found himself on North Claiborne Avenue. He drove past St. Bernard and Esplanade, both busy cross streets. He suddenly felt an urge to turn down the next intersection, Ursuline Avenue. He slowed as he spotted Saint Ann's Shrine, then stopped, remembering Lenten visits to the shrine as a boy. He got out of the car and said a silent prayer that he would find his wife then hopped back in as soon as he was done. Daniel felt the need to visit another place of worship and remembered St. Peter Claver Church, was just around the corner.

After parking two blocks away, he walked into the church as the choir was singing a familiar hymn. The words twisted at his heart, wrenching a plea, "God, help get me through all this. Help me find my wife."

Before the song was over Daniel felt a change in himself, a confidence that he would find Cassie today. He left the church and continued searching on foot, his eyes moving in every direction, for exactly what, he didn't know. Up and down alleys, in and out of yards Daniel searched. He suddenly stopped. His nose detected the smell of smoke before he actually saw it. A fire truck and police car sped past him. People were coming out of their homes. Daniel moved with the crowd in the direction of the fire, his feet responding to some unknown pull.

"The line went dead," Cassie heard Joe whine. "There was static, I heard voices, and it went dead. The battery! I forgot to charge it!"

"Stupid, that was the contact signal," Red grumbled loud enough for Cassie to hear through the closed, still blessedly unlocked, door. "We were lucky the phone had enough juice so that we could get any call. I've got the caller ID number. I'm going to a pay phone. I'll be back in ten minutes."

Yes! Cassie gave a silent cheer that turned into a groan when Red peeked inside and said with a grin, "Can't forget to lock the door."

The click of the lock blocked her only chance of escape. Unless she could somehow manipulate Joe.

Cassie jumped from the cot and banged on the door. "Joe! Joe!"

"What's all that yelling for?" he asked through the closed door.

"I need your help. I'm ready. I want to see the light."

"What do you mean?" he asked, a cautious excitement plain in his voice.

"I want to be de-programmed. When I see my cousin again, I want to be pure and white."

"Oooooo! Won't he like that?" The door unlocked and swung open. "And I'll be the one to take credit for it. I knew I was doing good before. Red shouldn't have stopped me."

"Red was jealous."

"You think so?"

Cassie nodded. "I like you better anyway," she lied.

"Well then, after we've got your mind set right, and that mud baby's taken away, you can show me just how much you like me."

Cringing inside, Cassie tried to keep any expression off her face. She was doing this to escape. Somehow she wouldn't allow Joe to get rid of her baby or touch her body. "Can we start?" Cassie asked, having no idea how soon Red would come back.

"Right. Sit over there on the cot and let's get started."

Cassie sat in the middle of the cot. Joe followed. He pulled out his lighter and flicked it. Nothing happened. He banged the lighter against his thigh and tried again with no success.

Disbelieving, Cassie stared at the lighter whose flame and heat had flickered at her during each encounter with Joe.

He played with it a few moments. In his frustration he laid the keys on the bed no more than three inches from her hand. "I think it might be out of fuel."

Cassie nearly jumped at the sound of his voice.

"My first chance to de-program and get in good with the General and look what happened."

The keys were within her reach and time was running short. "Let me see it?" she quietly asked.

He looked at her for a long moment. Cassie thought he wouldn't give it up until a grin eased onto his face. "Since you are partially de-programmed and bound to be my woman, okay."

Feeling sick at the image his words brought, Cassie reached for the lighter with one hand, at the same time sliding the keys into her palm with the other. She stood. "Let's see," she said, turning the lighter in her hand. For the first time, she noticed that there was a confederate flag embossed on the side. "It's beautiful," she said, pretending to admire it as she inched toward the door.

"My granddaddy gave it to me. He told me it was a symbol of our culture that was going to hell in a hand basket." He followed her, making Cassie's plan to get out of the room and lock him inside almost impossible. It was now or never.

Flicking it uselessly a few times, Cassie lifted her head and pouted. "It is broken." She tossed it back to him and awkwardly dashed through the door, hoping the element of surprise gave her enough time. As she pushed her body against the door to lock it, he pushed on the other side. Her feet slid on the floor as the door inched wider and wider. In concern for her baby and a last ditch effort to save herself, Cassie moved away from the door, ran into the bathroom and threw the keys into the toilet and flushed just as Joe burst into the room.

"You little liar. You little fake." He grabbed her by the arm and slapped her across the face before she knew what was happening. "Oh, no." Joe froze, his eyes wild. "I didn't mean to hit you."

Cassie's face burned. She turned and covered her stomach with both arms not knowing what to expect next.

"You—you—made me do it. But that doesn't matter. The General won't be happy. He wanted you back without a mark. Now you have a mark."

He reached over to touch her face. Cassie flinched, feeling

cornered and helpless, cradling her stomach to protect her baby.

Pulling his hand away, he slowly backed out of the room. "You are not going to be the cause of my punishment. I won't go to jail again, and I'm not going to be punished. You are," Joe said as he shut the door to the bathroom. "I can't lock you in, but I can do something just as good."

Cassie heard something heavy being dragged across the floor. She could hear Joe grunting and mumbling. Then absolutely nothing. Cassie pushed on the door. Whatever had been put against the door was heavy. She pushed then pushed again, the strain pulling across her abdomen. It couldn't be budged. Her opportunity to escape was ruined. She would never get away. All she could do was wait for Red to come back.

At the sink she threw water on her still stinging cheek, amazed that he had stopped at one slap. If she hadn't had her baby's safety to worry about, *he* would have suffered more than a slap. Not loyalty to T, but fear of punishment had stopped him from hurting her even more.

Thinking that she could still somehow get out of this before Red showed up, Cassie took a deep breath to clear her mind. Instead, her nostrils filled with smoke.

Smoke. She sniffed again, turning toward the door. Wisps of smoke were coming under the door. It was warm to the touch.

Joe had set the house on fire!

That's what Joe had meant by punishing her. He was going to burn her alive. Not if she could help it. Her eyes went to the window. She might not be able to crawl out of it, but she could certainly yell out of it. Cassie took her shoe off and grabbed the towel that had doubled as a curtain. Placing her hand inside the shoe she wrapped the towel around it. Turing her head away from the window, she broke the glass.

"Help!" she yelled over and over again without any luck. She found herself competing with the sirens and the crowd of people she saw gathering near the house. The wisps of smoke became streams of smoke as the minutes passed. The door was no longer warm to the touch but hot. Her body shook with a hacking cough. Going to the sink, she wet the washcloth she'd used earlier and covered her nose and mouth. At the window, she yelled until the smoke racked her with coughs once again. Desperate, Cassie threw one shoe out the window, then her other. Grabbing the glass encrusted towel, she shook and waved it out the window. Finally, she heard a voice say, "There's someone in there!"

Hoping that she wasn't hearing things, Cassie continued to wave the towel. She didn't want to suffocate, she didn't want her baby to die. What would Daniel do without them? Her lungs burned and smoke was everywhere. Remembering that she should stay low to the ground where there was some clear oxygen, Cassie's dropped to the floor but still went into another fit of coughing. The heat was intense. Never again would she complain about a New Orleans summer.

"Anybody here?" Cassie heard a deep voice say.

"Here! I'm here! She crawled to the door, punching her fists against it. She heard the sound of something heavy being dragged away and soon after felt strong arms around her.

Cassie swayed in her rescuer's arms, as he guided her out, feeling light-headed and dizzy.

"Ma'am?" The fireman in full gear held her upright.

Cassie coughed uncontrollably.

"Is anyone else in there?"

Unable to speak, she shook her head no.

A police officer approached her. "Are you sure?"

"She was barricaded in the bathroom. Some bastard put a refrigerator against the door," the fireman said, leaving her with the police officer.

"Possibly the guy someone saw race out the front door a few minutes ago. Do you know him?"

Cassie shook her head yes, then no. Another coughing fit hit her. She pointed to her belly, a plea in her eyes.

"Come with me, ma'am, to the ambulance."

As the officer guided her to the front of the house where the ambulance was parked, Cassie's eyes grew wide with fear. Not twenty feet away, walking purposely toward them, was Red. "What happened here?"

"Isn't it obvious? A fire," the officer said.

"I can see that."

"Are you okay?" Red asked, coming close to her, laying a heavy hand on her shoulder. She shook her head side to side, shrugging her shoulders wildly to rid herself of his touch.

"She needs oxygen." The police officer continued to walk her toward the ambulances.

As the emergency medical technician gave her oxygen and checked her vital signs, Red stood quietly talking to the police officer.

This didn't look good. Cassie could breathe now, but her throat felt too raw to talk.

The police officer walked over to her, a sympathetic expression on his face. He patted her shoulder and said, "I'll leave you to your husband now, ma'am. He'll take good care of you."

Cassie ripped the oxygen mask away from her face and forced sound past her raw throat. "No!"

Every person, emergency workers and gawkers, turned toward her. Good, she wanted attention. She would not be handed back to Red. Cassie searched all the faces, looking for one that was likely to help her. One stood out, giving her blessed relief in an instant. Recognition and a silent message to stay calm reached past her panic.

He walked toward them. "Is there a problem?" Her savior stood between her and Red.

"No Officer, this is my wife." Cassie could detect an instant change in the manner that Red talked to this man.

"Really?" The Officer turned to Cassie, a twinkle in his eye, as another officer stood behind Red. "Ma'am, are you married to this gentleman?"

"No," Cassie answered, her raw throat in no way hindering the clear and steady tone in her voice.

At that moment, the officer who had spoken to Red earlier came over. "It's okay, Randy, the woman's confused. That man is her husband. She's a little off."

"Is she now? Then I must be way off because I think she's telling the truth."

"I should know, I'm the one who's married to her," Red insisted.

"That's kind of funny, considering the fact that I was at her wedding, and you look nothing like my cousin, who *is* her husband."

Red stood stunned. And trapped.

"Cuff him, Frank. You're under arrest for kidnapping, bud."

As Frank took him away, Cassie fell into Randy's arms. The other officer looked on, dumbfounded.

"Cassie's face has been plastered all over the news. How could you not recognize her?"

"I don't know, Randy..."

Their voices faded away as Cassie eyes spotted and focused on a small figure over a block away, a figure she knew without a doubt was her husband. She did not move until her eyes connected with his. Then she flew from the shelter of Randy's embrace into the arms of her love. No obstacle, whether a misunderstood word, outside interference, or a possible brush with death would keep her away from him. Cassie was in Daniel's arms, where she belonged.

EPILOGUE

"She's beautiful, Cassie, Daniel," Jacqueline Jordan gushed as she walked into the hospital room.

Cassie acknowledged the compliment given to her firstborn with a smile before answering.

"You bet she is, Grandma."

Daniel nodded in agreement. "She looks like her mother."

Cassie was pleased with the short interaction she had just witnessed. Those five words were the most Daniel had said to Jackie since her return to New Orleans yesterday.

Miss Jackie's efforts to keep Daniel sane during Cassie's experience had been relayed through Melanie, who hadn't known a thing until after the fact. Daniel had also confided that having Jackie in the house and unavoidably in his face had forced him to look at his mother in a new light, cracking a door to a new beginning for them.

Melanie burst into the room. "My niece is gorgeous. I now forgive you for keeping me in the dark."

"It's about time, Daughter."

"I had no say in that," Cassie defended.

"And there's not much I remember about that time except wanting my wife back."

Cassie squeezed his hand.

"We know, Daniel," his mother said. Mother and son held eye contact for the briefest second. This was a momentous instant that both Cassie and Melanie witnessed and celebrated with identical grins.

"Back to the baby," Melanie commanded. "She is so long. I

didn't know a premmie could be so long."

"She gets that from her daddy, thanks to the gods." Cassie laughed.

Daniel laughed along, too, obviously remembering the day Cassie had begged the gods to give their child height.

"Private joke, right?"

"Right, Sis."

Melanie went on to shower the baby with countless compliments, the proud parents and grandmother agreeing with every word.

"Let's go see her again," Melanie suggested.

"You and Grandma go on ahead. I need to get my robe and slippers."

"Take your time," Melanie told them before dragging her mother away. "Come on, Mama, let's get our fill. They get to keep her."

Daniel took Cassie's robe from the foot of the bed and held it out for her to put on.

"So it's not just us? Our baby's really cute?" Daniel asked.

"We could even say gorgeous."

"How about lovable?"

"Another trait taken from her daddy."

"Me?" Daniel asked, pulling her to the edge of the bed with her feet dangling over the side.

"Yes, you."

"You've got it wrong, Cass. My wife is the most lovable person in the world." Daniel paused a moment, a ridge of thought on his forehead. "But if she thinks I'm lovable, it's because she loved me enough to let me see it, even when it stayed hidden inside."

"Not from me. It's always been plain as day."

"Then from myself."

Cassie laid her head on his shoulder and put her arms around his neck. "Daniel, do you think that's why you've had such a hard time reconciling with Miss Jacqueline? You thought that she didn't love you?"

"M-m-m-m. What took you so long to ask me that question?"

Cassie hadn't mentioned his mother in the past month—since before the kidnapping. She could finally say that word without vivid images of the entire episode flashing in her mind. Instead, those images had been replaced with hours in Daniel's company in this very hospital room, talking, reading, playing board games and cards and just being together as Cassie followed her doctor's orders to be hospitalized until the birth of their child, which had happened two days earlier.

"I was giving you that time you kept asking for."

"Well, almost losing you and the baby helped me put things into perspective. I loved Jackie once. I think she loved me at one time, too. After getting you back from those crazy people, I felt that God was giving me a second chance."

"So..."

"So, I figured Jackie might deserve one, too. At least a chance for me to hear her out. One of those evenings while you were lying here incubating our baby, Jackie and I had it out."

"And?"

"She admitted her faults. She was selfish and young and deserted me because she felt that I didn't deserve such a mother. She knew I'd be loved and cared for by family until she got her act together."

."Which she did," Cassis interjected.

"Yes, by marrying a preacher and starting a whole new family. She told me she never could admit to having a son. But it was her guilt from leaving me behind and denying me that made her a better mother for her other children. She still claims to love me, Cassie."

"I'm sure that she does," Cassie said, unable to imagine leaving her baby with someone else now that she was finally here, healthy and strong.

"I'm giving Jackie the benefit of the doubt. She had her reasons, though I doubt that I'll ever truly understand them. But I hope we can have a decent relationship because you know we're never going to get rid of Melanie. My half sister's proof enough that Jackie has done something good in her life."

"I can say the same about you." Cassie gave him a quick kiss. "And the baby should know her grandmother."

"Yes, she should."

Daniel and Cassie headed to the open door of the room. "Cass, about your cousin T."

"He's missing, I know."

"You heard?"

"The other night when you were talking to Devin on the phone."

"I thought you were asleep."

Cassie shook her head.

"Then you know we hired another investigator, and he couldn't find a trace of your cousin."

"Yes," she answered simply, not feeling much of anything about T's disappearance.

"But both of your kidnapers were caught, Cass. Too bad it happened before I was able to get hold of the bastard who slapped you."

Cassie traced a finger down the lines on his forehead. "I'm okay now. There are no lasting marks. I'm just relieved to know that they were caught. It's one thing knowing there are people somewhere in the world with such bigoted opinions, but it's another to actually hear them speak, look into their eyes and know their hatred.

"I know how terrifying that experience was for you, Cass—"

"You don't have to say any more, Daniel. Experiencing first-hand some of the warped views of people like Joe and Red makes me appreciate my family and the people I know even more."

They walked out of the room with arms around each other. As they rounded the corner, Cassie and Daniel found the entire nursery window blocked with family members. Cassie's aunt and uncle were the first to see them.

"We came back to get another look at our great-niece," Aunt Margaret told them.

"We had the whole window for ourselves for about two minutes." Travis laughed. "You were right about this baby being loved."

"We know, we're lucky." Daniel pulled Cassie closer to his side.

"There they are. It's the parents!"

"Not so loud Uncle Cal, this is a hospital," Daniel warned.

"We know that. This is the place where babies are born. That's why we came to the hospital, to see the baby. Everybody had the same idea at the same time. At least everybody except Devin and Monica. Those triplets are keeping them busy."

"I'm sure they are," Cassie answered.

"We've got a question for you. What did you finally decide to name the baby? We've been saying the baby this, the baby that. She's got a name, right?"

"Yes, she does, Aunt Joyce," Daniel answered.

"Something you thought about long and hard, right?"

"Yes, indeed. The baby's name is Jax."

The hall became instantly silent. Cassie and Daniel could barely hold in the laughter at the look on everyone's faces.

"Those two are up to something," Uncle Cal said in a voice that was the lowest Cassie had ever heard from him.

Unable to hold it in any longer Daniel announced, "Our baby's name is Jax- Jessica Ann Xena."

Soft sighs of relief filled the hall.

"Where are they going with her?" Melanie asked.

Everyone looked toward the window. The nurse behind the glass mouthed, "Home."

"That's right, we get to go home today." Cassie and Daniel hugged everyone goodbye and went back to the hospital room where the nurse waited with baby Jax.

Daniel lifted her from the crib and sat on the edge of the bed next to Cassie.

They looked at each other, then at the child they had made together. There were no more misunderstandings between them, just a future that looked challenging but happy.

"Jax, my little girl, you are loved."

"And so are you," Cassie said.

"And so are you," Daniel repeated.

"Speaking of love, Cass," Daniel said as he gently laid the baby back into the crib. "Sleeping alone these past few weeks has had my mind busy with some 'other ways.'"

"You, too?"

Nodding his head, Daniel asked, "How do you feel about marbles and a bucket of ice…?"

AUTHOR BIOGRAPHY

Pamela Leigh Starr was born and raised in New Orleans where she still lives and teaches elementary school. She is a graduate of Xavier University with graduate studies in mathematics at Loyola University. She is married and has three children.

Misconceptions is the third book in Pamela's Love Found Series. The other books in the series are Fate published in October 1999 and Chances published in December 2000. The fourth book in the series, Ironic, is due to be released in March 2005. Other titles by Pamela include *Illusions* released in October 2001 and *Icie* release in 2002.

Visit Pamela at http://pamleighstarr.com/

See her other titles at **www.genesis-press.com**

Excerpt from

I'LL PAINT THE SUN

BY

A.J. GARROTTO

Release Date March 2005

In the morning when I awake, I stretch my hands over my expanding belly, measuring the widening distance between my fingertips. I feel you move within me and I speak your name. Tobías. We'll call you Toby. How different your childhood will be than mine, lived in cramped quarters on heavily trafficked, windswept streets of one of the world's great commercial and tourist centers.

I've stepped back generations in time into an unfamiliar culture to live among a people I long to understand and become part of. I perch here free as a seabird, gazing out from the uneven flagstone terrace of our new home. My eyes feast on the South Caribbean's turquoise expanse while, at my feet, the serene Santa Magdalena shoreline stretches left and right. My lips taste the salty breeze which invites me to open my silk robe and let the mild, humid air slip across my swollen abdomen like your father's gentle hands in the night. My senses fine-tune to island sounds and tropical fragrances having no particular point of origin. The melodies and scents of happiness, I call them.

The waves await their turn to tumble shoreward with the rush of a première danseur leaping across a broad stage. Their sudsy fingers claw at the white-sand beach before returning to rest in deeper water before making another run at the shore.

With golden sunlight filtering through my closed eyelids, I marvel that healing and new life have replaced my vow of a year ago, never to trust another man as long as I possessed sound mental and emotional faculties. Healing. No other word describes our experience. I inhale...heal...caressing the silent sound and exhale...ing. My spirit breathes its gentle rhythm. The cadence anoints me with its sacred oil. You, Toby, are its fruit, its prize and celebration.

Your father's restoration during this time has been even more unlikely than my own. Scarred men and women—children too—make pilgrimage to the world's designated holy places praying for renewal of body and soul. Our miracle happened in the city of St. Francis. Quite by chance, if one believes in coincidence. I don't, not any more.

On the turbulent SFO-to-Miami flight, I read Message In a Bottle. Garrett Blake's love letters to his deceased wife brought such sadness to my heart that I exhausted my supply of tissues and soaked your father's handkerchief. When the book ended, I napped, head resting on his shoulder. I dreamed of sea-tossed bottles and sealed-in treasures. I remember saying to someone in my dream, "We're all corked bottles, each with our deepest truths sealed inside."

We devoted our first days on the island to patching the frayed cloth of your father's relationship with your grandparents. Amid tears and laughter, the principals of that divided trinity have let go of old hurts and reknit bonds of love like fragments of shattered bone. I've fallen in love with these good people who welcomed their prodigal home without question, if not without the lingering pain of his leaving them. They have drawn me, a stranger and foreigner not-yet fluent in their language, to their bosoms with such open-hearted hospitality that I have vowed to model my parenting after their example.

A local real estate broker found us this furnished beachfront mansion that belonged to international recording star Eduardo Colón, whose name is spoken with reverence on this island.

"The only item Señor Colón and his new bride took with them to Paris was the grand piano," the broker told us. Minus the massive instrument, the conservatory looks like a glassed-in ballroom. You'll love playing in it. Why the Colóns left everything is a mystery to me. Did some tragedy scar the tables, chairs, beds, and mirrors, sending the newlyweds in pursuit of fresh dreams far from home? If so, I identify with their need.

It will take me years to integrate the events that brought me to this place. I began this year in despair, facing bankruptcy. Can it now be true that every brick and nail and pane of glass in this villa estate belongs to us, paid for in cash? The deck I stand on? The spacious bedroom in which we sleep? The broad pool we swam in last evening and made love in the night before? If you've paid attention, you'll come into the world knowing all about the birds and bees. What a relief that will be to your father.

Okay, Toby. That was a certifiable kick.

I'm your bottle, aren't I? Impenetrable green, like a liter of rich red wine. You, the unreadable message. Are you running out of patience with the sealed safety of my womb? Are you ready to embark on the adventure we earthlings call Life? I want to know you, learn your deepest desires, discover what makes you happy and sad. How I'd love to fast-forward, to see how you'll fulfill your destiny.

Not true.

I'm an impatient woman but I'd rather walk that unpredictable road with you, each day marking a single step along your life-path. I'll thrill with your every new discovery, rejoice in the measured unfolding of your inner spirit. Will the stories you tell your children come close to matching the ones we'll tell you on nights when tropical storms lash at the windows testing the endurance of our house? I can't bear the thought of you suffering, of ever losing your way as we did.

Two mourning doves just landed on the fountain in the corner of the terrace. I wish you could see how the jacaranda trees have spread a soft lavender welcome mat for them. These loving creatures remind me of a TV show in the States about divine messengers with the mission to heal the wounded, restore sight to those blind in spirit. If there's one thing your mom knows about, Toby, it's angels. I have two of my own. Let me tell you the miracle story of how our little family came to be.

2005 Publication Schedule

January

A Heart's Awakening Veronica Parker $9.95 1-58571-143-9	Falling Natalie Dunbar $9.95 1-58571-121-7	

February

Echoes of Yesterday Beverly Clark $9.95 1-58571-131-4	A Love of Her Own Cheris F. Hodges $9.95 1-58571-136-5	Higher Ground Leah Latimer $19.95 1-58571-157-8

March

Misconceptions Pamela Leigh Starr $9.95 1-58571-117-9	I'll Paint a Sun A.J. Garrotto $9.95 1-58571-165-9	Peace Be Still Colette Haywood $12.95 1-58571-129-2

April

Intentional Mistakes Michele Sudler $9.95 1-58571-152-7	Conquering Dr. Wexler's Heart Kimberley White $9.95 1-58571-126-8	Song in the Park Martin Brant $15.95 1-58571-125-X

May

The Color Line Lizette Carter $9.95 1-58571-163-2	Unconditional A.C. Arthur $9.95 1-58571-142-X	Last Train to Memphis Elsa Cook $12.95 1-58571-146-2

June

Angel's Paradise Janice Angelique $9.95 1-58571-107-1	Suddenly You Crystal Hubbard $9.95 1-58571-158-6	Matters of Life and Death Lesego Malepe, Ph.D. $15.95 1-58571-124-1

2005 Publication Schedule (continued)

July

Pleasures All Mine Belinda O. Steward $9.95 1-58571-112-8	Wild Ravens Altonya Washington $9.95 1-58571-164-0	Class Reunion Irma Jenkins/John Brown $12.95 1-58571-123-3

August

Path of Thorns Annetta P. Lee $9.95 1-58571-145-4	Timeless Devotion Bella McFarland $9.95 1-58571-148-9	Life Is Never As It Seems June Michael $12.95 1-58571-153-5

September

Beyond the Rapture Beverly Clark $9.95 1-58571-131-4	Blood Lust J. M. Jeffries $9.95 1-58571-138-1	Rough on Rats and Tough on Cats Chris Parker $12.95 1-58571-154-3

October

A Will to Love Angie Daniels $9.95 1-58571-141-1	Taken by You Dorothy Elizabeth Love $9.95 1-58571-162-4	Soul Eyes Wayne L. Wilson $12.95 1-58571-147-0

November

A Drummer's Beat to Mend Kay Swanson $9.95	Sweet Reprecussions Kimberley White $9.95 1-58571-159-4	Red Polka Dot in a Worldof Plaid Varian Johnson $12.95 1-58571-140-3

December

Hand in Glove Andrea Jackson $9.95 1-58571-166-7	Blaze Barbara Keaton $9.95	Across Carol Payne $12.95 1-58571-149-7

Other Genesis Press, Inc. Titles

Acquisitions	Kimberley White	$8.95
A Dangerous Deception	J.M. Jeffries	$8.95
A Dangerous Love	J.M. Jeffries	$8.95
A Dangerous Obsession	J.M. Jeffries	$8.95
After the Vows (Summer Anthology)	Leslie Esdaile T.T. Henderson Jacqueline Thomas	$10.95
Again My Love	Kayla Perrin	$10.95
Against the Wind	Gwynne Forster	$8.95
A Lark on the Wing	Phyliss Hamilton	$8.95
A Lighter Shade of Brown	Vicki Andrews	$8.95
All I Ask	Barbara Keaton	$8.95
A Love to Cherish	Beverly Clark	$8.95
Ambrosia	T.T. Henderson	$8.95
And Then Came You	Dorothy Elizabeth Love	$8.95
Angel's Paradise	Janice Angelique	$8.95
A Risk of Rain	Dar Tomlinson	$8.95
At Last	Lisa G. Riley	$8.95
Best of Friends	Natalie Dunbar	$8.95
Bound by Love	Beverly Clark	$8.95
Breeze	Robin Hampton Allen	$10.95
Brown Sugar Diaries & Other Sexy Tales	Delores Bundy & Cole Riley	$10.95
By Design	Barbara Keaton	$8.95
Cajun Heat	Charlene Berry	$8.95
Careless Whispers	Rochelle Alers	$8.95
Caught in a Trap	Andre Michelle	$8.95
Chances	Pamela Leigh Starr	$8.95
Dark Embrace	Crystal Wilson Harris	$8.95
Dark Storm Rising	Chinelu Moore	$10.95
Designer Passion	Dar Tomlinson	$8.95
Ebony Butterfly II	Delilah Dawson	$14.95

Erotic Anthology	Assorted	$8.95
Eve's Prescription	Edwina Martin Arnold	$8.95
Everlastin' Love	Gay G. Gunn	$8.95
Fate	Pamela Leigh Starr	$8.95
Forbidden Quest	Dar Tomlinson	$10.95
Fragment in the Sand	Annetta P. Lee	$8.95
From the Ashes	Kathleen Suzanne	$8.95
	Jeanne Sumerix	
Gentle Yearning	Rochelle Alers	$10.95
Glory of Love	Sinclair LeBeau	$10.95
Hart & Soul	Angie Daniels	$8.95
Heartbeat	Stephanie Bedwell-Grime	$8.95
I'll Be Your Shelter	Giselle Carmichael	$8.95
Illusions	Pamela Leigh Starr	$8.95
Indiscretions	Donna Hill	$8.95
Interlude	Donna Hill	$8.95
Intimate Intentions	Angie Daniels	$8.95
Just an Affair	Eugenia O'Neal	$8.95
Kiss or Keep	Debra Phillips	$8.95
Love Always	Mildred E. Riley	$10.95
Love Unveiled	Gloria Greene	$10.95
Love's Deception	Charlene Berry	$10.95
Mae's Promise	Melody Walcott	$8.95
Meant to Be	Jeanne Sumerix	$8.95
Midnight Clear	Leslie Esdaile	$10.95
(Anthology)	Gwynne Forster	
	Carmen Green	
	Monica Jackson	
Midnight Magic	Gwynne Forster	$8.95
Midnight Peril	Vicki Andrews	$10.95
My Buffalo Soldier	Barbara B. K. Reeves	$8.95
Naked Soul	Gwynne Forster	$8.95
No Regrets	Mildred E. Riley	$8.95
Nowhere to Run	Gay G. Gunn	$10.95

Object of His Desire	A. C. Arthur	$8.95
One Day at a Time	Bella McFarland	$8.95
Passion	T.T. Henderson	$10.95
Past Promises	Jahmel West	$8.95
Path of Fire	T.T. Henderson	$8.95
Picture Perfect	Reon Carter	$8.95
Pride & Joi	Gay G. Gunn	$8.95
Quiet Storm	Donna Hill	$8.95
Reckless Surrender	Rochelle Alers	$8.95
Rendezvous with Fate	Jeanne Sumerix	$8.95
Revelations	Cheris F. Hodges	$8.95
Rivers of the Soul	Leslie Esdaile	$8.95
Rooms of the Heart	Donna Hill	$8.95
Shades of Brown	Denise Becker	$8.95
Shades of Desire	Monica White	$8.95
Sin	Crystal Rhodes	$8.95
So Amazing	Sinclair LeBeau	$8.95
Somebody's Someone	Sinclair LeBeau	$8.95
Someone to Love	Alicia Wiggins	$8.95
Soul to Soul	Donna Hill	$8.95
Still Waters Run Deep	Leslie Esdaile	$8.95
Subtle Secrets	Wanda Y. Thomas	$8.95
Sweet Tomorrows	Kimberly White	$8.95
The Color of Trouble	Dyanne Davis	$8.95
The Price of Love	Sinclair LeBeau	$8.95
The Reluctant Captive	Joyce Jackson	$8.95
The Missing Link	Charlyne Dickerson	$8.95
Three Wishes	Seressia Glass	$8.95
Tomorrow's Promise	Leslie Esdaile	$8.95
Truly Inseperable	Wanda Y. Thomas	$8.95
Twist of Fate	Beverly Clark	$8.95
Unbreak My Heart	Dar Tomlinson	$8.95
Unconditional Love	Alicia Wiggins	$8.95
When Dreams A Float	Dorothy Elizabeth Love	$8.95

Whispers in the Night	Dorothy Elizabeth Love	$8.95
Whispers in the Sand	LaFlorya Gauthier	$10.95
Yesterday is Gone	Beverly Clark	$8.95
Yesterday's Dreams, Tomorrow's Promises	Reon Laudat	$8.95
Your Precious Love	Sinclair LeBeau	$8.95